WAREHOUSING
VIOLENCE

FRONTIERS OF ANTHROPOLOGY
Series Editor:
H. RUSSELL BERNARD, *University of Florida*

The **Frontiers of Anthropology** series is designed to explore the leading edge of theory, method, and applications in cultural anthropology. In rapidly changing times, traditional ways in which anthropologists work have been transformed, being influenced by new paradigms, methodological approaches beyond the use of participant observation, and field settings beyond the world of primitive peoples. Books in this series come from many philosophical schools, methodological approaches, substantive concerns, and geographical settings—some familiar to anthropologists and some new to the discipline. But all share the purpose of examining and explaining the ideas and practices that make up the frontiers of contemporary cultural anthropology.

Books in This Series

FAMILY VIOLENCE IN CROSS-CULTURAL PERSPECTIVE
by **DAVID LEVINSON,** *Vice President*
Human Relations Area Files, New Haven
Frontiers of Anthropology, Volume 1
ISBN: 0-8039-3075-5 (cloth)   ISBN: 0-8039-3076-3 (paper)

WOMEN'S POWER AND SOCIAL REVOLUTION
Fertility Transition in the West Indies
by **W. PENN HANDWERKER,** *Humboldt State University*
Frontiers of Anthropology, Volume 2
ISBN: 0-8039-3115-8 (cloth)   ISBN: 0-8039-3116-6 (paper)

WAREHOUSING VIOLENCE
by **MARK S. FLEISHER,** *Washington State University*
Frontiers of Anthropology, Volume 3
ISBN: 0-8039-3122-0 (cloth)   ISBN: 0-8039-3123-9 (paper)

CAPITAL CRIME
Black Infant Mortality in America
by **MARGARET S. BOONE,** *George Washington University,*
School of Medicine and Health Sciences
Frontiers of Anthropology, Volume 4
ISBN: 0-8039-3373-8 (cloth)   ISBN: 0-8039-3374-6 (paper)

WAREHOUSING VIOLENCE

MARK S. FLEISHER

Frontiers of Anthropology   Volume 3

SAGE Publications
International Educational and Professional Publisher
Newbury Park   London   New Delhi

For information address:

SAGE Publications, Inc.
2455 Teller Road
Newbury Park, California 91320
E-mail: order@sagepub.com

SAGE Publications Ltd.
6 Bonhill Street
London EC2A 4PU
United Kingdom

SAGE Publications India Pvt. Ltd.
M-32 Market
Greater Kailash I
New Delhi 110 048 India

Printed in the United States of America

Library of Congress Cataloging-in-Publication Data

Fleisher, Mark S.
    Warehousing violence / by Mark S. Fleisher.
        p. cm.—(Frontiers of anthropology ; v. 3)
    Bibliography: p.
    ISBN 0-8039-3122-0   ISBN 0-8039-3123-9 (pbk.)
    1. United States Federal Penitentiary at Lompoc, California.
    2. Prison administration—California—Lompoc. 3. Rehabilitation of criminals—California—Lompoc. I. Title. II. Series.
    HV9474.L65F54   1989
    365'.97949—dc19   88-27624
                                                                CIP

96   97   98   99   00   01   02   03   10   9   8   7   6

Contents

Foreword

by H. Russell Bernard   7

Acknowledgments   10

Preface   12

1. Ethnography and Social Policy   14

2. USP-Lompoc   32

3. Systems of Control   64

4. Fieldwork   93

5. Rapport with Inmates   113

6. Life Inside   131

7. Sex   156

8. Scenes of Discipline   174

9. Scenes of Violence   197

10. Mainline Talk   220

11. Custody: A Growing American Industry   234

Glossary   241

References   246

About the Author   256

Foreword

Cultural anthropology is changing quickly, adding new methods of data collection and analysis, and new problems to the repertoire of the discipline. Until recently, cultural anthropologists relied almost entirely on participant observation as *the* method of data collection, and on qualitative exposition of results. Today, in addition to participant observation, anthropologists commonly use more formalized methods for the collection of quantitative data; and, in addition to qualitative methods of data analysis, they use statistical techniques and nonmetric scaling. Until World War II, anthropologists studied almost exclusively non-Western peoples, particularly preliterate societies. Beginning a half century ago, anthropologists extended their use of participant observation to the study of small agriculturalists and fisherfolk—what came to be called "peasant" societies.

Now, anthropologists have turned their attention to the study of occupational groups and modern bureaucracies, as well as to the study of social problems like family violence, teen pregnancy, drug abuse, civil war, and forest depletion. The study of new problems has led to the development of new theories, and anthropologists are finding new ways to apply the discipline's theories and findings—in helping to determine the historical legitimacy of Indian tribes, for example, or in building better workplace environments, or in marketing new commercial products. The *Frontiers of Anthropology* series explores all the exciting edges of the discipline, and provides an outlet for some of the most creative and controversial work in the field.

In this volume, Mark Fleisher presents an insider's account of life in a major federal penitentiary. Using traditional anthropological methods, such as long-term participant observation and open-ended interviewing, Fleisher addresses two important social issues in contemporary America: What will America do with an increasing number of violent criminals? What can be done to lower the cost of operating maximum-security prisons? Fleisher's book is at the frontiers of anthropology because it demonstrates the intuitive power and appeal of ethnography in illuminating social problems and in formulating potential solutions for those problems.

Fleisher was asked by the Research Division of the Federal Bureau of Prisons to look at why correctional officers at the United States Penitentiary at Lompoc, California, appear to experience a lot of stress, and why they have such a high job turnover rate. When Fleisher accepted the assignment, he asked to be allowed to participate fully with the guards in their daily routines (Fleisher is an ethnographer, after all), but there was a problem: no one would be allowed by the Federal Bureau of Prisons to "walk the mainline" of a major penitentiary for a year without credentials as a certified prison worker.

Fleisher went for training, received his credentials, and spent a year at Lompoc as a true participant observer. He studied staff stress, and wrote several training manuals that help new guards understand and cope with the problems they confront. But in the course of his applications work, Fleisher came to understand how the prison at Lompoc operates, and why it has a relatively low rate of violence, despite being populated by many violent convicts. They keys to Lompoc's success are 1) an institutional culture that rewards peace and quiet rather than violence; and 2) a prison factory that actually runs at a profit and that provides inmates with the opportunity to make their lives materially easier in prison. Both of these keys to success depend on a particularly effective leadership style in top management. Fleisher's ethnography shows how "heavy thugs" can be controlled without armed or abusive correctional staffers, and without expensive correctional technology. In short, *Warehousing Violence* shows how an employment-based system of social control can be effective in keeping down both prison operating costs *and* prison violence.

Fleisher's findings have broad policy implications. His position is that, whatever the cause, American society produces a certain number of very violent criminals, mostly men. These men are not insane, but neither can they be "rehabilitated" by applying well-meant programs in prison. Instead, according to Fleisher, we must admit that the best place for otherwise sane, violent criminals is a well-run prison—one that keeps them away from the rest of society and one that provides them with a secure, nonviolent place to live themselves. It costs about $25,000 a year to keep one repeat criminal in a secure prison. By contrast, the cost of allowing one repeat criminal to leave prison is, by some estimates, about $400,000 a year, including the costs of extra law enforcement, an expanded judiciary, and the costs to victims. Fleisher concludes that safely warehousing violence is better than our current system of allowing violent, repeat criminals to go free, and he advocates the greatly expanded use of facilities like the Lompoc penitentiary to deal with one aspect of violence in America. He also advocates the use of profits from prison factories to support victims of violent crime, and to support the development of community-level programs that may prevent desperate young people from turning to violent crime in the first place.

This is a controversial book. Fleisher takes a strong position, based on nearly 20 years of studying prisons and the men who live and work in them. Whatever your own ideas may be about how to deal with violent criminals in America, Fleisher's ethnography provides first-hand data on how one maximum-security penitentiary actually works, from day to day, as the keepers and the kept struggle to live out their lives together.

—H. Russell Bernard
University of Florida

Acknowledgments

Since the late 1960s, I had only dreamed of doing full-participation research in a major, maximum-security penitentiary. Helene Cavior made my dream possible, and Robert J. Christensen opened USP-Lompoc to me. H. Russell Bernard has been my friend and teacher for almost twenty years. He has been a very patient, caring mentor; without him, this book wouldn't have been written. Each one has helped me satisfy my dream. *Warehousing Violence* is for them and for the tens of USP-Lompoc correctional workers and inmates who contributed to it. Without them, this book would have remained a dream.

As I prepared to conduct my fieldwork at USP-Lompoc, Professors James B. Jacobs, New York University, School of Law, and James F. Short, Jr., Department of Sociology, Washington State University, listened patiently to my research strategy and invested their time in reading drafts of my research proposal. Because of conversations with them, I was better able to organize my thoughts and to develop an ethnographic strategy for studying correctional officers. They helped me immensely, and I am most grateful.

During my research at USP-Lompoc, I met many employees of the federal prison system. Without exception, each person was knowledgeable, friendly, and highly professional. In Washington, D.C., Norman Carlson, Director of the Federal Bureau of Prisons, Dr. Peter Nacci, Chief of Research, and Harriet Lebowitz were more than generous with their time during research for this book and in my subsequent research at USP-Lompoc. Mr. Ogis Fields, the Federal Bureau of Prisons' western regional director (now retired), opened the administrative door to USP-Lompoc. Mr. John Sams, Mr. Gene Gill, and Captain Mel Collins, USP-Lompoc's senior executive staff, became my friends; that was sincerely appreciated. Mr. Richard Rison, USP-Lompoc's warden since June 1987, graciously assisted me whenever I needed something; his kindness and support, even though we didn't meet until after this book was finished, made writing *Warehousing Violence* much smoother.

Carole Bernard also made my writing smoother by carefully editing this book; she did a terific job. Mitch Allen, my editor at Sage Publications, had faith in my ability to write an ethnographic study of a penitentiary that would interest a wide audience, long before I had the vision that I could do it. He improved this book by making many insightful suggestions, and I am most grateful for his help.

One final comment. I became fond of many men at Lompoc's federal prisons. Some of those men were on the government's team, and some weren't. USP-Lompoc's correctional officers did a tough job and did it very well. And, for the record, many inmates at USP-Lompoc, who had spent years or decades of their lives committing violence on the streets of America, were always friendly and kind to me. These men never failed to answer my questions, and they always let me hang around and join in the fun.

This investigation was supported in part by funds provided by the Washington State University Graduate School, by the Washington State University Research and Arts Committee, and by a Washington State University, College of Science and Arts' Completion Grant. Dean John Pierce has been generous, and I am most appreciative. I am grateful for the financial and academic support of the Federal Bureau of Prisons and of Washington State University.

So that I could work at USP-Lompoc, my kids, Emily and Aaron, had to give up their friends in Pullman, Washington, and my wife, Ann McGuigan, had to postpone the start of her Ph.D. program. Ann, Emily, and Aaron listened patiently, day after day, month after month, year after year, while I talked about my research and my writing. Now, that was "doing hard time," according to them.

The views expressed in this book are mine, and don't necessarily reflect the attitudes, opinions, and ideas of the Federal Bureau of Prisons and the U.S. Department of Justice.

Preface

In *Warehousing Violence,* I distinguish between correctional officers and hacks, and inmates and convicts. This is done intentionally to convey a sense of staffers' and inmates' mutual attitudes and feelings toward each other.

The Federal Bureau of Prisons houses inmates and employs correctional officers. It doesn't house "convicts," "thugs," or "fucking-thugs," nor does it employ "hacks," "cops," or "screws." However, the terms "convict" and "hack" are heard most commonly among staffers, and present a more honest view of the internal system than do the bureaucratic designations, "inmate" and "correctional officer."

Staffers and inmates use these terms differently, in different social contexts, among different people. When a convict sits in front of the Federal Parole Commission, he refers to himself demurely as an inmate. When he leaves the room, returns to his cellblock, and tells his cellblock partners of his experience, he refers to himself as a "'vict" or "convict." The parole commissioners are no longer, "sir," but "assholes."

When an inmate is being verbally reprimanded by a senior correctional lieutenant, the inmate will address him as "boss," or "lieutenant." But when the inmate leaves the lieutenant's office and tells his partners of his experience, he may refer to the lieutenant as "a pig motherfucker."

In formal social situations, correctional staffers refer to inmates, not convicts. But, at the monthly Friday afternoon beer party at the institution's training center, correctional officers refer to themselves as "hacks," and inmates become "thugs" and "fucking-thugs."

In writing *Warehousing Violence,* I sometimes use prison terminology as it is used socially and informally, and sometimes as it is used bureaucratically. Be aware that my switch in terminology is purposeful, and meant to signal a switch in emotional value appropriate to each situation described.

Some staffers and inmates were involved in highly sensitive situations in which, if their surnames or nicknames were disclosed, or even if the details of those situations were disclosed, their personal safety in the institution, and/or their careers might be jeopardized. In these cases, even with their informed consent, I have used pseudonyms, and, when necessary, omitted potentially damaging information from their accounts.

At times, this is a very personal story, and one which provides insights into a well-managed penitentiary. But at bottom, this book is about men living out their lives in a warehouse of violence.

—Mark S. Fleisher
Pullman, Washington

—1—

ETHNOGRAPHY AND SOCIAL POLICY

INTRODUCTION

Prisons, like other human communities, are socially complex places. Most studies of prison life have been based on data collected by scholars using survey questionnaires, short-term formal interviews, and casual walk-abouts (see, for example, Carroll, 1974: 11; Jacobs, 1974b; Sykes, 1958: 135; Wooden and Parker, 1982: 5-10), rather than by close-up, long-term observation (Marquart, 1986a; and see Adler and Adler, 1987). By design, and by constraint of data resources, outsider research tends to focus on particular issues, usually of managerial interest, such as overcrowding, gang violence, and so on.

M. Silberman (1986), who did research at a maximum-security penitentiary, noted that "The most useful and informative aspect of my research was the opportunity to walk freely throughout the institution and to interview whomever I pleased. In this way, I came to know a number of inmates and staff members, and to know *intimately* how they felt about the prison experience" (p. 3; emphasis added). Davidson (1974), in discussing his research at San Quentin, realized the importance of intimate familiarity with prison culture. "As the prisoners would say, this study 'tells it like it is.' This is not an ideal, or partial, or distorted description of prison life. This is not an idealized view of the prison. . . . Instead, it is a presentation of the real prisoner culture" (p. 2).

The sociological perspective generally produces reliable data, data that can be replicated. The ethnographic perspective focuses on validity, often at the expense of reliability. This makes ethnographic data strong on internal validity—the researcher knows what he's talking about insofar as his community is concerned. But ethnographic data are low on external validity—the results may not generalize beyond the ethnographer's community (Bernard, 1988; also see Campbell, 1984, 1986; Read, 1980). In order to develop external validity—the kind that permits inference on how to solve problems—we need both reliable and valid data, and the comparative perspective.

From August 1985 through September 1986, I did participant observation fieldwork as a certified federal correctional staffer, employed full time, at the United States Penitentiary (USP) at Lompoc, California. When I began at Lompoc, I had been studying prisons, on and off, for almost 20 years, but this was a once-in-a-lifetime opportunity to get a long-term look inside a major federal penitentiary from the perspectives of staffers, inmates, and executive administrators. My work at USP-Lompoc relies on the many excellent studies by sociologists and criminologists for the reliable, hard data about prison life in America, and I offer an ethnographic perspective in addition.

According to officials of the Federal Bureau of Prisons (Bureau), new correctional officers (COs) at the Lompoc penitentiary were suffering from high stress and low morale, and, according to the Bureau's central personnel office in Washington, D.C., the penitentiary was experiencing a higher-than-average staff turnover rate, particularly among new COs.

Correctional officer stress, low morale, and related issues have been well studied (see Crouch and Alpert, 1982; Jacobs, 1974a, 1974b, 1976, 1977, 1983; Jacobs and Grear, 1977; Jacobs and Kraft, 1978, 1983; Lasky et al., 1986; Lindquist and Whitehead, 1986; Philliber, 1987; Poole and Regoli, 1980). However, few researchers have actually worked among maximum-security convicts, assumed the daily responsibilities of a full-time correctional staffer, and experienced the stress and anxiety, the danger and exhilaration, of a major, maximum-security penitentiary (see Marquart, 1986a).

I was hired on contract by the Federal Bureau of Prisons to investigate the pressures affecting the performance and turnover of new COs and to develop intervention programs that might alleviate those pressures and improve retention. To accomplish these goals, I became, and worked as, a federal correctional worker. This included complete participation in formal correctional training programs and on-the-job CO training. As a trained correctional staffer, I was able to participate freely in all penitentiary activities, even including on-the-scene involvement in violence.

In the eyes of staff, just being in the penitentiary month after month isn't enough to justify making suggestions for improving correctional officer training or for new supervisory techniques. I had to fight hard against the staffers' perception of researchers as being "all brains and no balls," as one of my favorite hacks enjoyed saying. Building my reputation was as vital for my success as a contract researcher as establishing one's reputation is for a new line hack.

Penitentiary custody staffers are cynical about research and the sincerity of researchers. Over the years at USP-Lompoc, and in other prisons where they have worked, line staff have encountered researchers who stayed a short time, collected their survey data, and left quickly, without learning about the staff as individuals or about day-to-day life in the institution. The warden told me on my first day of work that "researchers come in here, spend a few days, leave, and call themselves experts." He laughed.

Outside researchers' second- and third-hand data about prison violence can't match the experience of actually participating in it. I was there when violence broke out. I ran with other men, feeling the anxiety of never knowing what we would find when we arrived. I saw the blood of inmate-inmate and inmate-staff violence. I felt the emotional highs of a violent scene, and the anxiety of wondering if I, too, would get "hit" sometime. I was able to watch staffers react during and after assaults and a killing. I was able to talk to hacks as we worked together, shaking down inmates in their cells after cellblock violence. I watched inmates and then watched them watch me. I watched their reactions to violence, listened to their comments, and questioned them, formally and informally, after a violent incident.

Although I've spent thousands of hours working as a penitentiary correctional staffer, often sharing daily responsibilities with USP-Lompoc's correctional officers, this book isn't about federal hacks. Rather, *Warehousing Violence* is an ethnographic evaluation of the formal and informal forces of social control that make the Lompoc federal penitentiary a relatively peaceful, humane, and profit-making maximum-security penitentiary.

During my research, I talked to inmates about many things, but I was particularly interested in their family lives, experiences in prison, and difficulties on the street. Gradually, I became aware of inmates' views on these issues. In Chapter 1, inmates talk for themselves about crime and prison and street life. And I discuss my social policy recommendation that the long-term incarceration of high-risk, violent offenders in humane institutions, like USP-Lompoc, can benefit them and us.

Chapter 2 presents an overview of the Federal Prison System (FPS) and discusses the organizational structure and correctional culture of USP-Lompoc. Chapter 3 is a detailed description of USP-Lompoc's system of formal and informal social control. In Chapter 4, I present my research techniques and discuss issues which affected my research. Following this, six chapters of ethnographic description offer an insider's view of prison life. In Chapter 5 I discuss my relationship with several inmates and they talk about their lives. In Chapter 6, I describe inmate life at USP-Lompoc. In Chapter 7, inmates discuss sexual behavior, sex-related violence, and the implications of AIDS for staff and inmates. In Chapter 8, I offer an insider's view of informal inmate discipline. Chapter 9 presents a close-up look at scenes of inmate violence and staffers' response to it. Chapter 10 presents staffers' reactions to violence and the role that violence plays in staff culture. And in Chapter 11, I offer suggestions for improving prison management.

GOING TO THE STREET

Despite our justified fears about releasing violent criminals, most convicts eventually walk away from maximum-security prisons, and USP-Lompoc isn't an exception. One mid-week morning I was standing with correctional officer Gary Charles, a ten-year veteran of state and federal prisons, and watching convict Burrell as he prepared to leave the penitentiary on his way to a Community Treatment Center (a "CTC," as it's called, is a privately operated halfway house, used by the Bureau of Prisons as part of federal inmates' reintroduction into society; see Glaser, 1969: 277-282). "If it weren't for us [federal prison]," said Charles, "these motherfuckers would be sleeping under bridges in Los Angeles. I'm glad to see Burrell leaving, but he'll be back. It seems like they all come back." I now believe there's some truth in that notion.

Most inmates at Lompoc, about 60% according to an executive administrator, eventually regain their freedom. The Federal Prison System gives each one $100 "gate-money." If an inmate is prudent in his prison job selection, in his behavior (by not losing his job and by not earning a disciplinary transfer), and in his commissary and illegal spending, he may have thousands of dollars saved by the time he is released. There are, however, few prudent ones among them, according to inmates and staffers alike.

Although they're free and heading back to their home turf, they're still uneducated (or undereducated), unemployed (or underemployed) and without positive family ties. They must fend for themselves, perhaps for the first time in 10 or 15 years.

Leaving prison makes inmates nervous. "Parole jitters," convict Slim called it.

It gets 'em all. Yeah. The ones who yells the loudest about getting out are always the ones who don't wanna leave. Ya know Crazy. That mother-fucker went up to Lt. Washburn—I don't like that motherfucker—and got right up into his face and called him a "White Woman." Can you see that, Mark, calling Washburn a "White Woman." Washburn didn't do nothing though. He knew Crazy was getting out soon and he knew what

Crazy as up to. Man, Crazy wanted to get charged with some bullshit so he didn't have to leave. Some dudes, they have a tough time out there. Not me, though.

Lompoc's inmates have good reason to be nervous about going to the street. Most walked away from prisons many times before, and most didn't stay on the street for long.

FREEDOM ISN'T PAINLESS

We are constrained by a sense of justice: when many are unemployed, it seems unfair to give criminals or would-be criminals priority access to jobs [Wilson, 1985: 247].

The streets aren't paved with gold for former convicts like Burrell, Frenchie, Slim, Fat-Boy, Crazy or any of my other convict acquaintances who left USP-Lompoc during my research (see Irwin, 1970: 86-148 for state inmates' views of readjustment and reemployment). Twenty years ago, Glaser's (1969: 225; also see Beck, 1981) federal inmates said they needed "no more than $25 'to get by with' during their first month out of prison." Today, federal inmates say they need a lot of money. Convict Willie had been in and out of maximum-security prisons since the late 1960s before coming to USP-Lompoc about three years before I got there. Willie says,

A guy needs $6,000 to $10,000 when he's paroled, for clothes, a car and an apartment. After three years in here I saved about $1,500 working [at an institution job] paying $.38 an hour. Other guys working at better jobs out back can save maybe $2,000 to $3,000 in about five years. If you parole and don't have enough money in your pocket, you're in trouble before you get to the corner. I know, maybe, a hundred guys here alone who were paroled, violated, and now they're back.

Willie estimated that among the several hundred inmates he knows at Lompoc, 35% to 45% don't want to leave the penitentiary. He said, "They have a lot of time in state and federal prisons. Now they don't want to live on the street. A lot of them don't know how to live on the street. . . . Some of them never knew how, that's how come they're in here."

The last time inmate Frankie was on the street, he had finished doing a long stint in San Quentin, Folsom, and several other California prisons.

I had a good job in Oakland, cooking in a nice place. I was doing all right. I had an apartment, and I had an old lady. It was OK. After a few years of that shit, though, man, I just got bored. I started hanging around with some guys, and we pulled a job. Yeah, I just got bored I guess. I needed some excitement.

At the end of 1985, Slim was near the end of his federal sentence for selling stolen government checks to an undercover Treasury agent. One morning we talked about his upcoming parole (see Glaser, 1969: 231-238).

"Slim, what are you going to do when you get out of here?" I asked. He laughed, and said: "I going back to Vegas. I met a guy in the Vegas county jail who told me I had a job whenever I wanted one. He worked for the Gambino family. Ever hear of them, Mark? Shit. [He laughed.] I worked for them before. It's good money, if you got the stomach for it." "Oh, yeah," I said, "doing what?" "Whatever they wanted," he replied smugly.

"Slim," I said, "you're going to end up right back in this joint, if you don't stop that gangster stuff." That remark annoyed him. He leaned back in his chair, lit a Camel, took off his sunglasses, and glared at me.

Now what the fuck do you expect me to do, Mark, teach college? The only things you know you learned sitting on your ass, reading them faggot books of yours. I been in these joints all my life. Who's going to hire me? I'm a convict, remember. I got a choice: sweep floors for $3 an hour, or take contract hits for $25,000 each. What would you do, if you were me? I ain't working for $3 an hour. I'm a gangster. I like being a gangster. I got BMWs, clothes, women, and good times. Do you have a BMW? You know, Mark, I'm real good at what I do. When I kill somebody, I don't leave no evidence. And in America, they need evidence to put you in prison, hard evidence. America is a great place. I love America. I love America.

Slim said that he had two women; one was a common-law wife with whom, he said, he had a 12-year-old daughter, and his other "wife" was a businesswoman in Nevada. Neither one of these women would make his street life easier.

Shit, I don't know where I'll go. I think I'll go back to L.A. for a while, take it easy, ya know, and let the ol' lady keep working. Somebody's gotta work. It takes money to raise up these kids today. Marriage is hard, ya know. They always wanting shit from ya. My ol' lady in L.A. don't like me fucking around with drugs. She says it makes her nervous, and she don't want me bring that shit in the house, around the kid. Shit. Mark, when I was a kid, my mother used to yell at me for dealing dope, then she started using that shit, and liking it. Shit. She'd come to me for her joints. She liked the money I made, too. She got used to that, alright.

I called Slim's Los Angeles "wife," a few weeks after his release, trying to track him down. His wife said: "He came down here after he got out, but then he took off. I think he's in Vegas. But I'm not sure where he is."

When Cowboy was released from San Quentin, after serving ten years, he said,

The only person I knew that was left on the street was my cocaine dealer. Before going to Quentin, I had a $1,000-a-day coke habit. I kicked it in Quentin, and I started using again when I got to the street. Before I knew it, I was doing it again. I needed money, and there's only one place to get it, the bank. I've been out 72 days in the last 11 years and now I've got 25 more [years] to go.

Maintaining family ties during imprisonment, to ensure that an inmate has a family available to him on his release from prison isn't an easy solution to keeping a former convict out of trouble (see Canon, 1988c). In Glaser's study (1969: 242), he found that federal inmates in his study count on family ties to their parents, brothers, sisters, among others, at the time of their release, but that this is "largely a matter of expediency" (p. 245; see Fishman, 1986; also see Fishman and Alissi, 1975; Fleisher, 1981, 1982, 1985a; Hower, 1978; Holt and Miller, 1972; Morris, 1965; Schafer, 1978; Schwartz and Weintraub, 1974; Weintraub, 1976; Zemans and Cavan, 1958).

"Men whose first residence is with their wives," wrote Glaser (p. 249), "have the fewest failures, and those living alone have the most." But Fishman (1986: 53) found, in her ethnographic study among medium-security prisoners, that "wives do not appear to have much influence on whether or not their paroled husbands participate in criminal behavior, get rearrested, and returned to jail."

My research from 1979 to 1985 among maximum-security convicts and their families at the Washington State Penitentiary shows that an inmate's parents, friends, or wife are at worst negative influences on him at release and at best neutral influences on his post-release behavior (see Glaser, pp. 249-253). In my participation in inmates' family lives and in interviews with inmates and their wives, I found that wives, parents, and friends had often contributed to an inmate's criminal behavior before he went to prison, by encouraging it and by getting involved it themselves. Some wives, in fact, particularly those who were prostitutes and drug dealers on the street, perpetuated their husbands' in-prison criminal activity by smuggling drugs to them. Post-release street life for convicts whose criminal record was long and strong enough to land them in a maximum-security joint is never easy and often simply terrible, according to my inmate sources. Common problems include alcoholism, drug abuse, wife beating, and the ability to pick up their criminal careers and the high personal safety risks that that entails.

At USP-Lompoc I was involved in processing inmates' requests to add visitors, such as girlfriends or wives, to their visiting lists. "NCIC (National Crime Information Computer) checks" often reported that potential female visitors had "rap sheets" (criminal records), which were almost as long as their boyfriend's or husband's.

Convict John-John said that his previous experiences with postprison family life have been consistently difficult. He's been released from prison before, and he isn't anticipating a warm experience the next time, either.

> The street is tough. Your family isn't interested in hearing your stories about Lompoc, but that's all you got to offer them. This is only place I been for the last 7 years. What else do I got to talk about. They don't want to hear nothing about prison; they hate the idea that you were even in prison. Shit, what else do you got to talk about after 5, 6 years in here. There's guys been in here for 10, 15 years. This is your whole world. Your family thinks you just get out of the joint, get a job and start where you left off. But that ain't the way it is. When you don't run right out and get that great job and start looking middle class, they get on your case. They pick at you: "Get a job," or "Why you sitting around the house all day?" You get tired of that shit, and you start hanging around the bars with your old buddies. Or you may run into a guy you knew from Lompoc while you're riding a bus or just walking down the street. Then you start to feel good again, you know. Somebody understands you. He knows what you're going through. You talk about the cell block and who was doing what. Then, before you know it, you talk about money and start planning a job . . . and you're back inside.

Comments like these about doing time and post-release street life aren't unique to convicts at USP-Lompoc. I've listened to similar remarks from young inmates, too. In Fort Lauderdale's modern Broward County Jail, over New Year's weekend 1988, felony inmates told me they didn't mind doing time there. "Food's good, it's clean and the staff are pretty nice. I like it in here," said one detainee.

Another detainee, whom I interviewed over four days, said: "This place saved my life. I was on coke and in trouble. If they hadn't pulled me in off the street, I woulda done something dumb and got my ass killed, man. In here, man, they helped me kick it and get my life together again. I was in a treatment program; I've gained weight. I feel good, now."

In February 1988, in the fifty-year-old Fresno County Jail, I interviewed inmates housed in the "serious-felony tank," a high-security living area for detainees charged with serious felonies such as murder. I talked to Don, a young Hispanic man about twenty-four years old, who had bright sparkling eyes, about going to jail and then to prison.

Don: "You worked for the feds, huh? No, shit. I got a friend who did some time with the feds, man, out there in the desert. You know where it is?"
I replied: "That's Boron."
Don: "Yeah that's right, that's it. He loved it out there, man. Yeah. He said there wasn't no shanks . . . no violence . . . no killings . . . nothing man, everybody left him alone. I can't wait to get to the feds."

As he talked about getting into the Federal Prison System, his face beamed with excitement and a broad smile covered his face.

THE STREET'S TOUGH

Not only society but also governmental leaders need to remember the character of those who come to the doors and gates of America's prisons . . . they are the poor, the stupid, the inept, the flotsam and jetsam of society. Fifteen percent are illiterate; 90% are school dropouts; 65% come from broken homes; 40% had no sustained work experience prior to their incarceration; 20% are mentally retarded. . . . they stumble from one mud puddle of life to another [George Beto, director of the Texas Department of Corrections, 1962-1972, as quoted by Jackson, 1984: 218].

Prison is a relief from the burdens of street life. Inmate Dannie Martin, USP-Lompoc's inmate author, wrote in the *San Francisco Chronicle* (October 18, 1987) that

many criminals, drug addicts and alcoholics outside the prison can't deal with their lives or their habits. Their waking hours become a foggy maze of pain and lawless destruction, blended with intermittent moments of peace and gratification. They are forever tortured by the knowledge that the release they seek will only bind them more securely in the cage they build for themselves.

One day they are shoved into a real cage, and the iron doors slam shut behind them. The most common look in their eyes at the moment the last door cranks firmly shut is a strange mixture of resignation and relief. Suddenly they are able to handle their habits and to get a grip on their lives. The choice isn't theirs anymore.

[Prison] restores order and certainty in a person's life. Meals are served according to a rigid schedule, laundry exchanged at definite times; sick call, mail call and visits are all at fixed hours on designated days.

We can't see out the windows . . . but we see the future stretched before us in a rigid, orderly fashion. From lives of chaos, uncertainty and danger, we are thrust into order, security and boredom.

When our routines are disrupted, chaos is once again among us. The future seems fragmented, uncertain.

Freedom for former convicts means freedom to be out of work, freedom to be out of money, freedom to be without clean clothes, freedom to be without an apartment, and freedom to resume an alcohol or drug dependency, or both.

A senior clinical psychologist at USP-Lompoc estimates that 75% of Lompoc's convicts are psychopaths for whom life is comfortable in a tightly run institution (see Hofer, 1987). Prison for psychopaths, he said, is a psychologically comfortable place to live, because the factors which contribute to their violence (drugs, strains on personal responsibility, and interpersonal conflict) are tightly controlled. And, here, too, the persistent socioeconomic pressures of street life are absent.

When these inmates are released from a secure, custodial grasp, they commit or participate in the commission of violent crime. Their need to return to a comfortable penitentiary environment, free of street pressures, social problems, and life's persistent ambiguities, is acted out in symbolic behavior when they commit crimes.

On the street, it's too easy to get into trouble: There are banks to rob to get cash to buy a day's supply of heroin or coke; there are old ladies to assault, at knife point, to get a few bucks to buy cheap wine; and there are teenage girls to rape and dismember (see Jennison, 1986: 64; Elder, 1985; Hagan and Palloni, 1988: 98; Petersilia, 1980). When that happens, each criminal is given his own "ticket home." Then, after years in prison, they're released again. Back to street life, back to poverty, back to crime, back to prison. So the cycle continues for high-risk offenders, but at whose expense?

HUMANE PRISONS

Prison life at USP-Lompoc is an example of warehousing violence as well as it can be done. Lompoc's financial, correctional, and industrial success lies in its personnel, not in its high-cost, modern correctional hardware. Lompoc was built in the 1940s, and it isn't an example of a "new generation" ultramodern prison. Only one cellblock had electronic locking devices when I began my research. But obviously that didn't make a difference, since there weren't any escapes, and since the few incidents of serious violence that occurred during my research couldn't have been prevented by even modern correctional technology. At Lompoc, cost efficiency was achieved with careful planning and with competent prison administration and management.

Maximum-security penitentiaries are often highly violent places, but Lompoc isn't. There have been very few inmate killings in Lompoc's history; no staffers have been killed, and very few have been seriously injured; and there have been no escapes. There has never been a riot or a "total-institution lock-down," during which all inmates are locked in their cells around the clock until staff have regained control. Convicts have never burned their cellblocks in protest of bad food, or against crowded and filthy living conditions. Neither prison gangs nor prison branches of street gangs rule daily inmate life at Lompoc; there has never been a "gang war."

Further, there are no "hard-line guards" who abuse convicts; there are no back room beatings with rubber hoses or fists. There is neither a "hole" nor a "strip-cell" where disruptive convicts are sequestered in the dark, month after month, sleeping naked on a cold, concrete floor. None of the stereotyped conditions of a major, maximum-security prison, filled with violent, dangerous men, are in evidence at Lompoc.

Instead, each inmate's private cell is clean and warm. Good quality food is available in such quantities that inmates worry about their waistlines. Inmates have easy access to medical and dental care. Staffers are polite and responsive to inmates' needs. Gainful employment, vocational training, and adult education are available to inmates (if they don't violate the rules).

USP-Lompoc is a maximum-security penitentiary, and has its share of fights, stabbings, and assaults. The unexpected finding of my research is that Lompoc's rate of serious violence, including fights and assaults with and without weapons and homicide, was the lowest among penitentiaries in the Federal Prison System (see Table 1.1).

At Lompoc, social conditions usually found in prisons such as overcrowding and the predominance of predatory gangs, idleness, and sexual aggression were not tolerated; this penitentiary is neither over-crowded nor packed with idle inmates, or street or prison gang members. Manifestations of racial prejudice among inmates were also discouraged. Lompoc's administration, management, and cellblock supervisory staffers were intolerant of even minor instances of physical or verbal sexual "come-ons" or open aggression toward homosexuals. Sexually motivated assaults were virtually absent; there weren't any homosexual rapes or homocides during my research. Even so, keeping peace among violent criminals is not an easy task.

WAGES AND SOCIAL CONTROL

To put people behind walls and bars and do little or nothing to change them is to win a battle but lose a war. It is wrong. It is expensive. It is stupid [Chief Justice Warren E. Burger, as quoted in Funke, 1986: 23].

TABLE 1.1
Comparative Assault Rates for United States Penitentiaries, 1985.
(Per 100 Inmates Per Year)

U.S. Penitentiary Inmate Population	Inmate-on-Inmate					Inmate-on-Staff					Combined Year-End Rate
	Armed Rate	Armed (n)	Unarmed Rate	Unarmed (n)	Yearly Rate	Armed Rate	Armed (n)	Unarmed Rate	Unarmed (n)	Yearly Rate	
USP-Lompoc (n) = 1,208	.66	(8)	.41	(5)	1.07	.17	(2)	.25	(3)	.42	1.49
USP-Leavenworth (n = 1,073)	.75	(8)	.37	(4)	1.12	0	(0)	.47	(5)	.47	1.59
USP-Marion (n = 345)	.87	(3)	1.16	(4)	2.03	.29	(1)	.29	(1)	.58	2.61
USP-Terre Haute (n = 1,104)	1.63	(18)	.45	(5)	2.08	.09	(1)	.54	(6)	.63	2.71
USP-Lewisburg (n = 1,171)	1.28	(15)	.43	(5)	1.71	.34	(4)	1.02	(12)	1.36	3.07
USP Yearly Rate	1.06	(52)	.47	(23)	1.53	.16	(8)	.55	(27)	.71	2.24

SOURCE: Correctional Services Report, July 1986.
NOTE: The rate of serious assault for the Federal Prison System in 1985 was 1.1 per 100 inmates.

My ethnographic evaluation of Lompoc's social control suggests that Lompoc isn't very violent because the basis of social control is Unicor, formerly called Federal Prison Industries, which is strengthened by a swift, effective discipline system and intensive, face-to-face management. My long-term, on-the-job evaluation shows that when a warden and his staff accept the responsibility of maintaining order among potentially violent prisoners as their personal mission, daily life in a maximum-security prison doesn't have to be "painful" for inmates, life threatening for staff, or grossly expensive for taxpayers.

Unicor was established by Congress in 1934 and is a U.S. government-owned, profit-making corporation operating within the federal prison system. At the Lompoc penitentiary, Unicor operated numerous factories and employed over 700 inmates in 1986, or about 60% of Lompoc's inmate population. Most of the remaining 500 inmates are employed in "institution jobs," as they're called by staffers. These inmates work in the kitchen, preparing about 3,500 meals daily, or they work in the dining hall, cleaning up after meals. Others work in mechanical services, or on a painting, plumbing, or electrical-repair crew. Still other inmates work as orderlies, sweeping, mopping, and polishing every floor in the prison; washing windows; and wiping bars.

The success of this maximum-security factory-town relies on strong but passive social control. USP-Lompoc's convicts are Unicor or institution employees and also violent men serving long sentences. To keep Unicor factories humming and to ensure smooth daily operations in the rest of the institution, a firm but unobstrusive system of social control operates to keep peace in this "factory with a fence," as Chief Justice Burger called factories within prisons. Without rapid, effective means of maintaining convict discipline and reliable day-to-day social control, Unicor factories would grind to a halt.

In this factory-prison where every inmate works, they all have something to lose by breaking the rules, even "lifers" (see Crouch, 1980). Inmates and staffers alike have a stake in avoiding actual violence, and it is the inmates themselves, whose capacity for violence is unquestionable, who work hard at keeping violence down to a minimum.

Don't misunderstand this. I don't mean to imply that these convicts aren't dangerous. They are very dangerous. An inmate's reputation for violence is often an important part of his self-esteem (see Bowker, 1980). But in a well-managed industrial-prison, an inmate doesn't have to be violent, unless he chooses to be. A convict who makes this choice pays a high price for losing self-control, and he pays immediately: he relinquishes his income; he disrupts his regular daily lifestyle; he loses what measure of freedom he might have gained as a result of good behavior; he runs the risk of being transferred to a penitentiary where the climate is less desirable than Lompoc's year-round southern California sunshine (see Megargee, 1977); and he loses "good time"—time awarded to each inmate by policy, which can reduce his time served (see Schafer, 1982). The casual and rather pleasant ambiance of this factory-town suddenly becomes "penitentiary-cold" for a convict who chooses violence.

Day-to-day life for inmates in this industrial-penitentiary is, of course, different from street life. At Lompoc, an uneducated criminal who was unemployed or unemployable on the street must get a job. He earns a steady income, and he can have a decent lifestyle. USP-Lompoc is less violent than their former urban neighborhoods, according to many inmates (see Jacobs, 1976: 79), and, they add, Lompoc is less violent than other maximum-security prisons where most of them have already done time.

The material and nonmaterial rewards and comforts that are available to inmates in this industrial-penitentiary is the driving force of social control. Earning a reliable income, having a decent personal lifestyle, and enjoying the social freedom that comes in a peaceful prison community are the valued results of conforming to prison rules.

PEACE AND PROFITS

There is really no such thing as a "good" prison, but there is now momentum in the direction of more enlightened prisons—momentum to make them "factories with fences" [Chief Justice Warren E. Burger].

A low rate of serious inmate violence and smooth daily operations have permitted Unicor to develop at USP-Lompoc and in the Federal Prison System. At Lompoc, Unicor operates a business office, a warehouse, a quality control office, and four light industries, whose customers for products of the print, the electrical cable, the sign, and the custom furniture factories include the General Services Administration, United States courts, the Department of Justice, the Federal Bureau of Prisons, the Defense Department, the United States Forest Service, the National Park Service, the Bureau of Land Management, and the Bureau of Indian Affairs.

In 1984, Unicor employed 42.7% (485) of USP-Lompoc inmates, and 22.9% (100) of inmates at the Federal Prison Camp (FPC), also at Lompoc (Federal Bureau of Prisons, USP-Lompoc 1984 Anniversary Celebration). In 1985, Unicor at USP-Lompoc and FPC-Lompoc had combined operational earnings in excess of $40,000,000 (USP-Lompoc Freeway, January 15, 1986). Each of Lompoc's inmates produced a profit of over $30,000 at his Unicor job in 1985.

The FY '86 annual institution budget for the FPS Lompoc installation (the United States Penitentiary and the Federal Prison Camp) was $15,502,000 (USP-Lompoc Internal Memorandum, January 10, 1986), or a yearly operating cost of about $9,119 per inmate, or $24.98 a day. The FY '87 annual institution budget was $15,340,000, or a yearly operating cost of about $11,808 per inmate, or $32.35 a day. Daily per-inmate care, excluding the cost of staff salaries and overhead was $3.19: $2.31 for food; $.35 for daily medical and dental care; and $.53 for everything else (United States Penitentiary, Lompoc, CA 1987: 10). Even on $3.19 a day, there were infrequent complaints from inmates about the food or the medical and dental care.

In California state prisons such as Soledad, the 1986 per-inmate cost averaged $14,250. The California Men's Colony, a medium-security facility housing over 7,000 inmates, spent 10% to 15% less than the 1986 California Department of Corrections' average, and was recognized by DiIulio (1987) as an example of successful correctional management. From this example, and that of USP-Lompoc, the apparent cost of running a major, medium-to-maximum security prison well is about $12,000/inmate/year in 1987 dollars. The trick, of course, is running them well.

SO NOW WHAT?

Slim, Magic, Eddie, and other self-proclaimed gangsters at Lompoc have said that maximum-security penitentiaries haven't rehabilitated, punished, or reformed them. I believe them. Crime has paid them dividends. They said they've enjoyed the excitement and the power of crime; they've made money in the gangster world; and they don't mind doing time. They also say that prison "rehabilitative" programs and group therapy are worthless (see Irwin, 1970, 1980; Schmalleger, 1979: 55). Magic:

> All the hoops you jump through are just bullshit. A man will only change if he wants to change. I'm happy. And I don't give a fuck if you or anybody else don't like what I do in here or on the street. Fuck 'em if they don't like it. What are they going to do, Mark, put me in prison! That might stop you, but it don't stop me from anything.

At age 16, convict Lou served six years in a state penitentiary. Now at 29, he thinks that he's "invincible":

> Beating the system is the best game in town. Middle-class Americans will never understand it. You know, I feel "extracultural." I live on the same

planet you do. We speak the same language, but that's where our similarity ends. That's right, I live outside this culture. This is your culture. This is your prison. You have to live with all the fucking rules in this society. I don't. You have to obey the rules, Mark. That's how you live. But I don't have to obey anybody's fucking rules. The worst that can happen to me is that they put me back in prison. And who gives a fuck! When they do that, you got to pay for me. I win. If this is all this society can do to me, then I'm gonna do whatever I want to do. How you going to stop me? I'm invincible.

As the Federal Parole Commission was hearing cases in September 1985 at USP-Lompoc, three inmates were sitting around, waiting to be heard. They were smoking cigarettes and laughing, but they looked anxious. I was standing among them, laughing at their stories and listening to their talk. The conversation was about bank robbery, a topic they all discussed from personal experiences.

Smiley, one of three inmates, was a handsome man in his early forties, with short greying hair cut close to his head. Smiley had sat before the board on many other occasions, trying to convince them of his rehabilitation. On the street, however, Smiley was a heroin addict and notorious bank robber. Smiley was doing a sentence for 29 bank robberies, though, "they [FBI] think he pulled about 50 bank robberies," said a parole commissioner.

Shorty, who was sitting next to Smiley, said: "I hear the FBI won't bother looking for ya if you do one or two jobs. There are too many guys who've done 20 to fuck with the others."

Smiley: "Yeah, you can do six, seven, eight jobs, before they can even get a good picture on you. The bank cameras suck."

Shorty: "I did almost ten when they got me. Next time, I'll use a disguise."

I heard Smiley's parole hearing. He sat politely, and said, "I've been in drug rehabilitation and got my problem under control." A parole commissioner asked Smiley: "You needed the money from the bank robberies for heroin?" Smiley: "Yeah, but now I've got that licked." During his years in Lompoc, Smiley had picked up a few minor infractions and several more serious ones for alcohol use. But otherwise, Smiley had been a "good inmate." The parole commissioners decided that Smiley wasn't as "rehabilitated" as Smiley claimed, so they told Smiley that he'd have to stay at Lompoc a while longer.

The talk of Lou, Slim, Willie, Magic, and others doesn't indicate a keen interest in becoming vested members of the American middle class. I didn't know one inmate at USP-Lompoc who didn't enjoy thinking of himself as a gangster, a tough guy, a rogue, a free-wheeler, a man who lives outside the normal set of controls by which the middle class must live. And, since these men live in a familiar inmate culture of their own creation, it's rather short sighted to think of prison either as rehabilitation, as a deterrent, as punishment, or as an object lesson in morality, at least for high-risk criminals.

Among offenders like those, whom do we release? Goodstein's (1979: 265, 267) study of the relationship between prison adjustment and post-release success found that there is

> no credence to the widely held assumption that poor prison adjustment leads to difficulties after release. On the contrary, they indicate that the inmates who adjusted most successfully to a prison environment actually encountered the most difficulty making the transition from institutional life to freedom. . . . It appears that the prison . . . does not prepare inmates for a successful transition to freedom through its routine administration of rewards and punishments. It is ironic that institutionalized inmates, who accepted the basic structure of the prison, who were well adjusted to the routine, and who held more desirable prison jobs . . . had [the] most difficulty adjusting to the outside world.

Irwin and Austin (1987: 13) allege that convicts who aren't management problems also aren't as dangerous as the public thinks they are: "While imprisoned, most inmates do not commit crimes or become management problems. More than 80 percent of inmates released from prison have no serious disciplinary record while imprisoned."

This isn't the safest or surest way of assessing or predicting the dangerousness of a criminal (see Blumstein and Cohen, 1987, and Greenwood and Turner, 1987). One of my closest convict acquaintances committed two minor offenses (one for refusing to work and another for insolence to a staffer) in 36 months at Lompoc, but his criminal career shows more than 20 years of violence on the street, including street gang violence and drug-related killings.

The problem of predicting violence is far more complicated than is suggested by Irwin and Austin's glance at in-prison offense rates. Wilson and Herrnstein (1985: 208) wrote that

> crimes may be committed by people with other sorts of deviance than psychopathy, or by utterly average people, if the circumstances push the rewards for it high enough. . . . For someone addicted to drugs, the rewards of more drugs may swamp the rewards for noncrime. . . . Uncommonly strong or bizarre sexual urges may cause sex crimes by people who are otherwise normal. . . . The practical . . . difference between someone who breaks the law because of provocative circumstances and someone who does so because of deviance is not in the behavior itself, but in its predictive implications. . . . Age, sex, physique, a history of academic or socioeconomic success or failure, impulsiveness, fearfulness, cruelty,

momentary need, and longstanding habits and values are among the factors that may distinguish the potential offender from his victim. The offender offends . . . because of enduring personal characteristics, some of whose traces can be found in his behavior from early childhood.

When the gates of our prisons slide open, we must *know,* not guess at, which criminals are highly likely to commit violent crimes over and over again. We must be careful in releasing inmates who are already in prison for committing violent crimes on the street. We must balance an offender's freedom, the suffering of potential victims, and society's needs for safety (Megargee, 1976: 15-16). I wouldn't want to be personally responsible for releasing high-risk violent criminals from prison just because they didn't kill anybody while in prison, or because it's cheaper not to keep them behind high walls or razor-wire fences. Who will be accountable for the "mistakes" (killings, rapes, armed robberies) that are made?

The violence of high-risk offenders is a product of the poverty-ridden slums they called home, of their abusive parents, of their alcohol and narcotics addictions, of their street-gang violence, and of the streets that took the place of parents who abandoned them (see Kotlowitz, 1987). Those conditions that have been breeding violence in America aren't likely to change soon. In the meantime, industrial prisons can solve at least a small part of the crime problem by housing high-risk criminals.

In a penitentiary such as USP-Lompoc, staffers and inmates are more or less safe and satisfied. Criminals who have long proved themselves to be violent men generally live out their lives in a relatively peaceful environment. As ironic as it might sound, putting criminals in humane, industrial prisons like USP-Lompoc, for very long terms, gives them a chance to live a decent life, and it saves others from the pain and anguish of being their prey.

2

USP-LOMPOC

THE FEDERAL PRISON SYSTEM

The Federal Bureau of Prisons operates a network of 46 Federal Prison Camps (FPC), Federal Correctional Institutions (FCI), United States Penitentiaries (USP), Metropolitan Correctional Centers (MCC), an Alien Detention Center (ADC), administrative facilities, and supporting facilities that include staff training centers and a medical facility (see Hershberger, 1979, and Potter, 1976, for brief histories of the Federal Prison System).

> The Correctional Philosophy of the Federal Prison System stresses a balanced combination of deterrence, incapacitation, rehabilitation and retribution. . . . The mission is to protect society, to carry out judgments imposed by the courts, to provide a safe and humane environment for those committed to our custody, and to increase the number of inmates who return to the community as law-abiding citizens by providing them with opportunities to change their behavior [Federal Bureau of Prisons, 1985 Correctional Techniques Training Manual, Federal Law Enforcement Training Center].

As America's corrections agency, the Bureau has complex social depth and wide geographic dimensions. Its central offices are in Washington, D.C., and there are five Bureau regions in the country, each with a central administrative office: Northeast—Philadelphia, Pennsylvania; North Central, Kansas City, Missouri; Southeast—Atlanta, Georgia; South Central—Dallas, Texas; and Western Region—Burlingame, California.

Federal prisons are classified into six security levels, ranging from minimum security (Level I) to maximum security (Levels V and VI). Federal Prison Camps are Level I; Federal Correctional Institutions are either Level II, III, or IV; and United States Penitentiaries are Level V or VI.

The overall physical layout and architecture of a federal prison indicates the level of danger posed by its inmates. Federal prison camps, for example, house nonviolent offenders, often white-collar criminals, and, commonly today, men who were involved in drug distribution.

Camps don't require perimeter fencing or manned guard towers, and there are no armed patrol vehicles circling the perimeter. (See DeCordoba, 1987, for a light, succinct discussion of inmates' view of life in a federal prison camp.)

Federal correctional institutions are more security conscious, and are equipped with perimeter fences, guard towers, and secure housing facilities. Federal correctional institutions house offenders, usually eighteen to twenty-six years old, whose present offenses, histories of crime, and other factors don't warrant incarceration in a security level V or VI federal penitentiary. At lower security level FCIs, such as Level II, inmates aren't evaluated as high escape risks and aren't highly likely to commit in-prison violence. As the security level of an FCI increases, so do the inmates' formally evaluated potentials for violence and escape.

United States Penitentiaries require double or triple fences with attached detection devices or a wall, 24-hour manned guard towers, external perimeter patrol, secure housing units, and a high staff-to-inmate ratio. Penitentiary convicts, predominantly, are twenty-six years and older, have violent criminal records, are considered to be high escape risks, and have an evaluated potential to commit in-prison violence.

The largest federal prison installation in the United States is located at Lompoc, California, some 300 miles north of Los Angeles in northern Santa Barbara County. Here, about 50 miles from the California ranch of President Ronald Reagan, is a federal penitentiary and a federal prison camp, a minimum-security facility housing approximately 500 short-term offenders. Both facilities are about five miles north of downtown Lompoc, California, a community of approximately 30,000 residents.

In 1959, the U.S. Army Disciplinary Barracks at Lompoc became the property of the Federal Bureau of Prisons and was renamed a Federal Correctional Institution. Staff facilities, which were located about 300 yards southeast of the Army's prison, became a federal prison camp. In July 1981, the FCI at Lompoc was recommissioned as a U.S. Penitentiary, and became the sixth federal penitentiary. USP-Lompoc, USP-Leavenworth (Kansas), USP-Lewisburg (Pennsylvania), and USP-Atlanta are Level V penitentiaries; USP-Terre Haute (Indiana) is the only Level IV penitentiary; and USP-Marion (Illinois) is the only Level VI penitentiary.

The United States Penitentiaries at Lompoc, Leavenworth, Lewisburg, and Terre Haute are the Bureau's "mainline" penitentiaries, or "joints," housing "mainline convicts"; Table 2.1 shows inmate population levels at these penitentiaries. Mainline inmates don't require

TABLE 2.1
Average Daily Inmate Populations in United States Penitentiaries, 1985-86

| | Penitentiary Population | |
	1985	1986
Security Level IV		
USP-Terre Haute	1,104	1,100
Security Level V		
USP-Lompoc	1,208	1,167
USP-Lewisburg	1,171	1,180
USP-Leavenworth	1,073	1,117

SOURCE: Federal Bureau of Prisons, Statistical Report

special custodial treatment. They freely move in and out of their cells periodically during the day and night; they have the right to work every day, to attend educational programs, and to pursue vocational training; they enjoy recreational activities, inside and outside their cellblocks; and they have access to prison goods and services located inside and outside their cellblocks. They can also move about the prison during regularly scheduled periods of inmate movement (called "activities movements"). As a group, these inmates are called the "mainline," the "general population," or the "population." They are supervised by staffers called "mainline staff," "line staff," or, sometimes, "lines."

USP-Marion and USP-Atlanta aren't mainline joints. Each institution has a special purpose. According to a USP-Lompoc lieutenant, together these prisons house "killers, escape artists, and fucking pains in the ass." Official bureaucratic language labels them "difficult correctional cases," according to another staffer. USP-Atlanta, until it was destroyed in the Mariel riot, housed approximately 1,100 Cuban detainees.

As America's new Alcatraz (see Ward, 1986: 12), the ultra-secure USP-Marion "houses the nation's most hardened and dangerous criminals," write Olivero and Roberts (1987: 234), who call them "super prisoners" (p. 235). USP-Marion housed 345 super prisoners in 1985 and 335 in 1986 (Federal Bureau of Prisons, Statistical Report, 1986). USP-Marion inmates have earned their reputation. Ward (1986: 12-13) writes:

> During the period February 1980 to June 1983, along with 14 attempted escapes and 10 group disturbances, there were 54 serious inmate-on-inmate assaults, 8 inmates were killed by other prisoners, and there were 28 serious assaults on staff members. In July 1983, an institutionwide search following an assault on an officer turned up 79 homemade knives.

In September an inmate was killed and others were stabbed; two officers were taken hostage in the disciplinary segregation unit . . . one of whom was stabbed; two officers were attacked . . . one of whom was stabbed 12 times; in other incidents an officer was assaulted by an inmate wielding a mopwringer and a chair; another was attacked as he went to the aid of an inmate being assaulted by three other prisoners.

The bureau developed a segregation unit called the "control unit" to try to control the most ardently disruptive convicts at USP-Marion. In the control unit, convicts are locked down. Except for showers and carefully supervised recreation, they are locked in their cells twenty-four hours a day, every day. At USP-Lompoc it wasn't uncommon to find young convicts aspiring to commit violence serious enough to deserve a transfer to USP-Marion's control unit. After a staff-inmate brawl one evening in a USP-Lompoc cell block, one of the young convicts involved said he did it "to make Marion," that is, to bolster his joint reputation.

FEDERAL PRISONS AT LOMPOC

Lompoc (pronounced "Lom-poke" as in cowpoke) is the home of the Air Force's Space Shuttle project and calls itself America's Western Space Port. Lompoc's economy is supported primarily by NASA and Air Force contractors, including Boeing, Lockheed, Martin Marietta, and other companies that employ thousands of local residents at nearby Vandenburg Air Force base. Diatomaceous earth mining in the coastal hills also provides jobs. Local owners of and employees in restaurants, shops, and grocery stores, along with professional service workers and the like, round out the local economy. Lompoc's pleasant weather has also made it a popular retirement area.

Vandenburg Air Force base ("The Base") is Lompoc's prize possession. Few local residents pay much attention to Lompoc's federal prisons. Many Lompoc residents—whom I interviewed informally in grocery stores, in physicians' and dentists' offices, in shops, in restaurants and bars, and in my residential neighborhood—thought that the penitentiary (housing violent offenders and career criminals) was a federal correctional institution (housing nonviolent offenders and less violent criminals). One of the three Lompoc road signs displaying directions to the institution refers to it correctly, "United States Penitentiary." Another sign labels it, "Federal Correctional Facility," and the third one directs travelers to the "Federal Correctional Institution." I didn't meet any townspeople who knew the difference between a federal penitentiary and a federal correctional institution.

Many of them did insist, however, that the prison camp was much too nice for prisoners, "who we support with our tax dollars," as one of my neighbors said.

It isn't surprising that townspeople don't know much about the federal prisons in their backyard (see Canon, 1988a). It is strictly against bureau policy for prison employees to discuss daily prison events with nonemployees. An old-time officer said,

> I don't even tell my ol' lady, 'cause I know she'll tell her big-mouth friends, who'll tell their friends, who'll tell their friends. Then before I can turn around, the warden will call me into his office, and chew my ass royal! Fuck it. I don't say nothing to nobody. Anyway, what's the point; nobody understands what we do.

Warden Robert Christensen's executive assistant, Chuck LaRoe, is authorized to discuss penitentiary and camp events with outsiders. No one else can officially talk about prison business with the public, although I have permission to write this book.

These two federal prisons—one a major joint, the other looking more like a college campus—are tucked away on five square miles of federal land. Expansive commercial vegetable fields and beautifully fragrant fields of flowers (grown for their seed) abut the southern edge of federal land. To the east, west, and north the land is undeveloped and covered by wind-twisted trees, grasses, and low brush.

Lompoc is called the "The Garden Spot" of the FPS, by some employees whose bureau careers have taken them to less desirable locations. A well-traveled line staffer said, "There are federal prisons in a lot of shitty places. They put their prisons in spots where nobody wants to live. But to move up, you got to move out." Staffers say they have moved to southwestern deserts, hot-and-humid southeastern states, and hot-in-the-summer and frigid-in-the-winter heartland states of America to enhance their careers.

Not even convicts complain about Lompoc's climate. Daytime temperatures average 70 degrees. It rains during the winter, but only occasionally. Even though winter days often begin with dense, cold fog rolling over the nearby coastal hills, on most days by 10:00 in the morning the sun is shining brightly, and the day quickly warms. On Christmas Day, 1985, it was 88 degrees in my backyard, as hot air from the Mojave Desert blew across southern California.

The Garden Spot is divided into a west side and an east side by a Santa Barbara County road. On the east side—driving north—is a prison-staff housing area. "The reservation," as staff call it, provides 81 homes and many mobile home spaces for approximately 350 Bureau staffers who wish to live in cost-controlled housing (see Weber, 1988a).

Figure 2.1   Entrance to Club Fed

Fifteen institution employees are required to live there. These include the warden, the two associate wardens, and the captain; two lieutenants; the FPC camp administrator, the Unicor superintendent, and a unit manager; one staffer each from the safety office, the camp farm, food service, the business office; and two medical staffers.

On the west side, FPC-Lompoc (called "The Camp" or "Club Fed") meets the road. Club Fed's inmates are called "campers." No clear indication reveals that this bucolic setting is a federal prison, except for a sign (Figure 2.1). Its few buildings include a gym, a chapel, a visiting area, and two dormitories, which provide inmate quarters and staff offices. Club Fed is easily accessible to anyone who wishes to enter. The camp isn't security conscious. There are no gates, no check points, no bars, no guard towers, no visible security devices. On several occasions, during my research, people traveling past the camp stopped to picnic beneath the mammoth eucalyptus trees bordering its perimeter.

In cold, dramatic contrast to the collegiate environment of Club Fed stands the penitentiary, stark and grey beyond a field cleared of all obstructions, giving correctional officers who are stationed in perimeter guard-towers an unobstructed view (see Weber, 1988b). Figure 2.2 is an aerial photograph of the penitentiary, taken by the FBI in 1983.

Make no mistake: this is a maximum-security federal penitentiary housing experienced criminals. A demographic summary is shown in

Figure 2.2   Aerial Photo of USP-Lompoc

Table 2.2. These offense data apply only to current offenses, and are not necessarily indicative of USP-Lompoc's inmates' prior criminal histories. Diachronic offense data for this inmate population are not available.

After reading these inmates' dossiers ("jackets") and working among them for thousands of hours as a contract penitentiary employee, the absence of prison violence at Lompoc became even more striking to me. Despite decades of living in juvenile training facilities, jails, and warehouse prisons such as San Quentin, Folsom, Attica, New Mexico State, and Florida State, and despite having committed violent offenses including multiple murder, serial murder, contract killing, matricide and patricide, rape, rape and murder, armed robbery, terrorist acts, white slavery, kidnapping and murder, the majority of these violent men have chosen a path of nonviolence at USP-Lompoc.

ORGANIZATIONAL STRUCTURE

USP-Lompoc's executive staff includes Warden Robert Christensen, Associate Warden of Programs (AWP) John Sams, Associate Warden

TABLE 2.2
Inmates in USP-Lompoc by Selected Sociodemographic Characteristics, September 30, 1986

Characteristic	%	(N = 1,197)
Age		
Under 22	0.5	(6)
18 — 25	6.6	(79)
22 — 29	20.5	(245)
30 — 69	78.8	(943)
Over 70	0.3	(3)
(Median age 35.7)		
Race/ethnicity		
White	42.8	(513)
Black	37.7	(451)
Hispanic	14.3	(171)
American Indian	4.3	(51)
Asian	0.9	(11)
Highest grade completed		
12 or above	52.0	(623)
11	11.4	(136)
10	12.4	(148)
9	8.3	(99)
6 — 8	13.2	(158)
1 — 5	2.7	(31)
Marital status		
Single	39.8	(477)
Married	27.6	(331)
Divorced	18.7	(223)
Common law marriage	9.8	(118)
Separated	3.2	(38)
Widowed	0.8	(10)
Age at first arrest		
10 — 13	19.0	(233)
14 — 18	52.5	(629)
19 — 27	24.6	(295)
28 — 53	30.9	(370)
Prior arrests		
No prior arrests	3.2	(38)
1 — 4	18.6	(224)
5 — 10	40.0	(478)
More than 10	38.2	(457)
Drug history*		
Prior drug use		
Alcohol	26.1	(313)
Marijuana	37.1	(445)
Hallucinogens	16.0	(192)

(continued)

TABLE 2.2 Continued

Characteristic	%	(N = 1,197)
Narcotics	29.4	(352)
Barbiturates	16.3	(195)
Psycho-stimulants	14.3	(171)
Other drugs	10.4	(124)
At commitment		
Alcohol	9.5	(114)
Marijuana	10.1	(121)
Hallucinogens	2.0	(24)
Narcotics	15.6	(187)
Barbiturates	2.0	(25)
Psycho-stimulants	4.7	(56)
Other drugs	2.3	(28)
Sentence length		
6 months — 1 year	0.4	(5)
1 year — 2.5 years	0.6	(7)
2.5 years — 5 years	4.6	(55)
5 years — 10 years	19.3	(230)
More than 10 years	75.0	(898)
(Average number of months 253.8)		
Offenses		
Bank robbery	31.2	(373)
Assault during bank robbery	16.0	(191)
Robbery of post office or savings and loan	8.4	(100)
Drug law crimes	5.1	(61)
Kidnapping	3.3	(39)
Firearms	2.2	(26)
Military court martial	2.0	(2)
Assault	2.0	(24)
Larceny-theft	1.0	(2)
Fraud	0.7	(8)
Murder or manslaughter of a U.S. official	0.4	(5)
Explosives	0.4	(5)
Counterfeiting	0.3	(3)
Continuing criminal activity	0.3	(3)
Kidnapping/murder during a bank robbery	0.2	(2)
Burglary	0.1	(1)
Hijacking a commercial plane	0.1	(1)
Transporting false or forged securities	0.1	(1)
Violations of other federal laws	8.2	(98)
District of Columbia Inmates	4.5	(53)
Robbery		(13)
Homicide		(13)
Assault		(7)
Carrying deadly weapon		(5)

(continued)

TABLE 2.2 Continued

Characteristic	%	(N = 1,197)
Burglary		(4)
Rape		(4)
Larceny-theft		(3)
Drug laws		(1)
Other violations		(2)
Crimes committed on a government reservation, the high seas, or government territory, and state inmates transferred to Lompoc	14.4	(173)
Homicide		(90)
Assault		(24)
Rape		(18)
Robbery		(13)
Larceny-theft		(5)
Carrying deadly weapons		(6)
Burglary		(2)
Escape		(2)
Other crimes		(13)

SOURCE: Federal Prison System, Report 80.51.
NOTE: *Bureau data didn't account for simultaneous and multiple addictions as opposed to single or serial addictions.

of Operations (AWO), Gene Gill, and Chief of Correctional Services (CCS) Mel Collins (Figure 2.3). FPC and USP-Lompoc are administratively linked. The camp's executive administrator is never called or referred to as "warden"; he is always called the "camp administrator." In practice, the camp administrator is included in the executive staff, but since he doesn't play a role in penitentiary programs, operations, or social control, I have chosen not to discuss him.

Warden Christensen oversees penitentiary and camp programs, operations, and Unicor businesses. At the camp, he also administers the operation of a dairy with a herd of approximately 100 cattle, a ranch with about 3,000 beef cattle, and a meat-processing plant. Lompoc's ranch, dairy, and meat-processing plant provide milk and meat to federal institutions in the Bureau's western region. The warden also controls the budget and is always involved in personnel issues such as promotion boards, grievance procedures, and union matters. He offers final decisions in all cases of institution-level administrative remedy, and, in so doing, he monitors inmate-staff grievances and picks out problem areas in departmental management and staff-inmate rapport.

Associate Wardens John Sams and Gene Gill oversee the operation of institution programs and operations, except in Unicor, which is

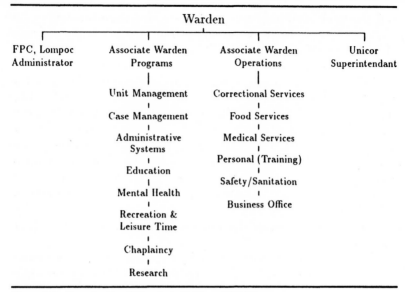

Figure 2.3   Organizational Structure, USP- and FPC-Lompoc

administered by a Unicor superintendent. John Sams supervises the smooth operation of five pairs of inmate living units and their five-unit management teams. This is his primary responsibility. He also oversees the case management office (which processes all inmate "paperwork"); the education, recreation, and leisure-time programs; the mental health department, including the drug and aicohol program; the research office; and the chaplaincy. He is responsible for "Administrative Systems," which handles the admission and orientation of new inmates, inmate transfers into and out of USP-Lompoc, and sentence-related time calculations. He is also responsible for the smooth administration of the FPS-inmate grievance procedure, called the "administrative remedy system."

Each unit management team, called a "team" or a "unit team," manages and supervises a pair of mainline living units (commonly called "cellblocks," "units," and, less often, "blocks"). (See Lansing et al., 1977, and Levinson and Gerard, 1973, for a discussion of the development of unit management.) Unit team members also handle the administrative and managerial needs of inmates who have been separated from the mainline and placed in I-unit. Unit team members provide all services to their own I-unit inmates; they deliver their personal and legal mail, process them through the discipline system, and offer personal counseling. Each team consists of a unit manager, two case managers, two correctional counselors (all with offices located in their cellblocks), a unit secretary (who is located in the administration building's case management office, well away from convicts), and a staff psychologist, who also has a cellblock office.

A unit manager (UM) is accountable for the smooth operation of his two living units, and is accountable to the associate warden for programs. Everything that occurs in his cellblocks, from disruptive inmate behavior to the units' sanitary condition, to sexual threats made between inmates, is his personal responsibility. He plays a significant role in the lives of his units' inmates. Special and personal requests often go through him; an inmate may go to him for an emergency phone call to his wife, for example. He is also the inmates' formal link to the executive staff, and I've heard unit managers give inmates advice about how to raise particular issues with an associate warden. A UM generally conducts Unit Discipline Committee (UDC) sessions, which hear nonviolent disciplinary cases.

A case manager's (CM) responsibilities make him, too, an important person in the lives of inmates. CMs prepare inmates' progress reports, correspondence with the courts, set parole hearing dates with the federal parole commission, and make sure that paperwork is current and complete before inmates' parole hearings. With more than a hundred inmates in eight of nine living units, CMs have to deal with a never-ending pile of paperwork.

For inmates, their most frequent face-to-face link to their unit team is their correctional counselor (CC). While I was at Lompoc there was a correctional officer shortage, and CCs functioned as unit correctional officers while maintaining their administrative and personal counseling responsibilities. CCs counsel inmates, negotiate their transfers to other federal institutions, manage their visiting lists, administer inmate property transfers to and from other prisons, arrange work assignments, and gather work evaluations from inmates' supervisors. They stay in direct and constant contact with unit inmates.

Associate Warden Gene Gill is responsible for the administration and management of the hospital, mechanical services, the commissary and food service, the personnel department (including training), and the safety/sanitation department and correctional services—the penitentiary's largest department, which employs up to 176 men.

Mel Collins (called "captain") is one administrative rung below the associate warden for operations, and is chief of correctional services. The captain sees to the smooth administration and management of the correctional services department (called "custody"), and is a key figure in all (formal and informal) inmate discipline. Custody is the most highly stratified department, with its officers ranked from probationary correctional officers, to correctional officers, to senior officer specialists, to junior and senior correctional supervisors, to chief of correctional services. In the speech of custody staffers, each rank is referred to by its GS level, the federal government's general wage scale. GS-6, probationary correctional officers are "6s," GS-7, senior correctional officers are "7s," and GS-8, senior officer specialists are "8s." Among correctional supervisors, GS-9, junior lieutenants are "9s," and GS-11, senior lieutenants are "11s." The chief of correctional services, a GS-13, is always captain, never "13."

Promotion between levels is competitive. Achieving a GS-7 from a GS-6 is virtually automatic, barring any major blunders or breeches of security; this promotion signals the end of an officer's probationary period. Potentially dangerous mistakes do happen occasionally. One GS-6 spent an eight-hour shift in a perimeter tower from midnight to eight. Tower work can be lonely and dull; reading, writing letters, or watching a portable television is forbidden. "This kid had John Wayne fantasies," said a lieutenant, "so he strapped on a .38, and just waited for a convict to hit the fence." (Tower officers aren't required by policy, as they are in some state prisons, to wear a side-arm.) During the early morning hours, so the story goes, he put on a thigh-length jacket that covered his waist-holster with a loaded .38 revolver tucked away inside. When his eight hours ended, the young officer left the tower and walked into the penitentiary and waited, along with other officers, for his shift to be relieved. But he forgot to take off his revolver before leaving the tower. Walking inside the prison among hundreds of convicts on their way to work, he stepped into the lieutenant's office, brushed his jacket aside with his arm, and exposed his weapon! "I almost shit," said the lieutenant in charge. "That stupid fuck could'a got us killed." He was given an opportunity to resign . . . and he took it.

In spring 1986, the Bureau initiated a new competitive status, a "nonsupervisory" GS-9. These were used only in high-cost-of-living areas such as Lompoc, Chicago, and Miami, in an effort to boost incomes of selected 8s. This increased their salaries, but it didn't enhance their prestige, since a nonsupervisory GS-9 hack isn't a lieutenant; consequently, 8s call these slots and the men in them "super-8s." The emergence of super-8s heightened tension between them and GS-9 lieutenants, since they were both paid the same salary, but "real 9s," as some lieutenants call themselves, have more responsibilities, according to them.

Promotions are made by a "promotion board." I attended a board meeting on December 20, 1985. This particular board chose new 8s, and was called a "GS-8 board" by staffers. The board offers promotion recommendations to Warden Christensen, who makes all final decisions.

GS-6s, GS-7s, and GS-8s are line officers. "Hack," the most commonly used term of reference for line officers, is used by convicts and staffers everywhere in the institution. Next to hack, "cop" is the most common term of reference used by convicts for all correctional officers. New correctional officers, GS-6s, are distinguished by staffers from 7s and 8s as "rookie hacks." Convicts frequently refer to rookie hacks as "fish pigs," "fish cops," or "fish police." But in everyday speech, convicts address line hacks as "boss," correctional supervisors as "lieutenant" or "boss," and the captain as "captain" or "boss."

The day shift at Lompoc is worked by 45 line staff and correctional supervisors (each shift is called a "watch") from 8:00 a.m. to 4:00 p.m., with 40 in the penitentiary (called "inside") and 5 at the camp (called "outside"); 33 work the evening watch, from 4:00 p.m. to midnight, with 29 inside and 4 outside; and 23 work the morning watch, from midnight to 8:00 a.m., with 21 inside and 2 outside. Each day's three, eight-hour watches are crosscut by 20 separate, eight-hour shift designations. Some correspond to the general watch rotation, such as 7:30 a.m. to 4:00 p.m., and others overlap two watch rotations, such as 6:00 a.m. to 2:30 p.m.

Each custody staffer is assigned a job (called a "post"), and a shift designation, with two days off each week; the yearly calendar is divided into four quarterly rosters. A correctional staffer usually spends his forty-hour weeks working four posts each year. All living units, perimeter towers, and common areas inside the penitentiary require custodial supervision twenty-four hours a day, seven days a week. One correctional officer is assigned to each cellblock; when hacks are in short supply, correctional counselors, who almost always came up as hacks, are assigned correctional officer duties.

Separate chains of command operate in programs and operations. Each department head and unit manager in programs, and each department head in operations, reports to his respective AW, who is then accountable to the warden.

CORRECTIONAL CULTURE

USP-Lompoc's organizational mission goes beyond merely warehousing violent men (see Fox, 1982; Jacobs, 1977; Duffee, 1980). The penitentiary has developed a strong correctional (organizational) culture, without jeopardizing or relinquishing security or safety precautions: "[a] pattern of basic assumptions that a given group has invented, discovered or developed in learning to cope with its problems of external adaptation and internal integration . . . to be taught to new members as the correct way to perceive, think, and feel" (Adler and Jelinek, 1986: 81, from Schein, 1984: 3).

USP-Lompoc's organizational culture stresses neutrality in evaluating staff-to-inmate and inmate-to-staff behavior; harmony in daily interactions among community members (staff and inmate); personal control of emotions (for staff and inmates); and public recognition and financial rewards for hard work (among inmates and staff) (see Adler and Jelinek, 1986: 76-81). This positive social "climate" (Toch, 1978), among other factors, has encouraged the emergence of a sense of a penitentiary community, as opposed to a mean-spirited, custodial warehouse.

Warden Christensen has had a personal effect on Lompoc's organizational culture, on its social control system, and on Lompoc's residents, both staff and inmates. I characterize Christensen as authoritarian, but not tyrannical; businesslike, but not stuffy; formal, but not stifled; bound by policy, but not pedantic; amiable, but not gratuitous in affect. He provided social and financial rewards for accomplishments, and was punitive toward rule violators. He was self-confident, free of ambivalence and ambiguity, and I found him to be strikingly free of personal bias. "Diamond" Jim Finley, a unit manager with more than fifteen years in the Bureau, said that "Christensen doesn't have any friends. He has lots of friends outside the institution, but here, everyone is treated the same. That's one reason they call him Chilly Bob—he treats everybody the same and he doesn't play favorites." I asked a senior lieutenant about Christensen's nickname: "He has to make the cold decisions and once he's made a decision, that's it." Staffers didn't call Christensen, Chilly Bob, to his face. They addressed him as "Boss."

Christensen was a highly visible leader. In his daily tours of the penitentiary, he visited staff offices; he walked the main corridor, checking its appearance and joking with hacks as he went; and he regularly visited I-unit, the isolation block. As he walked down each cell-range, he stopped to talk to any convicts who wanted to see him.

Christensen established face-to-face communication as Lompoc's first and primary means of problem solving. Old-time staff and inmates say this used to be unheard of in a maximum-security penitentiary. Joe Bannister, a veteran at FCI and USP-Lompoc, commented on the managerial style of a previous warden:

> I remember [a guy] who walked around here with a big cigar in his mouth and wouldn't talk to anybody. If you wanted to talk to him, he'd tell you to talk to your department head. The only way you could talk to this guy in his office was if he invited you in. In those days, convicts walked on one

side of the corridor and staff walked on the other. We didn't talk to each other unless we had to. If a convict came up to one of us and talked to us, the others thought he was snitching. You know, too, in those days, line staff didn't walk into the lieutenant's office unless they were going to get their asses chewed.

A large measure of respect for Christensen comes from his career path; he began as line hack at USP-McNeil Island, Washington, on July 18, 1966, and then worked his way to the top. From correctional staffers' viewpoints, a penitentiary warden ought to have a background in custody. "He's a no-nonsense custody man," according to Lt. Guy Baker, a senior lieutenant with fifteen years of Bureau experience, including five years at USP-Marion. Being tough, of course, is the most valued characteristic of a penitentiary warden.

In the men's world of a penitentiary, Christensen is the "head man": he is able to command and maintain authority. He has "juice," staffers say, and the power to back it up. Custody and former custody staffers say that "next to Carlson [Director of the Federal Bureau of Prisons], the boss has more juice than anybody in the BOP." Staffers enjoy being close to "real" power. Yet, "he is calm and decisive, and he can make decisions when other people are out of control," said another lieutenant. The boss is also admired for "knowing every word of Bureau policy and knowing how and when to use it," said a senior lieutenant. A unit manager also said that "the boss can recite policy, chapter and verse. He's memorized every word."

When staffers talked about the warden, which they did often at beer parties, Christensen became bigger than life. He took on folkloric qualities: part hero, part clever politician, part social psychologist, part hack, part fellow employee, and always a no-nonsense man in the tough world of penitentiary men.

Most experienced staffers voiced admiration and respect for Christensen, even when they didn't have to. Some staffers, usually program staff, found his management style overbearing; they said that his rule was too absolute, too controlling, too intolerant of change. Many agreed with these descriptions, but said they liked it that way. "That's a good way to run a penitentiary," said Lt. Guy Baker.

Inmates, to be sure, don't like the warden personally, but they respect his openness, his availability, and his tough attitudes. Inmates say they know what to expect from him, and they appreciate his management style: "Once he makes a decision, good or bad, he sticks to it." His emotions don't waffle: "He's the same man every day. Some guys come in here and they're hung over or pissed at their ol' lady, and they fuck us. Christensen don't do that. When he walks in, you know what you're going to get, every day," said convict Fat-Boy.

Warden Christensen believes that open communication with inmates keeps the lid on his penitentiary. John Sams, Gene Gill, Mel Collins, and other administrators and managers follow his lead, and are available to inmates during the noon meal and (if they are in the penitentiary) the evening meal as well.

As the hundreds of convicts pass by for lunch, many stop with problems. I regularly stood with Chilly Bob Christensen to observe his problem-solving style. On one occasion, a black inmate about thirty years old approached, with three other black inmates trailing behind. The point man looked a bit lost, not knowing which of us was the warden. He took a deep breath, blurting out the word, "Warden?" The warden responded, asking how he could help.

The inmate said that he and his companions had been transferred to Lompoc the week before from another federal prison, and they hadn't received all their personal property. The warden asked him his name and his living unit, then called to a midlevel administrator standing nearby; the warden summarized the problem for the staffer, saying "take care of these men." Problem solved.

As they walked away, Grey Feather, the leader of the American Indian brotherhood, the Tribe of Five Feathers, quickly filled the opening in front of the warden. He reached in his pocket and pulled out a crumpled letter that had been typed on a legal-size sheet of white paper and mailed to him from an American Indian acquaintance in Alaska.

Grey Feather explained that he wanted to have an elk shipped to Lompoc, at no cost to the Bureau, for a special ritual dinner for American Indian inmates and their guests. The warden listened carefully and responded by telling the inmate that he understood the importance of this to him and the others, but that Bureau policy doesn't permit meat that hasn't been government inspected to be issued to inmates. Grey Feather squabbled a bit. The warden reiterated the Bureau position, defusing a potentially difficult situation by remaining calm and reciting policy. Eventually, the inmate said that he understood the warden's position and walked away.

Christensen's attitudes have permeated his organization. "You've got to treat these guys like everybody else or you won't be able to work with them. You've got to forget what they've done, but always be aware of what they can do," said John Burland, a correctional counselor whose throat was cut by a Lompoc inmate's razor in 1978, when he was a correctional officer at FCI-Lompoc.

Lieutenant Jeff Bryan, a correctional supervisor with ten years of Bureau experience said it this way:

I don't care why they are here. I don't know why they are here, except the blue book inmates [pictures of especially dangerous convicts are filed in a blue vinyl three-ring binder called the "blue book"], and it's my job to know them. It's like going into a restaurant and having the waiter serve you, being pleasant with him and then leaving a tip. How do you know what he did that morning? You don't. You behave in a friendly way as you expect them to behave toward you. If they give me a reason to be tough, I will be; that's my job. A lot of guys come here just because it's a job; they don't have anything else. I like my job. I try to put it in perspective. Some [co-workers] are assholes. They hate convicts and bust their asses just because they're convicts. Then, too, [staffers] start giving each other shit. I try to get along with everybody, new guys and guys who have been around a long time. It's fun. I like it.

Interpersonal harmony and open communication (between staff and inmates, and among staff) are integrally tied values in USP-Lompoc's organizational culture. Verbal grease lubricates sensitive points of articulation between staff and inmates: "Either we come to work willing to talk to them, or we better be willing to fight them," stressed Christensen at a weekly warden's meeting of departmental managers and administrators. And for Christensen, this is not idle chatter; he ensures open communication between his staffers and inmates.

In September 1987, at a Monday afternoon warden's meeting, he heard that too few unit team members were visiting their inmates, who were isolated and forgotten in I-unit. His stern message to associate wardens, program heads, and unit managers was clear: Unit team members will regularly visit I-unit inmates as he prescribed, or he would take matters into his own hands. The room was very quiet.

Why place a strong value on talking to inmates? The answer is dangerously simple. A commonly used line-staff expression, "If the inmates want the place, they got it," reminds everyone that, anywhere, at any time, there are far more inmates than staff. On my first evening in the penitentiary, I helped supervise inmates in the mess hall during dinner. There were hundreds of convicts, and I wondered where the staff were, so I started counting: There were seven of "us." Those aren't great odds. Harmony, open communication, and rapport instantly took on new meaning.

Staffers and inmates share the pursuit of peace: Staff members work peacefully toward retirement, and inmates are given the chance to work peacefully toward parole. Peacefulness, as a theme in this correctional culture, was recognized at FCI-Lompoc by Moore (1978: 117). She reported that FCI-Lompoc had a reputation for being cleaner, less tense, and less violent than many California state prisons.

Doing "easy time" is important. Convict Slim says: "I just want to do my time and get out. If you fuck up in a federal joint, they'll never let you out." Staff utter similar sentiments. "We do time along with the inmates, and you have to be willing to talk to them," said Jim Finley.

But communication, harmony, and positive rapport are difficult values to build into a penitentiary's organizational culture (where machismo is an important and an opposing value, especially among line staff), and they are monitored constantly (see Toch, 1976: 48). John Sams and Gene Gill said that inmates tell them about staffers who are cold, inaccessible, unhelpful, impatient, and deceptive. When they, or other upper-echelon administrators, hear similar complaints from inmates, they confront the offending staffer with inmates' complaints.

By controlling overcrowding, drug smuggling, and gang activity, Lompoc's organizational culture can openly permit individualism and self-achievement among inmates. This further encourages and rewards open communication, rapport, and harmony with staff. USP-Lompoc operates with this message to inmates: Behave as you wish, but it's in your best interest not to violate the rules of the penitentiary. Every inmate is given an opportunity to contribute to the community, and to maintain his freedom and wage-earning capability. All inmates work, and they measure workplace success by salary grade, by dollar levels in their savings accounts, and by their purchases at the commissary. In getting inmates to the workplace, USP-Lompoc shares with other businesses many techniques for motivating its employees: Increases in pay and bonuses are the most important.

PHYSICAL LAYOUT

The fenced penitentiary occupies about 20 acres and is divided into four areas, oriented on a north-south axis. To the south stands the main administration building (called "up front" by staff) and inmate housing and services (called the "inside"). To the north (in the "rear compound") is the yard on the westside, and Unicor and mechanical services on the eastside (see Figure 2.4).

The penitentiary is surrounded by fifteen-foot-high double anchor fences; at the midpoint of the east and west side, the fences are triple deep. Placed at each corner and at the midpoint of the north and south side are perimeter towers, manned by an armed correctional officer, twenty-four hours a day, seven days a week.

Entering the penitentiary at the "1-tower sallyport," the south-facing main entrance, requires the 1-tower officer to open and close, one at a time, the sliding steel-mesh grills (Figure 2.5). An M-14 semiautomatic rifle and a 12-gauge shotgun stand erect in the tinted, sliding windows; towers also contain .38 revolvers, which are placed carefully next to bullet-proof vests lying on each tower's inside counter.

The 1-tower officer permits visitors and employees to enter and leave

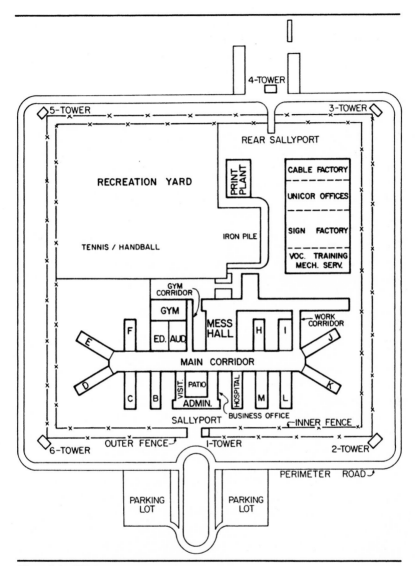

Figure 2.4   USP-Lompoc Institution Map

from behind the barricade of anchor fences. He leans out of the window, peering downward to make eye contact with each person, particularly unfamiliar men, entering and leaving the prison. On my first day of work, the tower officer questioned me: "Who are you, sir?" he asked, staring into my eyes. I responded, "I'm a new employee." He nodded.

As seen from inside the sallyport, fence 1 (the inner fence) and fence 2 (the outer fence) are topped by seven strands of barbed wire, attached in

Figure 2.5   USP-Lompoc Main Entrance (Showing 1-Tower)

parallel rows to a steel frame fastened to, and leaning inward on, the peak of each fence (Figure 2.6). On the inside of fence 1, a thin, unobtrusive wire is fastened about halfway up. This movement-sensing device triggers an alarm in the central control room inside the penitentiary if the wire fence begins to sway; it is sensitive enough for wind to trigger it.

Between fence 1 and fence 2 is a boundary zone approximately 15 feet wide, covered by a heavy layer of white diatomaceous earth. Not only does the white soil retain footprints, it brilliantly reflects light cast by high, overhead mast lights and each tower's spotlight, located on the peak of its roof. On foggy Lompoc nights, a shimmering white boundary adds to the security of the institution (Figure 2.7).

The inner side of fence 2 is heavily protected by six or more bales of razor-sharp concertina wire, wound in continuous spirals about four feet in diameter. The spirals are piled on top of each other until they reach the top, butting against the barbed wire fencing. Strands of each spiral bale are carefully tied with thin wire to maintain its shape; bales butting against the fence are tied to it, also with thin wire. The thin wire is a trigger mechanism in the razor-wire trap; should an inmate try to push through it, the thin wire releases, causing bales to spring up and around him, like a razor-sharp mousetrap.

A short sidewalk leads to the concrete-grey administration building and main lobby. Here, visitors are processed into the visiting room, off

Figure 2.6   Inside 1-Tower Sallyport

to their left (see Figure 2.8). To the right are the institution's business
and personnel offices, including the warden's office. Straight ahead,
looking through the lobby, is a ten-foot-high grill (a door constructed of
rectangular, two-inch-square steel bars arranged vertically), operated

Figure 2.7 Fence-Line (Looking Down From 1-Tower)

electronically by a lobby officer who is stationed in the lobby's security booth.

Beyond the grill is a visitors' patio, with its manicured lawn, neatly arranged flower beds, maturing trees, picnic tables and benches all permanently fastened to the ground, a children's sandbox, and several riding toys. On weekends, inmates' children are permitted to play here as their parents sit nearby. Looking to the left from the center of the visitors' patio is the visiting room, and to the right, on ground level, is the administrative services, or records office. One flight above the records office is the business office. Also one flight up, and directly

Figure 2.8 Visiting Room

above the main entrance (central control sallyport) leading into the main penitentiary building, is the case management office. All activity in the patio and all people walking through it are clearly visible from the windows of the lieutenant's office, straight ahead in the penitentiary's main facility.

Before going inside, everyone passes through another checkpoint, the central control sallyport. During the day watch, from about 7:30 a.m. to about 4:30 p.m., the control officer screens everyone passing into and out of the main corridor, checking the identification cards of people whom he doesn't know. He is surrounded by hundreds of numbered key rings, holding over 2,000 security keys neatly arranged in a wooden cabinet, and by a myriad of emergency communications and electronic sensing devices. He can be seen distributing and receiving institution keys, two-way radios, body alarms (emergency communications devices), handcuffs and leg irons from employees; answering a barrage of telephone calls and radio transmissions from staffers working throughout the prison; and working on a never-ending pile of paperwork. His is not a job envied by others.

Passing through the electronically controlled steel-grill doors of the central control sallyport, and now standing in the main corridor, visitors and new staffers are often overwhelmed by the sheer size of the institution. As I stand at this midpoint of the main corridor, I can look

Figure 2.9   Main Corridor (Looking East)

through barred windows in the north wall of the corridor toward the rear compound. There is the big yard, with its huge grassy area, dirt running track, iron pile (weight-lifting area), and handball and tennis courts to the west, and work shops of Unicor and mechanical services to the east.

The main corridor is a vast, 980-foot strip of polished terrazzo heading west and east. This is Lompoc's principal thoroughfare. Two floor-to-ceiling steel grills can be seen at each end, dividing the main corridor into three segments: one inmate residence area at the west end, one at the east end, and the dominant central portion, which is the focal point for staff business and the location of inmates' services (Figure 2.9).

As a locator aid, a sign is posted on the north wall of the main corridor, directly opposite the central control: "WEST END OFFICES" are listed and a large arrow points left; "EAST END OFFICES" also are listed, and a large arrow points to the right. The locator sign is hung to the right of the main corridor's entrance to the "gym corridor," which leads north to the gymnasium (on the left) and rear compound. The gym corridor is separated from the main corridor by a locked, grilled door. A metal detector stands just beyond the grill. To the west (left) of the gym corridor's entrance (on the main corridor's north side) is the five-hundred-seat auditorium. Every Thursday evening, members of the Tribe of Five Feathers, Lompoc's American Indian inmate organization, meet there for their native dances. Their drumming and singing of Plains Indian songs reverberates through the main corridor. Only rarely do staffers (even new correctional officers) stop at the auditorium door and peer into the dark auditorium, lighted only by red stage lights, to watch these convicts dressed in their native regalia dance in circular patterns, hour after hour, on the stage. A movie is shown here on Saturday and Sunday, afternoon and evening.

An unused ticket window, located next to the auditorium's entrance, is faced with a thick piece of bullet-proof glass taken from Alcatraz Prison after it closed, according to Wayne Ryun, a 26-year bureau veteran and Lompoc unit manager who began his career as a hack at Alcatraz in the early 1960s. Its lower-left corner shows the scar of rifle fire. The research office (which I used) is to the west of the auditorium, and is followed along the corridor by the chapel and the education department.

On the south side of the main corridor, moving west from central control, is the lieutenant's office, the captain's office (which is almost directly across from the research office), and the barber shop, which is behind the west-end grill. The lieutenant's office is divided into a large main room and a smaller office, and it leads to a maze of other rooms and offices. The main room holds two big wooden desks, set off to the left. Between them is a door leading to the smaller, operations lieutenant's office; he is responsible for all custodial activities during each watch. Windows in each room open the visitors' patio to their view; lieutenants can monitor all in-coming and out-going foot traffic and can watch visitors on the weekends. Four pale vinyl chairs are lined up along the right wall in the main room, and, just beyond the fourth one, there is a door leading into a toilet room. Just beyond the toilet door is a tattered orange vinyl chair, used in the inmate discipline process.

A door on the opposite side of the main room leads to the CO's mailroom, and to another door that opens into the "visiting corridor," a short corridor leading from the main corridor (now to the right) to visiting room, off to the left. The visiting corridor connects to the main corridor between the lieutenant's office and the captain's office. Turning left here leads also to the office of the special investigations supervisor (who is called the "SIS"). There are two at USP-Lompoc, Lt. Leonard ("Lenny") Lopez and Lt. Martin ("Marty") Lopez, both senior correctional supervisors, who investigate all significant incidents (assault and killing, drug trafficking and drug use, extortion, weapons possession, bribery of staff, and attempted escapes) and share their data with the FBI. USP-Lompoc's two FBI agents have an office next to the SIS office. Both are directly across the visiting corridor from the inmate "strip search" room, where all inmates undergo a body and a clothing search, before they enter the visiting room or reenter the penitentiary.

On the south side of the main corridor, moving east from central control, are the safety office, the AWs' offices, and the hospital; on the north side are the commissary and mess hall. The main corridor, catching cool breezes coming off the Pacific Ocean only a few miles to the west over California's coastal range, is illuminated by sunlight shining through south-facing windows which, along with north-facing windows, open the corridor visually to the front and rear of the institution. Because the main corridor is highly traveled, it receives constant attention from inmate orderlies. Small ash trays, built into the corridor's walls at regular intervals, collect only some of the cigarette butts, soda cans, and pieces of paper thrown at them. The floor is always dirtied by tracked-in dust and mud from the big yard. Orderlies busily sweep and mop the main corridor at least three times a day, and buff it with wax several times a week. Inmates, working off extra duty for minor behavioral infractions, clean, polish, and shine everything stationary in the corridor: windows are scrubbed clean; ledges and window tops are wiped; east-end and west-end grills are wiped free of accumulated dust blowing in from outside; vertical bars protecting the bullet-proof glass of central control are wiped; and stainless steel ashtrays are emptied in a continuous daily and weekly cycle. Scrubbing, wiping, cleaning, and polishing doesn't end in the main corridor. Every cellblock is polished and cleaned for weekly sanitation inspection; the visiting room and main lobby are mopped and polished every night; and the dining hall and kitchen are mopped free of grease after every meal. The lawns, flower beds, and trees decorating the inside perimeter are watered and cared for by the inside-grounds crew, while "campers" from Club Fed manicure the lawns and gardens outside the perimeter fence. Besides all this, there is a special cleaning, polishing, and painting once a year in preparation for annual community visiting day, a spit-and-polish event for Lompoc's community officials, Vandenburg Air Force Base's high-ranking officers and their families, and staffers' spouses and children. For six to eight weeks before the public tour the full attention of several inmate crews is given over to repainting everything that can be painted, cleaning every window again, polishing every floor, and scrubbing the broad grout lines in the dining hall floor until they gleam like polished teeth (see Figure 2.10).

CELLBLOCKS

Cellblocks are designated by a letter and are paired: B and C, D and E, F and M, H and L, and J and K. Staffers refer to each unit with

Figure 2.10 Mess Hall

military designations such as "baker-unit," "charlie-unit," "dog-unit," and "echo-unit." Inmates usually don't do this.

There are five general cellblocks, C-unit and F-unit on the west end, and J-unit, K-unit and L-unit on the east end. On the east end, too, is I-unit, an ultra-secure cellblock housing inmates who committed rule violations. H-unit, on the east end, prohibits loud radios, yelling, and other loud verbal interaction (it is the official "quiet" cellblock, and is available to those inmates who request it and who earn it). B-unit, on the west end, is the official honor cellblock, housing inmates with infraction-free conduct for at least twelve months. D-unit and E-unit, on the extreme west end, are dormitories housing inmates in the drug-and-alcohol rehabilitation program; and M-unit, on the east end, which, during my research, had mixed functions, sometimes housing "hold-overs." These are inmates who are designated to serve their sentences in other institutions but who are held over temporarily at UPS-Lompoc until transfer arrangements can be completed. When I-unit was filled to capacity, M-unit housed administrative-detention and disciplinary segregation inmates. (Lompoc stopped receiving holdovers in late spring 1986, and M-unit then housed some mainline and occasional spillover inmates from I-unit. Because of M-unit's multiple functions, and its varying inmate population number, I have excluded it from further analysis. Since the management of holdovers was distinctly different from the daily treatment of mainline inmates, and since holdovers didn't contribute to Lompoc's mainline violence, I will not discuss them here.)

Each cellblock has its own sounds, smells, and styles of staff-inmate interaction, and its own rule-violation patterns. Staff call units J, K, and L, as a group on the east end, the "low-rent district," with each unit having its own reputation as a tough cellblock.

Each living unit is a micropopulation in the bigger institution; these are the penitentiary's subcultures. In any cellblock, inmates might already know one another from other federal or state prisons, or from both. Some might have been members of a prison gang elsewhere. Others might have been members of the same or a rival street gang. Still others might have been street-crime partners, or they might have just hung around together on the outside; these men call each other "road dogs" or "running partners." Inmates who regularly hang around together inside are called a "tip" or a "clique." Road dogs or tip members might show their mutual solidarity by getting the same tattoo or by shaving their heads bald.

Each inmate in units B, C, F, H, J, K, and L has his own cell (called a "single cell"). The two floors in units D and E are divided into four rows of living-space "cubicles"; each one has a bed, a desk, and a small storage area. Adjacent cubicles are separated by a chest-high, wooden partition.

Except for H-unit and the dormitories, cellblocks are similar. There are six rows of cells (called "ranges") in each cellblock. There are three ranges, stacked on top of each other, along the two outside cellblock walls. Each cell has a solid, steel door and an outside window. The first, or ground-level, floor is called the "flats," the second level is the "second tier," and the third level is the "third tier." Each range, on the flats and on each tier, is labeled with a letter, beginning on the left side. A-range (left side) and B-range are on the flats; C-range and D-range are on the second tier; and E-range and F-range are on the third tier. Figure 2.11 shows the flats, ranges and tiers in B-unit.

In each cellblock, inmates have access to a full-size pool table; a coin-operated washing machine and a drier; and two color televisions, each with Home Box Office and Showtime. The pool table, one color television, and the washer and drier are located on the flats; the second color television is found in an upper-tier television room.

H-unit ranges are located along the center line of the unit. Tiers are back-to-back—"Alcatraz style"—and each cell faces large, barred, outer-wall windows that open the unit to fresh air and afternoon sunlight. Cells here have bar-grills rather than solid doors. (From the

Figure 2.11 B-Unit, Flats

west-facing cellblock windows, I have watched with inmates as Atlas and Titan rockets were exploded in the air after being launched from Vandenburg Air Force Base.) There is no pool table and only one color television in H-unit; these are accommodations to reduce cellblock noise.

I-unit, also called the "lockdown" unit, has no upper limit on the number of convicts who can be housed there; cell space is always available for disruptive convicts. The I-unit "trap," a sallyport between its steel, main corridor security door and an inner floor-to-ceiling barred grill-door, separates I-unit, its inmates and staff, from the rest of USP-Lompoc. I-unit is self-contained. It has its own recreation area, special security cells, and barred shower stalls, a disciplinary hearing room, its own lieutenant, and its own specially trained line staff.

I-unit's main corridor door must be opened by the main corridor officer, and its inner security grill is opened and closed only by I-unit staffers. All inmates entering the I-unit trap, either those going into administration detention (sober or drunk) or those performing repair work anywhere inside I-unit, are strip-searched. Even inmates' nostrils are checked for contraband; rumor had it that a USP-Marion control-unit convict was found with a piece of hacksaw blade stuck up his nose. Earholes are examined; mouths are opened, tongues are lifted, and cheeks are pulled away from the teeth; bottoms of feet and spaces between toes are carefully scrutinized; the penis is lifted so officers can inspect its undersurface, looking for taped contraband; and the scrotum is lifted for inspection of its undersurface. The anus is inspected, too, making sure that nothing has been inserted.

Figure 2.12 shows a cigar tube that can be keistered (inserted into the anus) with weapons and handcuff keys easily hidden inside it, along with drugs and messages. The I-unit trap is a real "hot" spot, and more than one drunk during my research had his clothes cut off after refusing to remove them. This isn't a picnic for I-unit staff, either. Drunks, say I-unit staff, often urinate and defecate on themselves during the wrestling match in the I-unit trap.

I-unit has only five cell-ranges. Four of them are arranged in two upper tiers in Alcatraz-style; these cells have open-front, bar-grills; together, these ranges are called "upper-I" (see Figure 2.13). The fifth range, on the flats, is called "lower-I." This range is the highest security living area in the penitentiary. Lower-I's single cells hold 13 of Lompoc's seriously violent and disruptive convicts, who are not only isolated from the mainline, but are also isolated from upper-I inmates, separated from them by four locked grills and a staircase.

All lower-I cells have "double-doors," an inner open-front, grill-door, and an outer solid door. Outer doors are locked with a security key and also can be padlocked on the top and bottom. Outer doors are supposed to prevent lower-I convicts from throwing debris or cups of urine or handfuls of feces at hacks, but they do it successfully anyway. When outer doors are closed, they help reduce the ever-present noise of screaming lower-I inmates.

Convicts who are temporarily housed here don't move freely as they do in all other cellblocks. All I-unit inmates are confined twenty-four hours a day, and are moved to the shower rooms and recreation cages by staff members, only after they have been handcuffed, with their hands behind their backs, while still in their cells. I-unit life permits each inmate a daily fifteen-minute shower and five hours of highly controlled recreation in one of three, specially constructed, completely enclosed, rec cages.

Figure 2.12   Cigar Tube with Composite Weapons and Cuff Keys

Figure 2.13   Upper-I, A-Range

3

SYSTEMS OF CONTROL

SOCIAL CONTROL

There is a rich history of studies on social control in prison. Clemmer (1958), Cressey (1968), and McCleery (1960) focus on formal aspects of social control systems. Schafer (1982) deals with good time and prisoner misconduct. Parisi (1982: 18-19) and McArthur (1974) examine inmate grievance mechanisms. Marquart and Roebuck (1986) reveal the role of "snitches," or inmate informants, on inmate social control. Carroll (1974: 115-122) discusses the disciplinary procedure and inmate punishment. A revealing look at inmate discipline is shown in two television documentaries, *Hard Time* (Dave Bell Associates, 1980), a study of prisoner life and social control at the Illinois Stateville Penitentiary, and *Shakedown in Santa Fe* (Hector Galan, 1988), a study of changes in the New Mexico State Prison since the February 1980 riot.

Cloward (1960) discusses formal punishments, such as isolation, for inmate misbehavior, and informal attempts by staff to nudge inmates into line with rewards, such as overlooking minor infractions (also see Crouch, 1986: 190-195; Davidson, 1974: 157-188; Fox, 1982: 46-50; Lombardo, 1981; Rothman and Kimberly, 1975). Nudging is one thing, but hitting and beating inmates into line is quite another. Bowker (1986), Crouch (1986), and Marquart (1986b) focus on this more aggressive side of staff-to-inmate social control.

Social control at USP-Lompoc is achieved through a combination of structural, organizational, personal, emotional, and cultural factors that check prison violence. Ultimately, though, social control rests on razor wire and on guard-tower officers who are armed with revolvers, shotguns, and high-powered rifles.

On a normal daily basis, Lompoc's social control begins with inmates' rights and freedoms balanced against strict and passive institutional control. A prison experiment giving maximum-security inmates freedom without strict control failed miserably at the Washington State Penitentiary (Fleisher, 1983; Stastny and Tyrnauer, 1982). The riots at Attica and the New Mexico State Penitentiary are reminders that convict violence and managerial malfeasance too often go hand-in-hand (see Mahan, 1982).

Social control at USP-Lompoc has three integrated components. One component focuses on the nature and effects of its formal discipline system, its administrative remedy system, and its formal inmate classification system. The second component is USP-Lompoc's organizational culture, which rewards staffers' and inmates' achievements and peaceful rapport between them, and sternly sanctions all forms of aggression and violence among or between members of these two groups. The last component deals with the social, emotional, and verbal interactions between staffers and inmates, and focuses on how speech patterns contribute to either aggravating or mitigating violence.

INMATE CLASSIFICATION

Upon entering the FPS, each inmate receives a numeric security and a custody score (see Levinson and Williams, 1979 for a detailed discussion of the Bureau's security and custody scoring procedures). An inmate's security score is "composed of variables which reflect inmates' social and criminal history, as well as characteristics of the present offense" (Janus et al., 1986: 40). Security factors include, for example, the severity of the current offense; the projected length of incarceration; prior commitment history; the nature of the most serious prior criminal offense; the history of escape or of attempts to escape; and the history of violence (see Federal Bureau of Prisons Program Statement 5100.2, CN-8).

Inmate Thom proudly gave me a portion of his security evaluation to use in this book, and to demonstrate to me that he was "bad":

I. Commitment History (continued):
    a. 01/72—violation of parole, returned to state custody, served approximately 7 months.
    b. 10/72—violation of parole, returned to state custody, served approximately 3 1/2 months.
    c. 09/73—burglary III, received 4 years imprisonment.
    d. 09/74—manslaughter I, received 10 years imprisonment, was conditionally released 07/31/81.
    e. Subject has 8 prior commitments of more than 30 days.
    f. Subject was 34 years old at the commencement of the current offense and does have five or more prior commitments.
    g. Subject was last released from a countable commitment less than 3 years prior to the current offense.
    h. Subject is a parole status violator.
    i. Subject has a history of opiate dependence. He has used heroin from 1963 to 1972.

II. Other Significant Prior Record/Stability Factors:
 a. Subject is a native of [any state] where his parents separated after he
     was approximately 1 year of age and the subject remained with his
     father but also resided periodically with an uncle and grandmother.
 b. He was reared in [any] city under modest economic circumstances.
 c. Subject began experiencing difficulty with the Judicial System at age
     13, at which time he received his first commitment to a Boy's School.
 d. Subject began using heroin at age 15, and in 1964, he was hospitalized
     for an overdose of that narcotic.
 e. Subject has been married on one occasion, but this marriage resulted
     in divorce.
 f. Subject has been continuously confined from 1973 until July, 1981,
     and was rearrested on the day of his release from state custody.

An inmate's custody score is "a systematic reflection of an inmate's
institutional behavior" (Janus et al., 1986: 40); custody is a measure of
how dangerous an inmate is to himself and to others, staff and inmates
alike. Custody levels are: maximum (MAX), in (IN), out (OUT), and
community (COMM). In figuring an inmate's custody score, these
factors are included: involvement with drugs and alcohol, mental/
psychological stability, type and number of most serious disciplinary
reports, frequency of disciplinary reports, levels of demonstrated responsibility, and family/community ties.

After arriving at his designated institution, a newly committed
inmate is automatically assigned a custody level. Security level I inmates
are OUT custody; security level II, III, IV, and V inmates are IN
custody; and security level VI inmates are MAX custody. All subsequent
changes in custody classification are made after an inmate's arrival and
in consultation with appropriate staff. After serving time, if an inmate's
institutional adjustment has been good, his security score may be
lowered, making him eligible for transfer to a lower security-level
institution. If, on the other hand, an inmate's adjustment has been poor,
his security level can be raised, and he may be transferred to a higher
security-level institution.

MAX custody convicts are dangerous, and require an intensive level
of control and supervision. Their in-prison movement can be restricted.
They can be excluded from some types of work, and they may not be
permitted to live in certain cells. At USP-Lompoc, MAX inmates aren't
permitted to live in D- and E-units (dormitories) or in B-unit. When
MAX convicts are taken outside a prison's secure perimeter, they wear
"full restraints" and are usually accompanied by three correctional
officers, one of whom may be armed (see Figure 3.1).

In full restraints, MAX convicts wear leg irons (which look like large
handcuffs); a Martin ("belly") chain that wraps around the waist,

Figure 3.1 Fleisher in Maximum-Custody Iron

permitting handcuffs to be attached to it; and handcuffs that are used with a lock-box (a hard-plastic, rectangular clamp, hinged on one end, clamped over the center of the handcuffs), which is padlocked in place. A lock-box prevents a convict from picking his handcuffs with a homemade key, concealed under his tongue or between his teeth and cheeks.

Figure 3.2 shows convict-made handcuff keys made from ballpoint pen refills; these cuff keys are designed for standard BOP handcuffs. The larger, plastic barrel keys are designed to pick a U.S. Marshal's handcuffs, according to Lt. Gilroy; U.S. Marshals transport federal prisoners. Inmates are strip-searched before being transported. A senior lieutenant said the following:

> When I worked at Marion, a convict refused to open his mouth for the Marshals. They were taking him to court on trial, and the Marshals thought there might be an escape attempt. A Marshal, a little guy, too, asked him a couple [of] times, and the thug still wouldn't open up. This little Marshal walked up to him—the convict was three heads higher than him—and told him to open his mouth, but the convict wouldn't. The Marshal hauled off and smacked him so hard, he spun around, and spit cuff-keys all over the room.

IN custody inmates are allowed to participate in all institution activities and programs under normal supervision. They aren't permit-

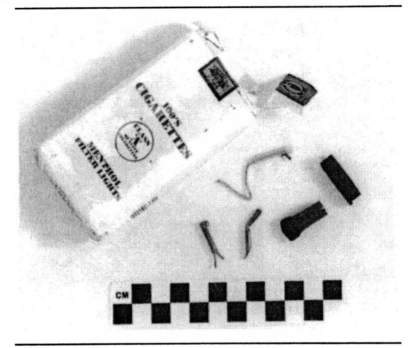

Figure 3.2   Handcuff Keys in Cigarette Pack

ted, however, to work at jobs or to participate in programs outside a prison's secure perimeter. OUT custody inmates are permitted to work outside the secure perimeter of an institution and are checked at least once every two hours. COMM custody inmates are eligible for community-based programs, for furloughs for job hunting, or to leave an institution to tend to emergency family problems.

In addition to custody classification, inmates at higher-security-level prisons (such as USP-Lompoc) who have assaulted or killed staffers, who have tried repeated escape attempts, or who have made successful escapes, and inmates who were high-ranking gang members and gang hit-men, have their photographs and brief criminal histories filed in a loose-leaf notebook. These convicts are called the "posted-picture," or "blue-book" inmates. All staff, especially line staff, make sure they know all blue-book convicts living in their cellblocks or working on their work crews. These convicts are carefully watched, and for good reason.

In daily conversation among themselves, correctional officers and work-crew supervisors use a shorthand version of inmates' custody/ security classification to quickly express a convict's dangerousness. I've heard staff say: "That shit-head is a MAX-6," and "That asshole is an IN-5." On July 1, 1986, 76.8% (909) of the inmates at USP-Lompoc were

IN custody; most of them were classified IN-4, 49.6% (585); IN-5, 20.9% (246); and IN-6, 3.9% (46). Also, 23.2% (274) were MAX custody; most of them were classified MAX-5, 12.4% (146); MAX-6, 5.6% (66); and MAX-4, 4.9% (58) (McCarthy, 1986).

The Federal Bureau of Prisons uses a Central Inmate Monitoring System (CIMS) to classify and monitor certain types of inmates into nine types, according to the 1985 Correctional Training Techniques Manual. On a day-to-day basis, CIMS classifications have no effect on the routine of line staff, nor do they affect interactions between line staff and inmates. In fact, line staff rarely learn which of their inmates are CIMS, unless a need to know is perceived by a superior. CIMS is an administrative effort to prevent violence by precluding violent situations. In August 1985, there were approximately 500 CIMS inmates at Lompoc.

(1) *Witness Security.* Government witnesses who are felons and in jeopardy because of their testimony against organized crime may be protected in a federal prison like USP-Lompoc. The identity of "witsec" inmates at Lompoc was closely monitored and guarded to protect these inmates from attempts on their lives. Some witsec inmates have been known to divulge their identity to other inmates for their own private reasons, however.

All incoming phone calls to witsecs are screened by a phone monitor; if information about an inmate is protected, the caller is referred to a locator center. Staffers are required to protect sensitive information and may not divulge information about any inmate. Unauthorized disclosure of information that is protected under the Privacy Act opens the offender to administrative or legal sanctions.

(2) *Special Security.* These are individuals whose safety may be in jeopardy because of their cooperation in sensitive internal investigations. These inmates are generally former witsecs who are back in prison and are good to tap as informants, or they are terrorists whose behavior is considered unpredictable and "fanatical."

(3) *Sophisticated Criminal Activity.* These inmates are "individuals involved in sophisticated large-scale criminal activities (drugs, property, white-collar) and were prime targets of law enforcement and prosecution efforts (R.I.C.O. [Racketeer Influence and Corrupt Organization law], C.C.E. [Continuing Criminal Enterprise])." Inmates in this category have realized substantial financial gain from criminal activity, as is the case, for example, with many convicts who are involved in drug-related offenses.

(4) *Threats to Government Officials.* Inmates who have committed a crime against a government official or who have a history of threats against government officials are placed in this category. These men are

considered a serious threat. For example, inmates in this category who were scheduled for parole from Lompoc during the 1984 Democratic National Convention in San Francisco, weren't released until after the convention ended, according to a senior lieutenant. An inmate with a history of threatening the president of the United States may face an additional five-year sentence, should he write a threatening letter from prison to the president.

(5) *Broad Publicity.* There are many inmates at Lompoc who have received national media coverage and repeated local coverage for their violent crimes or espionage. Public knowledge of the location of particular notorious criminals may jeopardize their lives.

(6) *State Prisoners.* State prison inmates who were strong-arming other inmates or were management and behavioral problems and state prisoners who cooperated in convicting federal or state inmates may be sent to federal prisons under CIMS.

(7) *Separation.* If two inmates have a serious fight, one of them will be transferred from Lompoc to another facility, and, from that point onward, the two of them will be classified under CIMS as separatees, thus limiting the potential for retaliation. Before any inmate is transferred from Lompoc to another federal facility, the receiving facility is checked for his separatees. This classification is especially important to maintain a separation of former and present prison gang members and inmates harboring grudges from previous conflicts. Inmates who cooperate in institutional investigations may also become separatees from all inmates who are the subject of that investigation.

(8) *Special Supervision.* "Inmates who require special management attention but do not meet the criteria for any other CIMS assignment, e.g., terrorists, hostage-takers, staff homicide, organized crime leaders, law enforcement background," are in this category. Other inmates in this category may include former judges and U.S. congressmen or senators who are serving sentences in federal institutions. These people are usually sent to prison camps rather than to maximum-security penitentiaries.

(9) *Disruptive Groups.* Members of five groups, monitored by the FBI, are considered potentially disruptive and dangerous and are monitored under CIMS to keep them away from one another. The groups are the Mexican Mafia (Eme), the Black Guerrilla Family (BGF), La Nuestra Familia (LNF), the Texas Syndicate (TS), and the Aryan Brotherhood (AB). (For additional information concerning prison and street gangs, see California Department of Corrections, Violence in California Prisons, 1985; Camp and Camp, 1985; Emerson, 1985; National Law Enforcement Institute Gang Manual, 1986; Rockey, 1987.)

A convict claiming membership in a disruptive group ("prison gang"), or one who has a history of prison gang associations, is investigated. If current or prior links to a disruptive group are verified, the convict is classified in his particular disruptive group. These five disruptive groups have earned an official place in Bureau classification. But there are many other convict criminal organizations that are not formally classified as disruptive groups that, because of their continuous criminal activity inside and outside the federal prison system, are also closely monitored.

These "collectives" include: The Aryan Nation, which includes affiliated groups such as The Order and The Convenant, Sword and the Arm of the Lord; Fuerzas Armadas de Liberación Nacional (FALN); Omega 7; the Wells Spring Commune; the Oregon Family; the New Mexico Syndicate; Los Carnales; the Texas Mafia and Texas Aryan Brotherhood (not to be confused with The Aryan Brotherhood); the Dixie Boys and the Dixie Mafia; the Hell's Angels, the Outlaws, and other biker gangs (see Rockey, 1987); the Mexikanemi; the Symbionese Liberation Army (SLA); the United White Peoples' Party (White Mafia) and the Supreme White People; the American Nazi Party; and numerous black and Hispanic street gangs (Bloods, Crips, Maravilla, and White Fence), all of which are represented in the prison system across the country.

To verify gang affiliations, staff search prison and street records, chart tattoos on each inmate's body, and look for distinctive gang emblems, which may appear on inmates' stationary and paraphernalia. Because tattoos are distinctive indicators of prison and street gang affiliation, new gang members tend not to be tattooed nowadays. Older members, however, reveal the distinctive "ink" of gang membership. Some among common prison gang tattoos are: EME, eMe, MM, M (Mexican Mafia); NF, or a sombrero resting on a knife dripping blood (La Nuestra Familia); BGF, BLA (Black Guerrilla Family); ESE, with T drawn through S (Texas Syndicate); and AB, 666, shamrock, lightning bolts and swastikas (Aryan Brotherhood). Extremist and terrorist groups also display affiliation with distinctive ink. These groups include the SLA, UWPP, WP, and White Mafia.

According to Lt. Rudy Marks, at USP-Lompoc in May 1987 there were nine or ten verified members of the Mexican Mafia, three members of the Black Guerilla Family, and six or seven members of the Aryan Brotherhood, with approximately 46 ABs in the federal prison system. Also according to Lt. Marks, the Aryan Brotherhood is the most violent of all prison gangs, and it has probably killed more of its own members than have been killed by other gangs.

"The AB kill for glory," said Lt. Guy Baker, who was SIS at USP-Marion, when AB convict Silverstein, second in command of the AB's nationwide organization, according to Baker, stabbed a control-unit correctional officer to death on October 23, 1983. Later that day at Marion, convict Fountain, an AB "want-to-be," killed a second correctional officer, also stabbing him to death. Fountain killed the second officer "to be like his idol, Silverstein," Lt. Baker said. After the killing, a special cell was built for Silverstein in the control unit; he was monitored twenty-four hours a day by a video camera, built into his cell, according to a Bureau official.

Silverstein surfaced again during the USP-Atlanta Mariel-Cuban riot in 1987. On November 29th, Cable News Network reported that an inmate Silverstein, who was threatening to kill hostages and was disrupting negotiations between Mariels and federal authorities, was turned over to the feds by Cuban detainees. I confirmed his identity with Bureau authorities.

The Aryan Brotherhood is extremely violent, and, because of its link to white supremacist and neo-Nazi groups, they are considered today's most dangerous prison gang. There is an unclear link between the ABs, which is exclusively a convict criminal organization, and the Aryan Nation, a white supremacist, separatist group that is opposed to the United States government. Although there are no apparent formal links between the two groups, Lt. Marks thinks that marginal ABs or Aryan Nation members may try to affiliate with the other group, if they feel socially more comfortable there.

Monitoring the social dynamics of prison gangs is vital to the safe operation of Lompoc. "Outsiders," said Lt. Will Merchant, a former Lompoc SIS, "don't understand the depth and danger of prison organizations and their street connections." Cultivating rapport with gang members, he said, is the most effective way to monitor them. Snitching (called "rolling-over") on a prison gang may, indeed, bring death to the rollover, but Lt. Merchant suggests that "the more you know, the more they'll tell you. If you know something, they feel comfortable telling you more. It's like watching sex through a keyhole; if you tell them you saw a little, they'll probably tell you a lot more." In May 1987, the Bureau was on the verge of expanding its disruptive group classification to include terrorist organizations like the Aryan Nation, said Lt. Marks.

EXTRAORDINARY GROUPS

Terrorist organizations aren't classified officially as disruptive groups, but some Bureau staffers consider terrorists in the federal prison system to be the most dangerous threat to the safety of inmates and staff, and to the security of federal prisons. Among these groups, the Aryan Nation is viewed as the most dangerous convict organization in federal prisons, according to senior staff.

The government's perception of The Order's dangerousness is summarized by the United States Department of the Treasury (1986: 28):

> The Order is an underground clandestine terrorist organization and very heavily armed with automatic rifles and shotguns, as well as all types of survival equipment. . . . FBI agents seized tens of thousands of dollars in cash, major stores of weapons, ammunition, explosives, disguises, and false identification papers. Reportedly there were also signed copies of a "Declaration of War" against the "Zionist Occupation Government of North America." The document calls for execution of police officers, reporters, U.S. and Canadian government officials, Jews, blacks, and other minorities and "traitors." This organization . . . refers to "The Turner Diaries," a fictional account of terrorist groups operating underground in the United States in . . . 1991-95. The Order . . . believes their criminal activity is justified by the fact they are members of "God's Army" and local and federal law enforcement officers are devils, who should be eliminated at any opportunity.

The dangerousness of these groups is illustrated by the extreme caution U.S. Marshals use when bringing members of The Order to USP-Lompoc.

In February 1986, 11 neo-Nazi members of The Order were transported to Lompoc by federal marshals from Olympia, Washington, where they had been tried in federal court. Two members were committed at USP-Lompoc. The others were held over in I-unit before being transferred to other federal penitentiaries. Although their trial had been broadcast widely, national news broadcasts didn't mention when The Order members were leaving Olympia, Washington, or where they were being sent.

One of The Order members, Gary Yarborough, had already received wide publicity for the June 18, 1984 killing of Denver talk-show host Alan Berg. Yarborough was a member of the White American Bastion and former chief of security at the Aryan Nation Church, Haden Lake, Idaho (see B'nai B'rith, 1986; Melnichak, 1986).

Using an unmarked bus, the penitentiary regularly delivers to and picks up inmates from U.S. marshals located at Vandenburg Air Force Base. The marshals' unmarked Boeing 727 aircraft flies into the base, where heavily armed staffers deliver already committed inmates for transfer to other prisons, and pick up new inmates who are being committed or transferred to Lompoc. The plane made a regular weekly run during my research.

The Order was considered so perilous that marshals brought them by small aircraft directly to Lompoc's town airport. To maintain tight security, institution staffers didn't know when the first planeload of about six members of The Order were to arrive at Lompoc, until just hours before they touched down. Just before landing, the marshals notified the penitentiary. A small, heavily armed and experienced contingent departed the penitentiary for the airport, but not before they notified local law enforcement agencies and the California Highway Patrol. The following day, the balance of The Order arrived at USP-Lompoc.

A senior correctional staffer told me, just before he left the institution for the Lompoc airport, that the staffers were readying themselves for an attempted break-out by groups affiliated with The Order. (Although I had participated in inmate transportation before, I was not allowed to join this time.)

As The Order members were processed into the penitentiary, each convict was given an anal examination. One of the convicts had keistered a plastic vial containing stick-on labels with the message, "The Order Reigns." The intent, apparently, was to stick these on the prison walls to incite racial violence.

And so The Order arrived at Lompoc, with two of its members, Gary Yarborough and Richard Kemp, walking the mainline (see San Francisco Chronicle, June 28, 1987, for a photograph of Yarborough and Kemp, and an interview with Kemp conducted by Dannie M. Martin). By spring 1987, according to senior staff, Yarborough and others in his cellblock had plotted an escape: they were going to drill holes in their cell's window bars, escape into the compound, and, using a homemade wire cutter, clip the perimeter fences, opening them to freedom.

Yarborough contracted with a convict who built a drill. A small motor, probably used in a refrigeration device, was set inside a circular-steel casing; the motor shaft had putty-like material built around it, forming a solid circular core in which a drill bit was inserted. A convict-made extension cord was to be attached to the drill; dummies were to be used to conceal their absence during morning-watch counts. The escape plan was thwarted after information about it leaked to staffers. Yarborough and others were transferred to USP-Marion.

Threats by white supremacist groups to attack federal prisons to free convict-members from the custody of the ZOG (Zionist Occupation Government) are taken seriously. Prisons are designed to keep people in, and aren't well prepared to defend themselves from outside attack by snipers shooting at perimeter-tower officers or from armored vehicles bursting through perimeter fences.

Prison gangs and neo-Nazi organizations pose serious threats to the security of federal institutions and to the safety of both staff and inmates. Since their recent entry into the federal prison system, the Cuban criminals from Mariel (Marielitos) and Havana (Havanitos) have also become serious threats to inmate and staff lives, and are an expensive custodial problem.

The April 1980 "Freedom Flotilla" brought 125,000 Cuban émigrés to the United States. Among them were criminals and mental patients sent by Fidel Castro. Nowicki (1987: 38) described these Marielito criminals as "some of the most vicious criminals the United States has ever known." About 7,600 Mariel Cubans are imprisoned today (*Wall Street Journal*, December 1, 1987). The FPS houses approximately 2,500 Cuban detainees (Los Marielitos and Los Havanitos), and others are housed in state and county correctional facilities throughout the United States. Lompoc staffers don't differentiate between Los Marielitos and Los Havanitos; they refer to both as "the Cubans."

Before the USP-Atlanta and ADC-Oakdale riot, USP-Lompoc housed some 30 to 35 Marielitos, according to Lt. Guy Baker. After the riots, Mariels from Atlanta and Oakdale were sent to USP-Lompoc, raising the Mariel count at Lompoc to about 290 by February 1988. To accommodate them, H-unit was renovated, transforming it into a high-security unit resembling I-unit. Almost all of the Mariels are housed in the former quiet unit; the overflow from H-unit is housed in I-unit and in a few cells in the hospital.

A Dade-Miami Criminal Justice Council study found that in 1983, "Mariel Cubans, who then made up 5% of Dade County, were responsible for 9% of felony arrests and 23% of the misdemeanor arrests" (*Wall Street Journal*, December 1, 1987). Cuban detainees in the FPS, who on July 29, 1986, made up 6% (2,497) of the inmate population (41,356), were responsible for 23% (10) of 44 assaults reported for that month, according to the Federal Bureau of Prison's Correctional Services Comparison Report (August 26, 1986).

Marielitos, like other prison and street gang members, have distinctive tattoos. Inscribed by the Cuban prison system in the fleshy web between their index finger and thumb, these green-blue tattoos denote their criminal specialties: one dot, nonsupporter of Castro; two parallel dots, larceny; three parallel dots, robbery; four dots in a square, murder; five dots in a square with a dot in the center, habitual criminal; a small heart with a "tail" extension, executioner; a star with three lines opening above it, coming from a common apex, kidnapper; and, a stick-like figure of a man without legs, enforcer.

USP-Lompoc's Marielitos often have long, knife-inflicted facial scars, earned in fights with other Cuban prisoners. Until retaliation is successful, these scars are signs of humiliation and shame, said a Cuban. One USP-Lompoc Marielito wears a particularly large, robust scar on one cheek. His shame, he said, lasted as long as it took him to kill his attacker.

Many USP-Lompoc line staffers have volunteered for 30 days' "TDY" (temporary duty station) at USP-Atlanta. Line officer Jim Rogers went TDY-Atlanta in August 1986. On his return, I asked about his trip:

> We had body alarms going all the time. There were two triple deuces and body alarms a day . . . you'd call for a lieutenant and 30 of them would answer. I got into a fight with one [Cuban] of them in the hallway, and the Atlanta staff stood there watching, while I was wrestling with this guy on the floor . . . they enjoyed it . . . then some TDYs jumped on top of me. It was an enjoyable experience. All officers should go there at least once.

Rogers and other hacks returned to USP-Lompoc, breathing a sigh of relief, and welcoming USP-Lompoc's peacefulness and relative scarcity of Marielitos. These hacks say Marielitos "kill because they enjoy it." Spanish-speaking line staff at USP-Lompoc had no serious complaints about their Marielito work-crew employees. Understandably, non-Spanish-speaking staffers have a more difficult time of it. They say they "don't understand them, they aren't like regular convicts." Line staff who can't speak to Marielitos and who don't know anything about Hispanic crime and culture are at a loss when trying to work with them.

Marielitos at USP-Lompoc aren't organized into groups; they seem to prefer doing their own time, and they tend to be left alone by other convicts. Since Marielitos speak little or no English, both English-speaking convicts and staff are suspicious of them. After serving time in Cuban prisons, some Marielitos said they were enjoying their time in this United States penitentiary. One told me that he was imprisoned by Castro himself, in the early '60s. He hijacked a passenger jet after it left Miami, taking it to Havana: "The jet circled and circled the airport and flew over Castro's house, and woke him up. He came to the airport so angry, he threw me in prison for two years. I was in a cell without windows." Compared to the brutality of Castro's prisons, this Marielito said, "This is good, here. This penitentiary is a vacation."

Homeboys are a black convict phenomenon at USP-Lompoc. Hispanic street-gang members who were violent competitors on the street tend to drop their mutual animosities in prison. But they haven't organized along geographic lines, as East and West Coast black inmates have done. At USP-Lompoc, "Blacks from east of Kansas City are East

Coast blacks, and those from other places are West Coast blacks," says Lt. Baker. Blacks have organized this way, Baker suggests, so they can retaliate against the Aryan Brotherhood, the Mexican Mafia, La Nuestra Familia, and the Texas Syndicate.

"Power on the mainline." This is what Dynamite, a leader of East Coast homeboys, meant when he said: "Street gangs are 1960s, 1970s action. That's all played out now. The big thing now is homeboys." Regional alliances serve as sources of quickly available manpower, should a need arise to fuse into a large social block of soldiers, with street gang leaders, like Slim, providing leadership.

Apparently, among the "East Coast homeboys," their need to unite is also personal. K. T., the leader of the "DC Mob" (District of Columbia), the politically dominant faction of the East Coast homeboys, told me that, at Lompoc, East Coast inmates are a long way from home, and, because they don't have social support mechanisms on the nearby street, they band together to help each other, when necessary. West Coast inmates, K. T. said, have social support nearby, so their desire to unite in prison isn't as intense as that of East Coast blacks.

The DC Mob has a few top leaders who are differentiated from others. K. T. is the one man at the top. The amount of time he has served in prison, his "accomplishments," his education, and his criminal history are his distinguishing criteria. As top man, K. T. is the highest node in the DC Mob's information network, and he has access to the most important information concerning social happenings at USP-Lompoc and elsewhere in the country. According to him, the DC Mob's information network is efficient and fast. "I know what's going on in D.C. before my mamma, who lives there." The East Coast blacks, with the DC Mob at their core, "can pull guys together in minutes, if we have to," said K. T. Dynamite agreed.

West Coast blacks are dominated by blacks from the greater Los Angeles area and San Francisco. The 415s (San Francisco's area code) are distinguished from Los Angeles area and San Diego groups; a DC Mob member called them all "California dudes."

Together, black homeboys can resist white and Hispanic pressure, but they also compete against each other. At USP-Lompoc, trouble from whites and Hispanics is limited by their low numbers, but the threats of the black gangs to fight each other have reached almost folkloric dimensions.

After a hiatus from the penitentiary, I returned in early August 1986. I was hitch-hiking to the prison late one weekday afternoon and was picked up by a correctional officer. As we chatted, I asked if the institution had been quiet over the past few weeks; he shook his head from side to side and smiled.

He asked me if I had heard about the recent riots at the Lorton Reformatory in Washington, D.C.; of course I had. He said, "we got a load of D.C. blacks after the riots," and trouble started soon after between them and the West Coast blacks. He cited two recent yard riots that broke out on weekends, when staffing levels were low, and early in the evening, after the 6:30 p.m. count, during the postdinner lull. He added that more riots were planned, and that the institution's riot squad had been alerted.

When we arrived at the prison, I headed straight for the lieutenant's office and began asking Lt. Hammer, then evening watch operations lieutenant, about the East Coast-West Coast black riots on the yard. He stared at me as if I was crazy: "It's been quiet for weeks. We haven't had any trouble." There had been no riots, no fights, no trouble at all between the black inmates.

West Coast-East Coast talk of rivalry and violence once led to a cellblock disagreement resulting in a stabbing, but the primary motivation for violence wasn't regional rivalry. It began on a personal level, in an argument over a pool game, then escalated into what appeared to be an East Coast-West Coast "homeboy thing."

Convict Henry, said Slim, was an East Coast homeboy, and he instigated the trouble against convict Gary, a West Coast homeboy. Henry, a blue-book convict in his early 20s, is known among staff as a violent man. He had been involved in killing a correctional officer in another federal institution. Here is Slim's account, with comments from Magic.

> It was behind bullshit over a pool game. The only reason Gary got scratched [as opposed to seriously injured] was because he was working that chair. The squabble started a few days ago over a pool game. All they was going to do was walk around each other and then let it die. They calls each other "sucker"; you never beat a person and talk bad while you're doing it. So like it lead to words. Instigation got into it and some people thought it needed more wood in the fire.

Magic:

> People pump people up: "Hey you oughta go get that dude." People wanna see shit happen, it keep things going. Them motherfuckers got nothing better to do with their time. Instigation righteously triggered it off; if you quit fucking with the dude, nothing will happen. If it can be ironed out, then you go for it.

Slim continued:

> Henry tried this homeboy thing before. They tried it on me and I went and got my shit [shank] and said "let's take care of it." If they want a homeboy

thing, they'll get one—I got mine [shank]. They [East Coasters] came and say, "Hey, cuzz, what's going on?" They all heard it and figured we [West Coasters] was ready for them, so they didn't start nothing. Then Henry did the same thing to Gary. Gary tried to talk to Henry. I don't condone it [talking to settle a problem], but I figure he was trying to settle it with talk. Not me, man, I would have said, "you got yours and I got mine, let's go!" I got Gary a piece, I gave him mine. When Gary thought it was safe, he gave it back. We [West Coasters] didn't want to get into it; if it's a one-on-one tip, that cool, but a two on three, or three on four, that different. Then we get our shit and roll on them, yeah!"

Thinking the problem with the East Coasters was resolved, Gary relaxed and put away his knife, but that's when Digger, an East Coaster, attacked him. Magic said: "Gary went to Henry and tried to talk things out. Gary put up his knife—he thought it was settled. Then he was sitting in the TV room watching the game and the dude [inmate Digger, another East Coaster] rolled on 'em. Gary grabbed a chair and worked it, that's why he only got scratched." Henry, the instigator, didn't want to be implicated in the attack and managed to place himself in a case manager's office as the assault was occurring.

The "scratch" Gary received, as Slim and Magic referred to it, was a chest laceration and a puncture wound that went through Gary's forearm. (Gary was disliked by some staff and many inmates; after the attack, a senior lieutenant said, sarcastically, "It couldn't have happened to a nicer inmate!")

By contrast, a small and noteworthy inmate bunch are "crazies," or "nuts," according to Dannie Martin (called Red Hog or Red by his friends):

Criminals are trying to make a living in the best way they know how. They're trying to make money, and if they're robbing a bank and have to kill someone, they have to deal with it. But that's different than some guy who beats a woman and her daughter to death, just for the fun of it. Living with nuts causes more pain than other things. Ax killers. Guys who murdered their daughters. You walk in your cell and there he sits. You know, there's a guy in Lompoc who killed four teenagers in Anchorage, after he stole their tape deck, and they wanted it back. He blew their brains out with a .44 magnum; he killed four of them. They put him in a mental asylum. They gave him a weekend pass and he killed his mother. I think that's what they built the gas chamber for. If you refuse to live with him, they put you in the hole [I-unit], you lose sixty days good time, and get three weeks in the hole. You can't trust these guys; they lie in business. You may give him money for dope, and he uses it to bring his wife here for a visit. When he does that, he spits on you. So what are my choices: I can beat him up, kill him or be a spit-on punk. If I beat him up, how can I go to sleep knowing I beat up an ax killer! So I kill him and another con sees; he'll testify against me, knocking off thirty years on his sentence, and I get life!

Dannie Martin publicly announced his opinion about crazies (*San Francisco Chronicle*, October 18, 1987).

The Federal Bureau of Prisons accepts convicts from state prisons and mental hospitals who are too unstable, violent, or sensational for local jails and prisons. The more violent of these are kept medicated on strong psychotropic drugs. They walk among us like zombies in slow motion. Others carry on lengthy conversations with imaginary companions or affect poses resembling the Statue of Liberty—they can remain motionless for hours on end. A mental patient here not long ago walked into a cellblock office where a guard was sitting and began cutting the officer in the head with a single-edged razor blade. They never exchanged a word. It took a multitude of stitches to close the wound.

There were 24 inmates at Lompoc on psychotropic drugs in May 1987. Inmates receiving psychotropics, or any other drug, must consent to treatment, according a USP-Lompoc official. Despite this low number, Red Hog said in a May 1987 interview with me that,

It's immoral of the Bureau of Prisons to use antiviolence drugs, because when these cons are released and come down, they may have ten years of hatred and anger built up which explodes on the streets. These cons rape and kill and then the courts and the Bureau of Prisons tighten their control over men who didn't commit crimes. It's not fair.

Red Hog recently commented on this latter point:

We are all treated like mental patients instead of convicts. Most regular officers aren't certain whether we are here because of insanity or criminality. In a cellblock with only one guard and 120 convicts, they can't afford any chances. This attitude breeds distrust and bad communication between staff and convicts [*San Francisco Chronicle*, October 18, 1987].

I spoke to Slim, Eddie, Cowboy, and some others about crazies. Their advice was simple: "Fuck 'em, just leave them alone."

THE DISCIPLINE SYSTEM

The Bureau's inmate discipline system, with its unambiguous structure of "prohibited (proscribed) acts," relies on the readiness of its discipline committees to impose "sanctions" (institutional responses to rule violations). But since a formal discipline system is only as effective as the people who use it, inmate discipline at USP-Lompoc depends on the common sense and skill of its staffers as they talk with violent inmates.

The formal discipline system includes four levels of prohibited acts: greatest severity (100 level), high severity (200 level), moderate (300 level), and low severity (400 level). Each severity level is accompanied by a series of formal sanctions, imposed by discipline committees according to policy guidelines. A list of prohibited acts, the sanctions for each, and a summary of the discipline system's operation (including inmates' rights) are published in Lompoc's Inmate Handbook (1987).

100-level offenses include killing, assaulting any person, escaping from either escort or a secure institution, setting a fire, rioting, encouraging others to riot, taking hostages, possession or introduction of hazardous tools—those which may facilitate escape or contribute to causing serious bodily harm to others—and possessing a gun, firearm, weapon, sharpened instrument, knife, dangerous chemical, explosives or ammunition. 200-level offenses include fighting, threatening staff, and engaging in sex. 300-level offenses include refusing to work, insolence to staff, and intoxication. And 400-level offenses include malingering, tattooing, and being unsanitary (see Table 3.1).

The two-tier discipline committee system is composed of a Unit Discipline Committee (UDC) and an Institution Discipline Committee (IDC). Staffers participating at each level must pass UDC and IDC certification examinations, recertifying every two years. All 100-level offenses are handled directly by the IDC, passing perfunctorily through the UDC. Offenses at the 200, 300, and 400 level may be heard and adjudicated by the UDC, or heard briefly and then referred to IDC.

All infractions except the most severe can be informally resolved. In this face-to-face negotiation between a citing staffer and an offending inmate, the parties try to agree on a mutually satisfactory sanction, such as 15 hours of extra duty cleaning windows. It is to both parties' advantage to come to terms on the spot. Staffers reinforce the fact that *they* are in charge and that *they* control inmate behavior. Staffers also reduce their paperwork this way—an important incentive not to be overly punitive, lest inmates refuse the negotiation and lodge their own complaint against them. By the same token, violations that are resolved informally don't reach either the UDC or IDC, and therefore don't become part of the inmate's official dossier.

Each discipline committee is empowered to levy severe sanctions against inmates. 100-level offenses may result in a parole date retardation, a forfeiture of earned statutory good time, a disciplinary transfer, time in disciplinary segregation of up to 60 days, or being forced to make

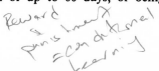

TABLE 3.1
Infraction Rates at USP-Lompoc by Severity Level, 1985-86

Infraction Level	1985			1986		
	(n)	Percentage of Total Infractions	Rate/100 Inmates Per Month	(n)	Percentage of Total Infractions	Rate/100 Inmates Per Month
Greatest (100)	(160)	9.19	1.10	(210)	10.25	1.50
High (200)	(500)	28.72	3.45	(531)	25.91	3.79
Moderate (300)	(967)	55.54	6.67	(1,206)	58.86	8.61
Low (400)	(114)	6.55	.79	(102)	4.98	.73
TOTAL	(1,741)	100.00	12.01	(2,049)	100.00	14.63

SOURCE: USP-Incident Report Logs, 1985-86.
NOTE: Average Incident Reports/100 inmates per month, from 1/81 to 9/84, at Security Level V prisons is 9.11, according to Janus, Mabli, and Williams (1986:36). Average Daily Population, 1985 (1,208), 1986 (1,167).

monetary restitution. 200-level offenses may be sanctioned by any of the 100-level sanctions or by a loss of privileges (commissary, movies, recreation), a change of living unit, a loss of job, or a restriction to quarters. 300-level offenses may result in any 200-level sanctions and the possibility of extra duty. 400-level offenses may be punished by all the above, or by a "reprimand" and "warning" (USP-Lompoc Inmate Handbook 1987). (This outline of sanctions doesn't account for restrictions on sanction use, cooccurrences of sanctions, and sanctions for repeat offenses; see Federal Prison System, Program Statement 5270.5, 1982.)

A minimum of two members of a unit management team comprise each UDC, and each one adjudicates any incident report (a legal document identifying a prohibited act or acts committed by an inmate and specifying the details of that act or acts) received by a units' inmates. The UDC passes on more serious offenses to the IDC. The UDC level of discipline is more personal than the IDC, which is composed of upper-echelon administrators whose daily contact with inmates is limited. The UDC system forces the offending inmate to face his unit manager, case manager, or counselor, explaining why he committed the prohibited act. UDC sessions often sound more like a "father-son" reprimand rather than a court of justice.

Convict Garrett celebrated his thirty-second birthday in late 1985 by getting drunk after work on a Friday afternoon and again the next morning. By the time he went to the mess hall for lunch at about eleven, he was barely able to walk. With his right elbow resting on a table-top and his drooping head held aloft in his hand, Garrett sat alone, not expecting any trouble.

Convict Shu, whom Garrett had punched out in the gym about nine months earlier, saw Garrett and retaliated. Shu sneaked up behind Garrett and smashed him in the face, knocking him down into a pool of blood mixed with water from the nearby ice machine.

Garrett was charged with fighting, and Shu with assault. On the Monday morning after the attack, Garrett was black and blue and seriously embarrassed for allowing himself to get decked. Garrett's UM ran the UDC session, and I was the second member of the UDC team. We met in I-unit.

"He sneaked me, that China motherfucker. I'll kill him, next time I see him," Garrett snarled.

"What! That's sure smart. You were told by Lt. Brand to stay away from Shu after the last fight. What happened this time? You know that you can get transferred out of here for this," said the UM.

"I didn't do nothing, man. That motherfucker kung-fooed me. I'll kung foo his motherfucking ass, when I get out of here," promised Garrett.

"Well, if that's how you feel, you're not getting out of here. You'll get transferred right from here," said the UM.

"I don't want to go nowhere, man," said Garrett in a calmer voice. "All right, then. If you promise not to go after Shu, I'll see if we can keep you here. But you have to promise me that you won't go near Shu. If you see him anywhere, you've got to promise me that you'll walk the other way. Well, what do 'ya say?" asked the UM.

"All right. I promise. But it's going to be hard to stay away from that China motherfucker," said Garrett.

"Does that mean you'll stay out of trouble?" asked the UM.

"Yeah, that's what it means. You won't ship me, will ya?" asked Garrett.

"I'll take care of it," said the UM.

At UDC sessions, the unit management team gets a sense of inmates' ongoing personal adjustment. For newly arrived inmates, their attitude toward prison life is a focus of attention for UDC teams.

Often, an inmate's reaction to his unit manager's or case manager's stern attitude is an apparent sense of embarrassment and contrition; this is part of a complex inmate-staff social game played out at every level of the organizational structure. Years of quasi-paternal concern fosters the development of social networks among team members and inmates. These networks are essential in gathering information after a violent incident.

It takes staff time and effort to adjudicate cases fairly at the UDC and IDC level. UDC and IDC members work together, sharing information and suggestions for sanctions that will "get the attention" of troublesome inmates. My observations of IDC and my participation in UDC suggests that UDC members, *because* of their personal involvement with inmates, sometimes pass cases to the IDC level, where a less subjective decision may be easier to make. The warden appoints the IDC with a minimum of three members, at least two of whom must be at the department head level or higher.

"A PERSONAL TOUCH"

The following factors enter into the operation of the formal discipline system, to affect inmate social control.

(1) Warden Christensen is directly involved in face-to-face inmate discipline.

(2) The captain, each lieutenant, and each unit team member takes personal responsibility for controlling problem convicts.

(3) Staffers use their acquired common sense to resolve conflicts with, and among, inmates. Successful staffers, particularly experienced line staff, don't hide behind the formal discipline system. They deal face to face with problem inmates.

(4) All male staffers (except Warden Christensen) respond to and participate in emergencies—that is, requests for back-up assistance. Since an inmate's personal safety often depends on staffers' quick responses to emergencies and their effective control of violence at the scene, inmates rarely interfere (physically or verbally) or assault them.

(6) All staffers are individually accountable for maintaining institution safety and sanitary conditions in their departments (and cellblocks). They are also responsible for the custody and safety of inmates. A unit manager who permits a dirty cellblock can and will be disciplined. If his team's performance doesn't improve, he may be demoted or fired. This is a powerful incentive.

(7) Inappropriate off-the-job conduct can lead to a staffer's dismissal as quickly as malfeasance on the job can. A new hack was dismissed in spring 1987 for drinking and fighting in a local bar, and a second one was dismissed for drug dealing, according to a correctional supervisor. All staffers who knowingly violate the Bureau's policies concerning inmates' rights or who fail to conduct themselves according to the Bureau's standards of employee conduct and responsibility (Federal Prison System, Program Statement 3420.5, 1981) are disciplined by Warden Christensen or a member of his executive staff.

The FPS and USP-Lompoc have other messages for staffers: "Don't exceed your scope of responsibility," and "Follow policy." If an employee exceeds his scope of responsibility by beating an inmate, for example, and is subsequently sued for malfeasance by the injured inmate, the FPS and Department of Justice will not provide cost-free legal help, and they will not pay the financial judgment against a staffer. Warden Christensen sent this message in the weekly employee newsletter:

> The Department of Justice has amended their policy to allow payment of judgment funds to indemnify DOJ employees who suffer adverse money judgment as a result of official acts or the settlement of personal damages by like payment of DOJ funds. This change in policy permits, but does not require, the department to indemnify a department employee who suffers an adverse verdict judgment or other monetary award provided that the actions giving rise to the judgment were taken within the scope of employment and that such indemnification is in the interest of the United States as determined by the Attorney General. . . . This is the best news employees have received in several years. In layman language, do your job according to, and within parameters established by Bureau of Prison

Policy and in case you are sued, you will be supported legally and monetarily by the Department of Justice [USP-Lompoc Freeway, September 18, 1986:1-2].

THE ADMINISTRATIVE REMEDY SYSTEM

Prison officials make the rules and there are no appeals. The rules exist solely to make the task of managing people easier for those doing the managing [Jackson, 1984: 222].

The formal discipline system controlled by staff places the accused inmate directly in front of staffers, permitting free verbal exchange and sometimes allowing the instant expression of controlled, verbal anger by the inmate. If an inmate is brought up on charges before a UDC or IDC, he can accuse the staffer of a biased judgment; he can resist the process by saying absolutely nothing and by refusing to sign the necessary paperwork. Staffers expect a degree of resistance and aggression, and tolerate it within reasonable limits. But at bottom, the UDC and IDC are clubs that staffers wield.

To impede improper use of the discipline system by staff, or excessive punishment by the IDC, or physical or emotional or sexual brutality by male staff toward convicts, inmates have recourse to the Bureau's administrative remedy system (ARS). Through the ARS, inmates have a mechanism for getting the attention of Lompoc's middle- and upper-echelon administrators and managers.

An inmate may raise the issue of using the ARS during informal problem-solving negotiations with his counselor. If informal resolution fails, the inmate is given "BP-8 paperwork," which he completes and brings to his UM, and informal resolution is attempted again. If this, too, fails, the UM gives the inmate "BP-9 paperwork," which the inmate files with the ARS clerk. (The ARS clerk was the research analyst during my time at USP-Lompoc.)

The BP-9 is the first and lowest level in the formal ARS procedure. BP-9s often describe grievances in meticulous detail, and frequently make requests for financial or other type of relief. The BP-9 is assigned to an institution program head for formal investigation and response. If, as is almost always the case, the institution's response doesn't provide the requested remedy or relief, the inmate may file an appeal, a BP-10, with Lompoc's regional office. If the BP-10 fails, the inmate may file an appeal, a BP-11, with the Bureau's Central Office in Washington, D.C. If his BP-11 is also denied, the inmate may initiate action in federal court.

TABLE 3.2
1986 Administrative Remedy Filings, United States Penitentiaries
(Rate Per 100 Inmates Per Year)

U.S. Penitentiary (Inmate Population)	BP-9		BP-10		BP-11		Total Number of Administrative Remedy Filings by Penitentiary
	Rate	(n)	Rate	(n)	Rate	(n)	
USP-Lompoc (n = 1,167)	36.2	423	14.1	165	5.4	63	651
USP-Leavenworth (n = 1,117)	60.2	672	27.5	307	13.4	150	1,129
USP-Lewisburg (n = 1,180)	63.0	743	26.6	314	15.9	188	1,245
USP-Terre Haute (n = 1,100)	80.0	880	22.8	251	9.3	102	1,233

SOURCE: Federal Bureau of Prisons Statistical Report, FY 1986.

The ARS operates to provide relief for inmates against a broad range of violations of institution policies, programs, and operations. In 1985, 439 BP-9s were filed by Lompoc's inmates: 35.5% concerned disciplinary matters; 13.4% concerned institution operations; 12.8% involved institution programs; 10.5% concerned legal matters; 7.3% were complaints against staff; 7.1% involved transfer issues; 8.4% had to do with community communications; 3.6% dealt with medical issues; and 1.4% concerned parole.

Of these, 6.4% (28) were granted either completely or partially; 73.8% (32) were turned down with a simple denial, or a denial due to repetitive filing, or denial due to improper subject; 16.2% (71) were classified as "other," including incomplete documents, previous grant of remedy, documents withdrawn by inmates, and Bureau requests for more information and explanation. Fifteen cases (3.6%) were classified as "missing cases" (McCarthy, 1987). Lompoc's ARS filings are relatively low compared to the other federal penitentiaries (Table 3.2).

The profile of 1986 ARS complaints at Lompoc was almost identical to that of 1985: 423 BP-9s were filed by inmates; 34.8% concerned disciplinary matters; 12.8% involved operations; 13% focused on programs; 9.7% concerned legal matters; 7.3% were complaints against staff; 4.9% involved transfer issues; 9.7% had to do with community communications; 5.9% dealt with medical issues; and 1.7% concerned parole. (There were no missing cases in 1986.)

Although only 6% of BP-9s were granted in 1985, and 11% were granted in 1986, the mechanism relieves pressure between staff and inmates. Invoking the ARS is in the inmates' control, and by means of it they have a legitimate and honorable way to challenge with impunity a variety of programs, operations, and staff behavior.

In contrast to the formal discipline system, the ARS is faceless and costly (in terms of time and effort) for staff. Inmates have nothing *but* time, and very little to lose by invoking it frivolously, although they are likely to suffer in small ways as their rapport with their counselors deteriorates. They might not be able to count on their counselor's support at parole hearings, for example. Still, in this system, the inmate is the accuser, and because it's faceless, the inmate gets the undivided attention of staffers, including the warden, whose time is spent investigating and responding to inmates' allegations.

Staff receive BP-8s and BP-9s daily; staff and inmates discuss cases, and inmates ask staffers about results. This continuous dialogue is almost always free of verbal anger and hostility and contributes to maintaining open communication across the staff-inmate boundary.

NONVIOLENT PROTEST

Tension, anxiety, and anger build daily in social interactions between staffers and inmates; line staff are particularly vulnerable to explosions of inmates' stress, and inmates are vulnerable to line staffers' anxiety, tension, and fears. The discipline system makes staffers feel that they have control over inmates—though it may not look like it as one correctional officer stands in a cellblock of 125 inmates. ARS, with its ultimate access to the federal courts, gives inmates a sense of control and a sense of not being lost in the vast bureaucracy of the federal prison system (despite those 15 BP-9 cases listed as "missing" in 1985).

A tennis racket lost in transfer to USP-Lompoc from USP-Leavenworth and a complaint about not being permitted to receive certain magazines are typical of grievances which, over time, may motivate inmates to assault one another or a correctional officer. The most dramatic use of the ARS during my research was initiated by American Indians.

In an effort to create a positive image and tone and to improve sanitary and safety conditions during meals, the warden enacted a dining-hall dress code. Prior to the new code, inmates came directly from recreation (weight-lifting, jogging, tennis, and handball) wearing sweaty and smelly work-out clothing. Some wore rubber shower shoes, which were safety hazards on the slippery tile floor; others wore shirts outside their pants, presenting a sloppy image; and some wore sweaty headbands.

The dress code went into effect on September 23, 1985. Inmates were required to tuck in their shirt tails; to remove their sweatshirts and replace them with green fatigue shirts; to wear steel-toed shoes; and to remove their head covering. Inmates were reminded of the coming dress code changes for about six weeks. The warden had memos posted prominently in each cell block, outlining the new code and its purpose. New memos posted on the unit office are a source of immediate and endless discussion. When the code went into effect, there wasn't an inmate in the institution who wasn't aware of its every detail.

One evening, an inmate who was shooting pool with four buddies in K-unit said to me: "You should do research into what's going to happen around here, when them new bullshit rules come down." They suggested that a food strike, as well as violence, were going to be likely consequences, if the warden didn't change his mind. "Go talk to the man . . . what they paying you for anyway," said the convict.

"This is our home," argued another convict, "and in a man's home, he can dress anyway he wants. If a man wants to go to the dining hall naked, he should be able to do it. The warden only works here, man . . . he's going to retire in a year anyway, so what the hell does he care."

When the big day came, there was lots of grumbling from hungry inmates, but they had a choice: Either follow the new rules or don't eat. Men who forgot to wear steel-toed shoes were turned away at the dining hall door by a lieutenant or the captain, only to return, properly attired, in a few minutes. Hundreds of men were stopped at the door and ordered to tuck in their shirts.

The only serious cries of protest came from Black Muslims, who had to remove their sufis, and from among American Indians, who had to remove their headbands. Rastafarians, who wore their colorful, hand-woven hats everywhere they went, removed them; bikers and inmates with shoulder-length hair took off their headbands; inmates coming in from the sunny yard removed their brimmed hats; individual Black Muslims threatened to file administrative remedies against the officer who ordered the sufis removed, but they took them off and entered for their meal. A barrage of verbal protests continued for about a week, then declined to a constant level of quietly muttered protests for about a month.

American Indian inmates, however, refused to remove their head-bands, claiming that removing them violated their religious rights. They wore circular headbands while eating to symbolize unity and wholeness with nature, they claimed, as prescribed by Archie Fire Lame Deer, a former convict and founder of the American Indian Prisoners' Sweat-house religion. Eighteen American Indians filed a BP-9, alleging a violation of their right to practice their religion; in each one the text was virtually identical. Then, after filing their formal protests, they and other American Indians refused to eat in the dining hall. Robert Wilson (a.k.a. Standing Deer, a coconspirator in the killing of federal agents on the Sioux Reservation, along with Leonard Peltier) and a leader of USP-Lompoc's American Indian group initiated a food strike. A year earlier, according to a lieutenant, Wilson organized a food strike at USP-Leavenworth.

In response to their food strike, the warden ordered kitchen staff to prepare sack lunches, including a baloney and cheese sandwich, fruit, cookies, and a drink for each protester, three times a day. The lunches were delivered by staff to their respective cellblocks, where each inmate received and signed for his meal. After several weeks of eating baloney and cheese, the number of protesters dwindled to a handful. Dozens of American Indians were again eating their meals in the dining hall, without wearing headbands.

Standing Deer went on a hunger strike and was hospitalized. He was fed by an esophageal tube, an unpleasant procedure. Another Indian was locked in I-unit for an unrelated offense. While locked down, he ate hot meals, according to I-unit officers. Indians on the mainline heard, via the convict gossip grapevine, that he was eating baloney and cheese and continuing his protest. Another Indian refused to enter the dining hall and was allegedly starving in protest. Actually, according to my inmate sources, he was eating food stolen for him by Indians who were eating in the dining hall. This continued for about a month, after which the hospitalized inmate was transferred to another federal facility, and the others returned, without their headbands, to the dining hall.

After the Bureau denied the Indians administrative relief, they contacted the American Civil Liberties Union, taking the case to federal court in Los Angeles. *The Lompoc Record* (November 6, 1985) reported this:

Denial of efforts to reverse a ban on wearing Indian headbands in the U.S. Penitentiary in Lompoc cafeteria is just a temporary setback . . . . Federal District Court Judge Edward Rafeedie Monday denied the preliminary injunction filed by the American Civil Liberties Union, leaving mixed opinions on the judge's ruling. Clarification of the "anthropological and historical significance" of Indian headbands will bolster their case, according to ACLU attorney John Hagar and private attorney Margaret G. Gold. Hagar and Gold will gather statements of cultural anthropologists and renew efforts to win the preliminary injunction, which would act as an extended restraining order against the Sept. 23 headband ruling. That step may not affect Rafeedie's ruling, said Assistant U.S. Attorney Joseph Butler. Rafeedie's upheld Warden Robert Christensen's views that failure to apply the new sanitary requirements—which cover all headgear, sweatsuits, and thongs—may threaten discipline and order at the institution, Butler said. Christensen said in his declaration to the court that inmate threats of "taking matters into their own hands," may make prisoners likely to "act out" violent behaviors. Cafeteria inspections of headgear could result in confrontations, Christensen wrote. "The possibility of staff/inmate confrontations in a confined and potentially highly volatile area is very real," he said. Whether the mealtime removal of Indian headbands represents a serious intrusion on religious freedoms was one of Rafeedie's concerns. . . . At issue is the unnecessary intrusion on inmates' religious rights by prison officials, Hagar said.

The insiders' view, however, was quite different, suggesting that this episode had little to do with headbands and religious rights. This was a contest of power and control between Warden Christensen and a group of inmates who challenged his authority and power. The challenge was lead by Grey Feather, who replaced Standing Deer as leader of USP-Lompoc's American Indian population after the latter was transferred. Grey Feather continued the legal battle in a personal quest to beat the warden and the Federal Bureau of Prisons.

Grey Feather brought his message to a small group of (mostly women) community supporters of the American Indian prisoners at USP-Lompoc, and to inmate members of the Tribe of Five Feathers, during a Friday evening meeting in the visiting room that I supervised. He hoped, he said, to win the headband case, to beat the oppression of the federal prison system, to end the tyrannical rule of the warden, to regain inmates' and Indians' rights at Lompoc, and to take control of the institution, program by program. After he won the headband case, he said, he was going to initiate legal action over the right of the institution to inspect mail.

After almost a year of legal jousting, the United States District Court for the Central District of California issued a summary judgment, in September 1986, in favor of USP-Lompoc. Eighteen American Indians, led by Standing Deer, appealed on August 4, 1987 to the United States Court of Appeals for the Ninth Circuit, filing suit against Norman Carlson (director of the Federal Bureau of Prisons), Warden Christensen, and Chuck LaRoe (the warden's executive assistant).

In his ruling of the appeal, Standing Deer v. Carlson (831 F. 2d 1525), Judge J. Clifford Wallace wrote the following:

> This litigation was prompted by a regulation promulgated by prison officials at Lompoc. The regulation prohibits all headgear by inmates in the inmate dining hall. Appellants, Native American prison inmates, claim that the blanket ban on headgear violates the Constitution and the

American Indian Religious Freedom Act. . . . In one declaration filed in support of summary judgment, the warden stated that prior to adopting the dress regulation, he had received numerous complaints from prisoners about dirty clothing and headgear in the dining hall and that several prisoners threatened to "take matters into their own hands" unless prison officials took steps to alleviate unsanitary conditions. According to the warden, the dining hall is the most potentially volatile area in the prison. . . . Viewing [the] evidence in the light most favorable to the inmates, we hold that the prison officials fulfilled their obligations under the Act to learn about and avoid unwarranted interference with Native American religious practices. The Act requires consideration of, but not necessarily deference to, Native American religious values. . . . We conclude that the dress regulation is reasonable related to legitimate penological interests. We therefore hold that the regulation does not violate the inmates' free exercise rights and affirm the summary judgment. . . . We also find that the prison officials complied with their duties under the Act and affirm the summary judgment on that claim.

This power play never got out of control: there were no staff-Indian fights; there were no obscenities shouted back and forth; there were no riots; and no other inmate groups came forward to support the Indians' cause.

Lt. Baker, in offering his comments on USP-Lompoc inmates' style of protest, said: "If Leavenworth or Lewisburg convicts stage a protest, staff would have to lock down the place. But Lompoc inmates just make noise."

—4—

FIELDWORK

GETTING STARTED

At 7:30 a.m. on August 15, 1985, I showed up for work. Institutional Familiarization Training (IFT), my first formal correctional training program, wasn't scheduled to begin until August 19th, the next Monday. I parked in the employee's parking lot, and tried to look like everyone else, walking sleepy-eyed toward the prison. Maury Waxman, USP-Lompoc's research analyst until October 1985, was supposed to meet me in the penitentiary lobby at 7:30. Waxman was one of the seven penitentiary staffers who knew why I was there. Warden Christensen wanted it that way, so that's the way it was. He was afraid that if staffers knew my mission was to explore new CO retention, I would be inundated by people with "axes to grind." He said that custody staffers would probably feel that I was intruding on them, and, because of that, they wouldn't talk to me (see Hilbert, 1980; Van Maanen, 1981). Along with the warden and Waxman, these other people knew my purpose: Captain Collins; Johns Sams; Gene Gill; the personnel director; and contract manager (he handled all contract business, whether it was buying a new carpet or renting a researcher). By the end of October 1985, I began telling hacks of my purpose.

I tagged along with Waxman on Thursday and Friday. He introduced me to staffers as we went from office to office on his daily routine; along the way, I met a few inmates. Waxman was assigned to the mess hall for mainline lunch (each general population meal is called "mainline") on Thursday, where he was supposed to supervise inmates waiting in line to get their meal; he had to stop "line-jumping" (cutting in line) and settle disputes among inmates, if they arose.

Standing with him for an hour, watching inmates stand in line would get dull, so over his protests, I left him and stood behind a steamtable between two inmate food servers. To my left, I chatted with "The Bear," an armed bank robber and killer (he had recently arrived at Lompoc after spending several years in USP-Marion's control unit), who was serving cheeseburgers, and to my right, with Stevie, a Sacramento bank robber, who was serving desserts. When they asked about me, I told them I was on a year-long "busman's holiday" from a university.

We talked and waited for lunch to begin. The mess hall doors opened at about 11:00. As hundreds of inmates came pouring in, my heart began to thump—for a moment I wished I was a historian. Standing between The Bear and Stevie, I tried my best to become invisible, but inmates saw me anyway. They asked me question after question (Where can I get a new diet card? Can I get on commonfare?), and I didn't know what they were talking about. They argued with me over food portions (Why can't I have another cheeseburger?). They asked me this and that, and I was lost—I had no answers for anyone. After mainline ended, I asked The Bear if I could talk to him later in his cellblock. "About what?" he asked. "Violence," I said. "Sure, any time."

After lunch, Waxman took me to the case management office, where inmates' files are kept. Mike Rizo, a former Lompoc hack, is the case management supervisor, and oversees the proper handling of inmate paperwork. All inmate files are kept in rows of fireproof file cabinets, secured by built-in combination locks and steel rods, locked over the drawer faces. Waxman gathered a tall stack of selected inmate files: "If you're going to be here, you better know something about the inmates you're around right from the start. These guys don't play."

I hung around the research office for the remainder of the day, reading files and meeting staffers who popped in briefly to shoot the breeze. I wasn't yet permitted to wander the penitentiary alone, since I hadn't been through Institution Familiarization Training. I spent Friday also hanging around with Waxman. This was getting dull.

INSTITUTION FAMILIARIZATION TRAINING (IFT)

Twenty years' experience as a "corrections professional" usually amounts to one year's experience twenty times over [Miller, 1988: 13].

My penitentiary life brightened quickly at 7:30 on Monday morning, August 19th, when I began six days of "classroom" IFT and four more days of on-the-job (OJT) training. As a researcher, I wasn't entitled to a hack's OJT, but I insisted on it. "All right," said Barney Halpern, the training officer, "If you really want to, it's all yours." He smirked.

Warren Roberts and Jimmy Young, new COs, were fellow trainees. Roberts had experience in an Alaskan jail and at the Arizona State Prison. "No matter where you go," Roberts said, "if you need work, there's always a prison or a jail close by. I don't worry about getting work." I called him a "correctional nomad." Jimmy Young, a local Lompoc fellow, was a "fish," like me, with no on-the-job experience in a prison. We met in the lobby that morning, and wandered upstairs together to find the training room. As I began to pry into their personal lives, Barney Halpern walked in at 7:30 sharp, and lit a cigarette. He told us that "Training starts at 7:30 sharp, not 7:32 or 7:35. I don't want your asses in the parking lot at 7:30, or walking up those fucking stairs or outside there in the hall, smoking a cigarette. I want your asses in this room at 7:30 sharp. We got a lot of work to do."

He was right! IFT is a general correctional training program. Federal prison employees are "correctional workers" first, then specialists at their individual jobs. All correctional workers (a male correctional officer in an FPC, a Ph.D. clinical psychologist in a USP, or a woman unit secretary in an FCI) must jump through the same training hoops: several written exams; a physical-fitness testing program; a practical correctional-techniques exam that tests proficiency at shaking down inmates and searching their cells; and accurately firing a handgun, a shotgun, and a rifle (physicians and clergy may request an exemption from firearms qualification).

Monday to Friday, from 7:30 sharp to 4:00 p.m., we listened to lecture after lecture, given by executives, lieutenants, and experienced hacks. There were lectures on staff-inmate relations; inmate mental health and chemical dependency; how to recognize and manage medical emergencies; inmate discipline, including incident report writing and the discipline committee procedure; administrative remedy; inmate classification and accountability; emergency fire procedures; body counts; contraband; public relations; tool and key control; inmate programs; legal responsibilities; firearms familiarization; and employee conduct and responsibilities. On day five, we had a written examination.

Day six began at the penitentiary's armory, loading .38-caliber handguns, 12-gauge shotguns, and M-14s into a prison van. Then it was off to the firing range, led by Mike Rizo, a certified firearms instructor; we were required to qualify with each weapon. Then it was back to the staff training center, located on campgrounds for an introduction to defensive Aikido (the Bureau doesn't teach offense moves).

ON-THE-JOB TRAINING (OJT)

Institutional Familiarization Training, I thought, had taught me enough policy and enough about working in the penitentiary to give me what I needed, until I went through my next correctional training program at the Federal Law Enforcement Training Center (FLETC) at Glynco,

GA, at the end of October 1985. But the very moment my keys were issued at central control, I realized that I didn't know what I was doing. Barney Halpern said he'd meet Young, Roberts, and me in the lieutenant's office, with our orders for the day. Armed now with a cursory knowledge of Bureau policy and procedures, I was very excited and equally anxious about OJT.

Halpern put me to work in L-unit with correctional counselor Barry Jeunesse, a retired Navy and Vietnam veteran, who had more than ten years of Bureau experience. Roberts and Young went elsewhere. I wasn't concerned about them. Roberts had prison and jail experience. Young is 6'9" tall and holds a karate black belt. Halpern actually told Young not to hurt any convicts who might make the mistake of harassing him: "I don't want you picking up a thug and throwing him head first into a cell grill," ordered Halpern. Young smiled: "Not even once, Boss?"

Inmates know that new hacks are scared, as convict Eddie explains:

> It scares new cops shitless. We ain't going to hurt them, but they don't know it. They're happy not to be screamed at. New cops don't know who to stop, what to say, and what to do! This is what they think: "I'm going to try to let these dudes do as much as they want so they don't kill me." Shit, 90% of the convicts won't kill anybody. They just bark, but it works. As long as you make them feel in charge, call them "boss," they believe it. Pretty soon, after they've been scared to death for weeks, they think that we're not so bad. We've left him alone, so he leaves us alone.

I was now in Jeunesse's hands, and Halpern made sure that I had a long list of activities to perform. I thought that I'd get some anxiety relief from Jeunesse. But instead, he cautioned me: "The toughest part of the job is dealing with these guys. They are gang members, and wheeler-dealers. Security is the big thing; even simple requests like exchanging laundry can mean a contract killing. Be careful." Then he handed me a fistful of oddly shaped keys: "Here, take these and watch the door," he ordered. He wandered off and left me alone. Now I knew what Eddie was talking about. As Jeunesse walked away, I heard a convict rap loudly on the cellblock door, and yell, "Door!" Convicts kept banging, and I kept letting them in.

At this point, I wanted to yell, "Time out, I'm just an anthropologist! Leave me *alone!*" Many years of research experience at the Washington State Penitentiary helped a little: "Just don't look as scared as you feel," I told myself. Right then, I knew that there was a world of difference between walking around a prison, talking to inmates and staff, and calling that research, and "carrying keys," that is, assuming real on-the-line responsibilities in a prison. "When you carry them keys on your hip,

I don't care who the fuck you say you are, you're one of them," said convict Monroe, who had arrived about a year earlier from USP-Marion's control unit. Lt. "Chilly Willy" Merchant, a senior IFT instructor, told us about watching the door. He made sure that we knew the seriousness of this fundamental custodial activity. While a cellblock door is open, inmates leave, others enter, but no one except inmates assigned to a living unit are permitted to pass beyond the unit's doorway; even so, it happens to some degree all the time.

That day I remembered Merchant's warnings; I must have been staring intently into inmates' faces as they walked into the unit. One inmate said, "Don't worry, man, I live here. Check you'll see." That was my first mistake—I believed him!

Watching the door keeps out foreign "locker-knockers," convicts from other cellblocks who steal inmates' personal items and leave. During my research in September 1986, a victim of a theft sliced the thief's forearm, causing a deep laceration.

Watching the door also prevents "runners" (inmates carrying keistered contraband from one unit to another) from moving drugs, drug paraphernalia, and weapons between living units. After an assault, an assailant may try to hide or dispose of an assault weapon by transporting it (or paying to have it transported) away from the crime scene. Figure 4.1 shows a keistered "hype-kit"; the hypodermic needle is made from a Bic pen shaft, pinched-tip rubber tubing, and melted into the end is the tip of a hypodermic needle—stolen by an inmate orderly from the hospital. A cover was made out of masking tape. The small container contained heroin.

Watching the door can keep out inmates wanting sex with a unit homosexual. "Guys try to slip in for sex," said Big Brother. "If a new cop is on the door and stops him, he'll try to tell him he's the unit orderly. Sometimes it works, sometimes it don't. If he gets in, he'll move out at the next [activities] movement."

Watching the door can stop a "hitter," a free-lancing, hired convict-killer or a killer sent by his prison gang to kill a convict. An assault like this can occur in a few minutes, as during an activities movement. An officer said: "I was standing on the front door and this inmate came up and said, 'Man, you better call an ambulance, get some help!' I seen this inmate full of holes and dripping blood. I helped him out [of the unit]. He walked to the hospital."

Lt. Merchant also told us, again and again, not to release convicts at their own request. Telling a convict, to his face, that he can't go somewhere is a world apart from knowing that he shouldn't go. Inmates

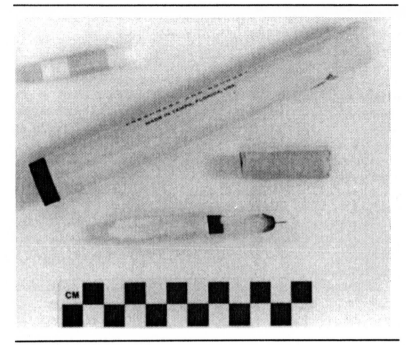

Figure 4.1   Keistered Hype Kit

always have urgent trips to make: "Man, I gotta get to the hospital," or "I gotta get to the laundry for some clean clothes. I got a visit coming up." The list of bogus requests seems endless. My response was the same: "You'll have to wait for Jeunesse. I don't know anything about it." Of course, this was partly true. Convicts grumbled and wandered off. Some of them argued, but I repeated my verbal defense, "Wait for Jeunesse." I knew these inmates were "gaming me," but I didn't how to cope with it. I was beginning to feel like a wimp.

About 8:20, Jeunesse told me to do the census count. Lt. Merchant had told us about the count and how to do it, but that was a week ago! I wasn't sure about it then, and I was less sure about it now, as I stood in one of Lompoc's "toughest" cellblocks. Jeunesse explained it again, and I pretended to understand. I was supposed to find every inmate in the unit. I had to walk down each range and look in every cell, in each day room, and in the tier showers. When I spotted an inmate, I asked his name and cell number, and then put an "X" next to his name in the census book, a looseleaf notebook filled with plastic-covered paper pages, listing each inmate's name, his cell designation, and his programming assignments (work, school, vocational training, or a combination of these). During the week, almost all inmates are either at work, at school, or at a vocational training program (called a "VT"), so there weren't too many inmates to count.

This was nerve-racking. I walked first into cell A-1. Three convicts were sitting around, and I knew only two were permitted in a cell at any time. I now had a problem: I had to tell one of them to leave.

They solved it for me. They also knew the rules, and when I stuck my head in, they looked at bit nervous. Immediately, convict Jimmy-John said: "Just leaving, boss." Whitey and the Greek barked out their names and cell designations; I didn't have to ask. Whitey, whose cell it was, had done time in Walla Walla at the Washington State Penitentiary, and, after we talked, we discovered that we had mutual "acquaintances" there. Whitey was a neo-Nazi with admitted leanings toward the Aryan Brotherhood. When Jimmy-John and the Greek heard I had some prison experience, they loosened up, and when they did, so did I.

I spent about twenty minutes with them, and now my confidence level had climbed to astronomic heights: I had talked to convicts (in my crypto-hack role) without inciting a riot or getting punched out. My census count continued. I slowly strolled down each range, peeking in each cell. When an inmate was there, he would automatically blurt out his name. When an inmate was standing on a tier, he would give me his name and cell number. My anxiety level was declining, until I arrived at a cell which had a blanket completely covering its open ("unracked") doorway. I knew this was against policy, but what was I going to do about it? I had to see inside, but I couldn't as long the doorway was covered. So I got down on one knee and carefully lifted the lower left corner of the hanging army blanket, secretly and quietly peeking in. I felt really stupid.

"Take it down," someone yelled, "Take the damn thing down. Yank it, man, pull the fucking thing off there." Still on one knee, I turned my head, looking for the anonymous voice. Across the cellblock, on D-range, a young black inmate was leaning over the rail, laughing at me.

"What?" I asked.

"Just tear it down," he repeated.

"But what if somebody's inside?" I quipped. He really started laughing then.

"That don't make no difference around here," he said.

"Thanks," I said. That was very embarrassing.

My first morning was hectic. I answered telephone requests from staffers, and had to figure out how to complete piles of cellblock paperwork. I dispensed toilet paper, matches, and single-edged razor blades. I denied inmates' occasional requests to use a screwdriver that was stored in the cellblock office. I answered their questions about getting "special" telephone calls. I learned how to write an "institution pass," which permits an inmate to move in the main corridor to meet a "legitimate" appointment after the end of an activities movement. And I gained confidence in telling convicts, who didn't have a legitimate appointment, that they weren't going anywhere, after a movement ended. There were always inmates hanging around the cellblock office, asking personal questions about me. At times, I felt like carrion being circled by buzzards.

By early afternoon, I lost the jitters. I started to understand that a penitentiary cellblock is a place of "images," where a convict's or a staffer's strutting walk and bravado talk can effectively mask his insecurity. An image of confidence, either from a staffer or convict, can have a strong influence on the people who see it. When I sounded and acted confidently, projecting a knowledgeable and strong image, convicts acted as though they believed it, and I had fewer arguments. I discovered, too, that when I waffled, acting and talking insecurely, convicts saw through my weak spots and arguments began.

Jeunesse gave the appearance of being an easy-going fellow, someone whom inmates might enjoy gaming. But after spending hours working with him, I began to appreciate his supervisory style and the effectiveness of his relaxed manner. Of course, I came into the cellblock long after Jeunesse had developed his rapport with inmates. His nonthreatening, easy interactions with inmates showed his confidence and demonstrated his control of the unit. That first day, a few telling incidents occurred, indicating clearly that Jeunesse had developed a unique style of inmate supervision, his own "cellside manner."

Just after lunch at about 1:30, an inmate plumbing crew, along with Micky, the crew's supervisor, arrived to do some work along C-range. I was standing on the flats near the cellblock office, and Jeunesse was busy inside it. In the midst of work, he left his office, walked onto the flats, stopped, and yelled an inmate's name.

As Jeunesse was standing there, the Greek, standing on E-range, three tiers and about thirty feet up from the flats, intentionally dropped a full metal trash can that zipped by Jeunesse's head, landing about six feet in front of him. The crashing noise reverberated in the concrete and steel cellblock. Jeunesse, nonplused, calmly looked up and spotted the Greek who was hanging over the tier railing, smiling and laughing at Jeunesse. Jeunesse yelled up to the Greek, "You fuckin' asshole." The Greek laughed even harder, and walked away.

Micky, who was watching this scene, said: "Who runs this fuckin' unit, Jeunesse?"

Jeunesse grumbled: "Convicts!"

Micky replied: "That's what we heard." Jeunesse just shook his head and walked into the office.

Inmate Maury came by Jeunesse's office later in the afternoon. He stopped for a moment to thank Jeunesse for helping him during a recent disciplinary hearing: "Listen, Jeunesse, thanks for helping me out with that." Jeunesse: "Yeah, sure. You owe me now, you bastard."

Inmate Callahan came sauntering by the office, after returning from his job in the kitchen. I had met Callahan earlier that day as I did the census count. He was lying on his bed when I walked in his cell, asking for his name. For whatever reason, we got along instantly and, within seconds of seeing each other, we were laughing about something. Callahan loved to talk, especially about robbing banks in New York City.

I'm from Brooklyn. Hey, do you know Spanish Eddy in B-unit? He's from Brooklyn, too. I'll have to introduce you. I worked at *Time Magazine* in the photo lab, doing the color front covers. I did that for years. One day I was sitting around the park having lunch, reading the *Daily News*. I read about some guy who had been holding up these fucking banks and jumping in the fucking subway and flying off; they never caught the bastard. So I said to myself, "Why the fuck am I working this hard?" I thought about it for a few weeks, and one day on my lunch hour, I walked into [a city] bank, handed some pretty teller a note, she gave me money, and I jumped on a subway. I did it for years. And I kept my job. I'd get a grand, $1,200 or sometimes a little less, every fucking time I went in. Then I got greedy. I tried to stick up Macy's.

Callahan went out of his way to walk by Jeunesse. "Hey, Jeunesse!" he said. "Yeah, what the hell do you want?" Jeunesse growled. "I'm going to take the rest of the day off," commented Callahan, "Why don't you?" Callahan laughed and headed down the flats for his cell on A-range. Jeunesse shook his head: "Fucking guys never leave ya alone. Some of these guys are assholes, but you have to be patient."

That one day was more significant for my research than I could have guessed. In eight hours, I met Eddie and Cowboy, along with Thom, Frankie, Callahan, the Greek, Whitey, and many other convicts, who became reliable sources (I prefer this term to "informants"). These men also introduced me to many inmates in other cellblocks. They enjoyed talking to me, and I enjoyed listening and talking to them.

My OJT continued. I worked in K-unit, H-unit, I-unit, and C-unit. Then I was posted with the main corridor officer, the recreation yard officer, the property room officer, and the officer working in corridor-2 (the portion of main corridor east of the east-end grill).

DAILY ROUND

After IFT and OJT, I was free to begin my research. My work day began at about 7:15 or earlier each morning, and ended temporarily about 4:00 p.m. I usually returned in the evening, for at least several hours. With the help of the quarterly roster (a list of all posts and personnel filling them) and the "rookie" roster (a list of all new hacks and their posts), I began my daily round, or survey, of the penitentiary. I followed its physical outline, beginning at the mess hall and then to each cellblock and each office. Along the way, if I met a new staffer, I'd introduce myself as the research analyst.

When I went into a cellblock, I never told anyone that they were being interviewed. We "just talked," as I accompanied a hack or a counselor working as a hack on their regular duties. Whenever possible, I volunteered to help. I wrote passes, answered the phone, and worked the unit door, when asked. Rookies were always thrilled to see me: "There's protection in numbers," one said. Since I had been on the job for a few months, I knew much more than they did, so I helped them with regulations and with handling overly aggressive convicts.

My daily round also included meetings and other events. Each Monday afternoon the warden held a meeting that brought together the executive staff and programs and operations department heads. At my first meeting, Waxman introduced me to the group. On alternate weeks, following the warden's meeting, John Sams, the associate warden of programs, met with program heads. On the third Thursday morning of each month I attended a lieutenants' meeting, chaired by the captain or, in his absence, a senior lieutenant.

At 3:10 on the last Wednesday afternoon of each month, there was Early Recall, an institutionwide staff meeting convened by Warden Christensen in the visiting room. Major items on the agenda: QSIs (Quality Service Increases) were awarded to several staffers each month for exemplary job performance (they received a plaque and a $1,000 increase in salary); retirements were announced and service pins were awarded at the 5-year, 10-year, 15-year, 20-year, and 25-year points; new staffers were introduced (I was introduced, too, as a "contract" research analyst); and staff transfers. When staffers transferred or retired, the warden called each one forward, asked his or her supervisor to say a few words, and he or she then said good-bye. Near the end of my research, AIDS information, along with the Bureau's efforts to protect staffers from AIDS, were recurring topics. Early recall usually ended by 3:40, and was followed by punch and donuts, provided by the USP-Lompoc's Employees' Club.

At the end of each day in the penitentiary, I organized my fieldnotes. I did this by updating my "contact" log (a list of all inmates and staffers with whom I spoke that day, where we spoke, and what we talked about and for how long). I also categorized my informal interview data: New Hacks (training problems; family troubles; personal history; work experience, etc.); Emergencies (where? when? parties involved?, etc.); Resolution of Conflict (cause? place? time?, etc.); Speech Data (how was speech used by different staffers in different situations?); Rapport (was I doing well? how did I know that?); Questions (whom will I talk to next? about what?); Networks (who introduced me to whom? how are they connected?); and so on. Armed with questions, I began the next daily round.

I never hid my pocket notebook and used it freely whenever I was talking with someone. There were times when using a notebook was impossible, as when I was performing a correctional task such as shaking down an inmate. Staff usually didn't balk when they saw me writing in my notebook, but convicts often got nervous when they saw me writing anywhere around them. They got used to it, though, as I got used to them.

THE MESS HALL

One of my most productive hangouts (interview spots) in my daily round was the kitchen and mess hall. On my first walk through there, I was startled by a young white convict carrying a long, glistening butcher knife in the waist-strap of his white, food-stained apron. He caught my attention, and I caught his.

"Who are you?" asked Frankie, Eddie's buddy from L-unit. "I'm an anthropologist," I replied. "There ain't no bones around here," said the inmate with the knife. "I'm a cultural anthropology professor," I responded. This was met with cynicism. Frankie: "Sure, I heard that shit before. I know who you are. You the FBI . . . CIA. You're sneaky, I can tell." I said: "Here, look at this. It's my university ID." That brought a chuckle from everyone. "Sure," Frankie said. "I seen those before, too." Inmate Kenny overheard this: "Hey, Frankie, the man can't be the FBI." "Why not?" asked Frankie. "'Cause look at him. He ain't wearing polyester, and you know they always wear them polyester suits," answered Kenny. A chorus of "Yeah, that's right," went up from around the kitchen. Up to my final day, some of these men still ribbed me about being an FBI agent. Among these men, I acquired my joint nickname: "Professa."

Beginning with them, the word spread quickly among other inmates that I was an anthropologist. Inmates whom I hadn't met approached me and introduced themselves, and starting asking me about the latest notions of human evolution, about the creation-evolution arguments, about flying saucers and pyramids. Dannie Martin told me his ideas about the "evolution of the criminal class," as he called it, beginning in the Lower Paleolithic with our cannibalistic ancestors, Homo erectus.

The kitchen also had good things to eat: delicious breakfast pork chops with mushroom gravy (on weekends, L-unit's Frankie, a head cook, saved these for me); wonderful puddings, particularly rice pudding. The bakery always had thousands of cookies (black walnut were my favorite) and hundreds of cinnamon rolls baking on Fridays for weekend brunch (their sweet smell wafted over the staff parking lots early in the day). Another one of my favorites, apple/mince pie was available at holiday time.

Staff could eat "inmate food," as inmates called it, if they bought a meal ticket ($1.25), otherwise they violated policy. Convicts took care of me, though. As long as no one "snitched me off," I knew that I wouldn't get into trouble. In the kitchen after meals were served, I got clues about lieutenant-inmate rapport (which inmates did lieutenants ask for food? which inmates offered food to which lieutenants?); this extended to other staffers, too.

There were about 175 inmates working in food service. Most kitchen inmates welcomed a chance to stop their work and talk to me; of course, I always made sure that the food service administrator didn't grumble at me or them.

THE FEDERAL LAW ENFORCEMENT
TRAINING CENTER (FLETC)

On October 22, 1985, I began a three-week correctional training program at FLETC; this training center is a law-enforcement fantasy world. All federal law enforcement agencies except the CIA and FBI, train their personnel at this southeast Georgia facility operated by the Treasury Department. U.S. Marshals and the Border Patrol are a "major presence," as FLETC personnel say, at the training center.

Before I went to FLETC, I heard via a prison-staff grapevine that Bureau administrators were concerned about my well-being there. Apparently, they were under the impression that a 38-year-old university professor might not be able to handle the rigors of correctional training and its physical fitness demands.

Three young correctional officers and I represented USP-Lompoc. Our class (BOPB-605) had 47 students, including a North Dakota state corrections lieutenant; an employee of Washington, D.C. corrections; and a sergeant from Fort Leavenworth, an Army stockade. Of my classmates, 16 were women; 29 students were COs, including 5 women. Everyone wore a Bureau uniform: grey slacks, white shirt, black shoes, burgundy clip-on tie, blue nylon wind breaker, and a blue hat with a Bureau patch proudly displayed on its front.

Living facilities at FLETC were full when our class arrived, so we lived "off base" in a local motel. At 7:00 each morning we were bused to class, and, depending on afternoon activities, we were bused back late in the afternoon. Every morning opened with a lecture at 7:30 sharp: employee conduct and responsibility; inmate discipline system; firearms and decision shooting; stress; inmate religious issues; institution disturbances; hostages; abnormal behavior and suicide prevention; sex in correctional settings; legal issues in emergencies; central inmate monitoring; correctional law and rights and responsibilities of correctional staff; custody and security; inmate program planning; inmate supervision techniques; gathering information from inmates; and practical exercises, including proper use of handcuffs, Martin (belly) chains and leg irons, and an (evening) escape simulation, using "dummy" weapons.

After each morning lecture, half of us attended Aikido training, and the other half went to the firing range. Following lunch (the food was terrific), we went back to our classroom for another lecture, and then to the firing range or self-defense, whichever we didn't have that morning.

The Bureau is very serious about achieving satisfactory performance levels and about evaluating new employees' ethics. Two people in my class washed out after failing on numerous attempts to qualify with a .38-caliber handgun. Three new employees (two men, and a woman whose husband was an FPS lieutenant) in another training class failed to pay a local restaurant dinner bill on their first Friday night in Glynco and were "sent home," said an instructor, at 7:30 the following Monday morning.

The training and evaluation was rigorous (Fleisher, 1986a). There were two written examinations on lectures and on material from a 1¼ inch-thick correctional techniques manual, filled mainly with Bureau policy statements. We had a sweaty, on-the-mat Aikido final. And we had firearms qualification with a .38 revolver, a 12-gauge shotgun and a .30-caliber carbine. Without exception, everyone enjoyed the firing range most. Least appreciated by those men and women who smoked too much, drank too much, or ate too much was the physical fitness examination.

We were timed in a mile-and-a-half run in the midday humidity of Georgia; we did bench presses; we ran an agility drill through an obstacle course; our flexibility was measured; and our instructors even brought out "fat-calipers" to measure everyone's blubber. Each score was charted by percentile, measured against age; to pass, everyone had to score above the 70th percentile. I graduated on November 7, 1985, with honors. After the ceremony, the deputy director of the Bureau's FLETC program approached me: "I got a few calls about you from the western regional office. There were some people there who thought you couldn't make it through this program. And they were worried about you! They should have worried about the kids in their twenties."

TEACHING CORRECTIONS

After FLETC, I developed a critical attitude toward Bureau training programs (IFT, OJT, FLETC). I knew a lot of policy when I finished my training, but I was very short on social and verbal skills that are essential in a correctional worker's daily interaction with inmates. These are a line hack's only weapons. Putting on handcuffs and using a radio are easy to learn. But knowing how to make prudent decisions quickly, particularly in face-to-face confrontations with hot convicts, would (I thought) keep a new hack on the job longer, and should keep his teeth in his mouth longer, too.

I thought that working as a trainer could serve me and the institution well, although it would be dangerous if done poorly. I volunteered my services to Barney Halpern, who agreed to use me. Training sessions gave me very high visibility in a responsible role. I taught correctional stress in annual training twice, a one-day session in October 1985, and a two-day workshop in September 1986. I conducted this training session as a focus group, trying to collect hacks' ideas about stresses on the job, and how they thought these contribute to low morale and high staff turnover. One correctional worker said that "giving us a chance to bitch, without worrying about the boss hearing it, is stress relief enough for me." A psychologist at USP-Lompoc called this "career fear," a general fear among correctional workers of administrative reprisal on them.

In January 1986, I became a regular trainer in IFT and in annual training. Every other week in IFT, I taught sessions on report writing and administrative remedy to new employees; groups ranged in size from about 5 to 20 or 25. I followed the Bureau's training lessons, but added ethnographic data. For example, I taught new employees how to complete an incident report form (which is the extent of the Bureau's prescribed lesson plan), but I also taught them how to verbally defuse hostile convicts; I told them how to make decisions about selecting among similar prohibited act codes; I informed them how to choose between informally or formally resolving an incident (using IDC or UDC); and so on. I also discussed the effects of "culture shock" on new hacks. I tried to stop future problems by telling new hacks that they would have emotional ups-and-downs but not to worry about them, because those reactions should go away.

I wrote an incident report handbook (Fleisher, 1985b). In my daily round, I spent hundreds of hours in the lieutenant's office, listening and watching. Too often, I heard lieutenants grumble about staffers who didn't prepare incident reports properly. "God-damn it, he's dumber than shit. Why the fuck can't he get this straight." Or, "Jesus Christ, you stupid fuck. How long have you been doing this?" Incident reports were a morale problem.

I decided to fill the void that existed between prescribed Bureau training and what hacks really needed to know about incident reports with ethnographic data, elicited from senior lieutenants. I used a time-honored, ethnographic technique: "O.K., lieutenant, what's the most important thing a (new) hack needs to know about incident reports?" And so on. I organized these data and added to them, creating an extensive set of carefully edited incident report descriptions. These provided hacks with a model for writing their own descriptions. I returned this manual to the lieutenants for their comments. Then it went to Barney Halpern, to both AWs, to the captain, to the warden, and to the regional office. It was included in postorders, and a copy was given to each new employee in IFT and to each employee in annual training.

I had to develop new lessons for annual training. Report writing in IFT was taught by the numbers; new hacks didn't know anything. But it's very different in annual training; experienced correctional workers are always a tough audience. I got some advice from an old-timer: "Too much of that university bullshit, and they'll walk out on you!"

Every annual training class had about 40 employees, many of whom were writing incident reports when I was still in high school. I prepared a series of ten study cases (Fleisher, 1986b); each included a controversial (by my definition) verbatim incident report description and the prohibited act code(s) selected by the staff writer. I turned these sessions into discussion groups by asking staffers a series of questions about these data. Is the prohibited act code correct? Should this incident have been informally resolved? Does the incident description substantiate the code violation?

Training sessions were never dull. The staffers almost always got into hot arguments among themselves. I guided the discussion with more questions, and took lots of notes. Each session gave me new data and more interpretations about how staffers make discipline decisions. Two and a half months and about 440 retrained and refreshed employees later, I reached the bottom, when I stopped hearing new information in the sessions. I incorporated all of these data in new employee, IFT training.

EARNING RESPECT

I began earning respect ("making my bones") by participating in every correctional activity, particularly in "emergencies"—fights, assaults, stickings, escapes, and a killing. Responding to emergencies was the most significant aspect of my daily participation in the penitentiary, of building rapport, and of understanding violence as it affects inmates and staffers alike.

Emergencies are signaled in several ways. A body alarm, a triple deuce (called "deuces"), and a metal whistle are "emergency communications devices," in Bureau language. A two-way radio transmission or a "regular" phone call will also get emergency help; those are used when a staffer anticipates an escalating problem but doesn't yet have a serious emergency. I kept a radio in my office so I wouldn't miss any action.

I carried a metal whistle, as did other staffers. I never heard anyone use a whistle to call for help; and I never heard a story about anyone using one in an emergency. My whistle was a good conversation piece, though. Inmates enjoyed teasing me about carrying it, particularly when we were getting to know each other. Some teasing was mild: "Do you really think that you're going to have time to get that whistle off your belt, if some stoned convict jumps your ass some night?" Other comments, like this one, were less friendly: "Somebody will take that stupid fucking thing and shove it up your dumb ass!"

A body alarm is an electronic sending device, encased in red plastic, about the size of a two-way radio. It attaches to a line staffer's belt. A small black button on its top, once pressed, flashes a red light on central control's body-alarm board; the light marks the emergency's location, and it sets off a loud, unmistakable screech that's clearly audible in the main corridor if it's quiet. Once alerted, the control room officer uses his intercom to call the operation's lieutenant. I didn't carry a body alarm. Men who supervise inmates carry it; all unit officers carry one. Women working in the hospital and the AW's secretary also have one, even though they never supervise convicts and are never alone with inmates. A staffer told me that an "AW's secretary was raped by a convict, right on top of her desk, back when the place was an FCI. That's why they carry a body alarm."

Dialing 2-2-2 is the universal FPS emergency number. When it is dialed from any regular, black penitentiary telephone, the call is received on red telephones in executive administrators' and security offices. Red triple-deuce phones ring differently than black telephones. A triple-deuce phone sounds-off in loud, oddly toned, difficult-to-miss rings. At USP-Lompoc, too, when a black telephone's receiver is off its hook for more than thirty seconds, an alarm is sounded in central control.

There are "false alarms," too. Some occur when an inmate dials a triple deuce without his supervisor seeing him. But most triple-deuce false alarms are attributed to the "old, fucked-up phone system," according to a lieutenant.

My emergency experiences include one killing in spring 1986; one serious assault in fall 1985 and a second one in spring 1986; five serious fights; one escape (from an I-unit rec cage); two assaults on staff; numerous "hot" incidents without bloodshed; and many false alarms. Reacting to violence was exhilarating, hair-raising, and exciting. After a few responses I looked forward to it.

Two days short of one month on the job, I saw my first cellblock violence, a minor incident. Just after lunch, about 12:50 p.m., a drunk white-racist, Aryan Brotherhood "want-to-be" assaulted a black counselor, a fifteen-year Bureau and Viet Nam veteran. A few cuts and a couple of bloody noses was the result.

But it wasn't until after my participation in a serious assault in 1985 that I began to see the positive social effects of getting involved in violence. Afterward, staffers reacted to me differently than they had before. Staffers who hadn't said anything to me before this, and staffers who hadn't before called me by name, now began paying attention to me. We now had conversations, and they addressed me by name. With a personal understanding of what happens in such an event, I was able to discuss and explore with hacks their experiences with, and attitudes toward, violence.

After having helped control a scene of cellblock violence, and having faced numerous high-stress situations among convicts, I felt a sense of belonging to the group, a sense of sharing in the ethos of penitentiary staff. I began to understand the pressure on new hacks who are awaiting this penitentiary rite of passage; the practical and emotional significance of experiencing violence; the snobbery of penitentiary line staff toward staff at less violent institutions; and the personal satisfaction that comes after coping with violence.

GETTING TOO INVOLVED

Despite rocky moments, I had good relationships with most inmates cited here. They told wonderful, colorful, and humorous stories about their criminal adventures, which were often recalled among other, more poignant and dramatic recollections of their youths and early family lives. These inmates didn't insult me or attack staff, though many of them landed in I-unit for fighting or drinking, for fighting and drinking, or for "dirty UAs" (drug use detected in urinalysis).

There were some convicts I didn't like. They were rude, nasty, and belligerent to me, to staffers, and to other inmates. I tried to initiate conversations with some of them, but it never worked. I'd usually either get a cold shoulder, no answer to anything I said, or a quick "Fuck you." I remember one of these guys well. He approached me: "What do you do here?" "Research," I said. He grabbed his crotch: "Here, research this, you silly fuck!"

Another convict always "threw me the finger"; whenever he walked by me, he would begin scratching his nose or cheek with his middle finger flying high. He always hid himself behind cardboard "3-D" glasses, so I never had a chance to look him in the eye. I never said anything to him, either; he was as big as a hillside. I told myself that this was research, and that I shouldn't take any of it personally. After all, these were all data! But I could only stand so much.

Convict Lowry had a very special place in my heart. From the instant I saw him in September 1986, I despised him. Several days after Lowry arrived from an FCI, I attended his unit in-take session in his CM's office. This was his first meeting with his CM and UM, and his second disciplinary transfer.

Lowry walked in without looking at any of us, and quickly sat down. He drooped his arms over the chairs adjacent to his, and hadn't yet looked at anyone when the UM began the meeting.

UM: "Lowry, this is Dr. Fleisher. He'll be observing. Is this O.K. with you?" Lowry grunted his approval, but then began talking.

Lowry: "You promised me a fucking phone call the day I drove up here, and I ain't got it. When am I getting my goddamn phone call?"

UM: "First things first. Let's take care of this, and then we can talk about that. O.K.? Have you thought about a job or VT program?"

Lowry: "Fuck that. When do I get my goddamn phone call. My ol' lady is sitting in a fucking federal prison, and I want to talk to her. When do I get my fucking call?"

UM: "We can talk about that later. I told you we'd talk about a phone call, and we will. Let's take care of business now."

Lowery: "Fuck you and your business. I want my call. All you fucking people are assholes. Federal prisons are full of assholes like you."

So it continued. He insisted on making his phone call from his UM's office, then and there. He didn't answer any questions or offer any information about programming interests. He turned each question and every comment into a complaint. The longer I sat next to him, the more I hated him.

When this session ended, I said to the UM and CM: "How do you put up with assholes like him?" They laughed.

CM: "It's part of the job."

"Yeah," I said, "a lousy part of the job."

I couldn't stop thinking about Lowry. I talked to his UM about him for weeks afterward with comments like this one: "I want to be there when he gets hit. And you know, somebody's going to hit him, unless he changes his attitude in one helluva hurry."

One Saturday afternoon, about a week before I left for FLETC, Lowry got drunk on homebrew in his cellblock and called a black inmate a "nigger." After the fistfight, both convicts were put in I-unit for three weeks.

At FLETC, near the end of October, one of my fellow USP-Lompoc trainees called the penitentiary and then reported the news to me: "There's been a couple of stickings in the last few days." I called my friend (Lowry's UM) that evening and asked about the recent violence.

UM: "One of them was an AB hit [a killing arranged, or contracted, by the Aryan Brotherhood, a prison gang], but they missed. The other one, you'll love. It was Lowry. The morning after he got out of I-unit at about 6:30 during breakfast, he got hit in his cell. They got him about 18, 20 times in the chest, shoulders, back, arms. They got him good."

I asked: "Is he still alive?"

UM: "Yeah, in fact he walked to the hospital, dripping blood all down the corridor. They got him with a short shank. Looks like they wanted to teach that young man manners!"

I said: "Shit! Maybe next time, they won't fuck it up."

Becomes his subjects

LOSING OBJECTIVITY

After many months of submersion in the penitentiary, it became harder and harder to keep my observations and thoughts separate from those of staff and inmates (see Rhodes, 1986 for a penetrating analysis of an anthropologist's role as institutional analyst). From September 1985 to January 1986, I lost touch with my role as research anthropologist and began to think of myself as a correctional worker. My thinking about penitentiary research started to fuse with notions, opinions, and beliefs of inmates and penitentiary staffers. I began to answer my own research questions, as if I were a correctional worker. In other words, I became my own informant. "I work here. I've been trained. I have to deal with thugs, too. I've seen what they have seen. Why isn't my opinion as good as theirs," I thought. I was becoming lost.

I had forgotten that I was a researcher whose role was to distinguish between what people say and what people do, and to put both in the holistic context of this massive government warehouse. My specific research, including new correctional officer training and retention issues, causes of violence, staff-inmate relations, and scrutinizing management strategies began to fade away in my mind.

I had become a "Bureau man," as hacks say, and a quiet advocate of the hacks, wanting to advance their "cause" (their complaint, gripes, and bitches) in my writing. What hacks did was "right," what convicts did was "wrong." Case closed. I defended the Bureau to my neighbors and friends. I found myself becoming more aggressive with impolite convicts, and, more than once I caught myself giving them etiquette lessons. My social reference group switched away from the university and toward the "Mash-like" world of penitentiary men. I thoroughly enjoyed working and partying among line staffers, managers, and administrators, and I developed several close friendships which have continued until today.

I recognized that I, too, had become an object of the prison socialization process that I had come to study. This recognition came only after I had a chance to open up, in February, 1986, to a close friend who was also an anthropologist (see Powdermaker, 1966: 229; also see Fujisaka and Grayzel, 1978: 178; cf. Levine, 1973: 388 and Giallombardo, 1966: 191). With the help of colleagues I regained my perspective, and from then on I kept my eye on research. I learned to be a more objective prison researcher, but I couldn't remain unaffected by the culture of staff and inmates.

RAPPORT WITH INMATES

SLIM

I met Slim in the mess hall. We got along instantly. Slim (a.k.a. The Pimp) was a member of the Los Angeles Crips in the early 1970s (see George F. Will's essay about "Sam," a Los Angeles street gang member, in *Newsweek,* March 28, 1988). He had a "CC" (Compton Crips) tattooed on one forearm and the PIMPING MAN scrawled in ink on his upper left arm. He had been a teenage heroin addict, smoked marijuana, but didn't like alcohol.

I first talked to Slim early in fall 1985. At about 10 a.m., I spotted Frankie as I was walking from the kitchen through the mess hall. I joined him at one of the 97 plastic-top tables. We were sitting near the two steel entrance doors. As we talked, Slim walked over, nodded his head and sat down with us.

He looked at me and, without hesitating, said, "What do you do here?" I replied, "I'm an anthropologist." "A what?" he asked. "What are you doing in here?"

I explained. We chatted for about fifteen minutes. I told him about my state prison research and that I really wanted to do research on prison gangs and street gangs at San Quentin or Folsom. At that, he just shook his head, quietly saying, "You like to think about dying, huh?"

I asked Slim if he knew any street or prison gang members at Lompoc; he smiled, saying nothing. I then asked if he had done time in other state or federal prisons; he looked across the table at Frankie, they smiled at each other.

Slim said, "Yeah, I've done a little time." "Where?" I asked. "You want serious joints or all of them?" he said. "Serious joints, for now," I replied. He rattled off the list: "San Quentin, Folsom, Soledad, California Men's Colony." Then he added, "I did time in county [jails] and juvie in LA [juvenile hall in Los Angeles]." That opened our first conversation. Slim became one of my most dependable sources about daily prison goings-on, and about Los Angeles street gangs and their operation in USP-Lompoc.

Slim never asked me for favors such as mailing a special letter, buying something for him on the streets and walking it in, or making a special phone call for him. He never asked for money or contraband. Best of all, he loved to talk about himself. He was bright and articulate, and had a well-developed and ironic sense of humor. He had a clear view of his future, undistorted by pipe dreams of achieving middle-class comforts or legitimate fame and fortune. He was honest about his chances of going straight after his parole, and freely admitted that he enjoyed being a "gangster," as he liked calling himself.

"Gangsterism has been good to me," he said; it was financially profitable; it gave him a sense of power over life and death, which he admitted enjoying thoroughly; and he anticipated returning to a gangster lifestyle once he was paroled in late 1986. Slim's self-reported criminal lifestyle was corroborated in his jacket. In fact, his admissions of violence just scratched the surface of his twenty-year spree of gangsterism.

Slim came into Lompoc wanting to do his sentence without picking up additional time for prison violations. He had a small cadre of acquaintances, but usually kept to himself.

Slim was almost able to make himself invisible among other inmates. He slowly and grudgingly walked to work in the mess hall, where he was supposed to pick up dishes left behind on tables, clean up spills, mop the floor, and so on. But he did as little as he could get away with. He would wander around the seating area and stop to say a few words and laugh with other inmates, until, eventually, his staff supervisor would round him up and drag him off.

Slim rarely appeared in public (outside of his cell) with his head uncovered. Just hanging around his cellblock, he almost always wore a white food server's cap or a clear plastic shower cap. He rarely uncovered his eyes, almost always wearing dark or reflective sunglasses as he sauntered slowly up and down the main corridor, back and forth from his cellblock to food service, to the yard, to the gymnasium, and to the auditorium for Friday afternoon Black Muslim services. His steel-toed black boots were always untied, the tongues folded forward, showing his institution-issue white socks. Slim was never without Camel regulars tucked away in the prison-issue green and baggy army fatigue jacket; his clothing always smelled of grease, the odor of the prison kitchen.

Though he found pride in adopting convict dress, Slim didn't like being "underdressed." Leaning back in his chair in my office he took a long drag on an unfiltered Camel.

> When I get out of here, you gotta see me at home. Yeah, my house is the one with the two new BMWs in the driveway. On the streets, man, I got some wardrobe. One of the worst things that ever happened to me was fucking up my $500 rain coat, tailored, full length. It was a real gangster

jacket. The cops came after me in this cocktail lounge; I ran my ass off through the alleys, hiding behind garbage dumpsters. That shit's beneath a man like me. Those L.A. cops don't fuck around; they shoot first and talk later. I jumped one of them anchor fences, you know with them wires sticking up on top there, and my coat hooked the top and ripped. Shit . . . that pissed me off. But I'll get another one. You should get one, Mark, you'd look good—but you can't afford one, huh?

As he passed my office, without fail he looked in, and if I was there he would bang on the door with his fist, make a "C" shape with his fingers, standing for Crips, smile and move on. Sometimes he shot me with his hand, shaped like a gun. That kid's game always caught my attention when Slim did it.

After we got to know each other, he would invite himself into my office and spend hours telling me about his family and his early life on the street. I enjoyed listening to his "gang-banging" [gang fighting] stories from his days as a Compton Crip; today there are some 2,400 Crips in the Los Angeles area and hundreds more in other major cities (Seattle, Portland, and Phoenix) in the western United States. As a teenager in the Compton District, Slim's criminal life began early.

I was sent to [Los Angeles] Central [juvenile hall] at 12, and Selmar at 13, and been rockin' and rollin' with it ever since. I was on the streets gang-banging, dealing drugs, pimping, pandering, contracting, collecting, jacking [stealing from criminals, such as drug dealers], and I was the trigger man in a drug operation.

He was a heroin junkie at 16, and didn't break his "stomach habit" (he was eating heroin) until 23. Later he became a coke addict, "shooting cocaine all night, until the police came to get me." Slim's violence goes back to his childhood.

Me and my cousin tore this girl's lip from here to here. We were about seven or eight. I remember the first time I cut a guy with a hook knife. I hit him from here to here [across the cheek]. At first, it opened, then blood rushed into it. It opened up and you could see the white flesh in it. I looked at the knife and said, "Damn, it works good!" When I was going to school, they sent me to a psychiatrist. I guess they didn't like my hostile ways. I guess I've always been a mobster. Violence is just a way of life. When I was a kid, I watched my uncle throw drinking alcohol on some woman and light it. When I was pimping, every woman I had got some [violence]. I chopped off Betty's finger with a machete and hooked her up to the circuits [he said he used live electric wires to torture his girls]. It was my form of discipline. The ones I put the circuits to, I had to do only one time. I did Joyce with a golf club, the putting iron. I was a barbarian then. I would tie them up and put the circuits to their titties, thighs, and toes.

They would say to me, "You're a cold motherfucker Slim." Yeah, those were the good old days.

Nineteen trips in and out of the L.A. County jail; two visits to the Clarke County jail; one time in the Culver City jail; two trips to the Englewood County jail; and two stints in the Las Vegas County jail were interspersed with time in the California Men's Colony; California Institute for Men; Deuel Vocational Institution ("the gladiator school," as he called it) at Tracey, California; Soledad; Folsom; San Quentin; and now USP-Lompoc. I corroborated these self-reported incarcerations, and there were others. In three years at USP-Lompoc, he was cited once for insolence and once for failing to go to work. But despite his peaceful record at Lompoc, he says that he is violent: "I'm dangerous if I have to be. Deadly if I have to be. I can be pretty ugly if the situation calls for it."

He admits to being a central figure in six hits in San Quentin, two in Folsom, two in Soledad, and numerous fights in other places. Slim:

> I was real violent. I thrived on it; I was looking for it. It was like a feeling of power to know you could stomp the other guy. It gives you a feel of false pride and power today. Fear is more powerful than love. You can love a person and fear them, too. Fear has a power all its own. In my neighborhood, neighbors are afraid of me. They think they could be next. Fear gives the gang power over that community. Fear can also get you killed. People will fear you to the point where they'll kill you.

I asked him about street gangs and prison gangs. He said he didn't know much about prison gangs, but he began recounting the history of the Crips in detail, and he claimed to be an original gang member. Slim gave me lesson one in Los Angeles street gang folklore one morning in the mess hall, just before lunch. I took notes on napkins.

In the early days of the late 1950s to mid-1960s, according to Slim, there were only a few gangs on the Los Angeles streets. These included the Gladiators, whom Slim called "pathfinders" because they started the L.A. gang movement. The Roman Pearls and the Businessmen were both chapters of the Gladiators. The Outlaws, the Slausens, and the Dell Vikings completed his list. As groups formed alliances among themselves, he explained, the Gladiators and Outlaws paired up against the Slausens and Dell Vikings.

Gangs recruited members from high schools, and became localized in neighborhoods. During his Freemont High School years, Slim was an Avenue, which was an Outlaw (Jefferson High School) splinter group; later, he said, the Crips emerged as a splinter group of the Avenues.

Wearing their "ace-deuce" (derby) hats and carrying canes, the Crips got their gang name, according to Slim, from the "Chicago man [who] came to L.A. in the '50s. He was crippled and used a cane." Thus, the name Crip, from crippled. (Camp and Camp [1985: 23] suggest that Crip is an acronym for Common Revolution in Progress.)

This Chicago man, said Slim, helped the teenagers band together into somewhat-organized street groups. The original Crips were from south central L.A.; there were the Eastside Crips, and later, as they expanded into western neighborhoods, the Westside Crips.

Today in Los Angeles, he said, there are the Main Street Crips, Insane Crips, Harlem Crips, Blackstone Crips, Bicentennial Crips, GQs [Gentlemen Quarterlies], War-Babies [young gang-bangers], Playboys, the Four-Trey Crips [Third World Crips], Five-Deuce Crips, Five-Deuce BGCs [Broadway Gangster Crips], Rollin' '60s, Eight-Trey Gangsters, Kitchen Crips, Cute 102s, Grape Street Crips, CCs [Compton Crips], Hoover Crips, Vaness Boys, Figueroa Boys, Bonzella Boys, and UGs [Underground Crips], among tens of other neighborhood gangs. (The Playboy Gangster Crips have recently become notorious; see the *Wall Street Journal* article "Los Angeles Seeks Ultimate Weapon in Gang War," March 30, 1988.)

Today's Crips mark membership with beenies and blue "rags," blue handkerchiefs worn as headbands or hanging out of a pant's pocket. Each Crip set, a neighborhood gang, uses a distinctive handsign: the Crip "C" is made by thumb and forefinger folded into a "C," with three remaining fingers curled and folded down on the palm. Members' sidewalk gait follows the rules of the Crip Walk.

"Cuzz" is the common greeting used among members of friendly Crip sets; it also is used as a friendly term of greeting among USP-Lompoc blacks who aren't necessarily members of street gangs.

Usually, says Slim, each set begins with some six to ten guys. As time passes and the group grows, it develops into a ranked organization: soldiers, gang members "out making their bones," corporals, and lieutenants. These ranks work under a set's council of five or six leaders who make decisions for the set's operations.

Gang-banging is initiated by predatory expansion for territory, to take on drug traffic, and to avenge "disrespect" by other sets. Membership, says Slim, is the only way that a teenager from the poverty areas of Los Angeles could "fight his way up out of there." The fighting among competing sets doesn't end when members leave the streets, however.

Opposing the Crips, according to Slim, are all other groups, including the Mafia, the BGFs [Black Guerilla Family], and the Crips' archenemies, the Bloods, who carry red rags and use the term, "blood," in mutual greetings. "They're slobs," said Slim. "Those punks couldn't make it into Crips."

The Pirus, one of numerous Blood sets, occupy a special place of anger and disdain for Slim (see National Law Enforcement Institute, 1986). The Pirus killed a close street companion of his in 1976, during a "drive-by" shooting in CC territory. Slim said a "slob car came by. Some guy stuck his head out the window, yelling 'Hey cuzz, guess who? Who? Piru!' And all shit broke loose." Little Country, Slim's closest boyhood companion, was gunned down and later died in an L.A. hospital. Slim's anger and frustration toward Pirus was heightened when, during Little Country's funeral, the Pirus "rode down on us, shooting up Country's casket. A couple Slobs jumped out of the car, dumped the body [out of the casket] and stomped it. The Pirus got their reputation behind that," Slim said.

Today, Slim still carries animosity toward street Pirus into dealings with them at USP-Lompoc. On more than one occasion, Slim said he armed himself against Pirus. He said he had a long shaft of brass, sharpened to a dangerous point, with tape wrapped around the handle for a sure grip. With this in hand, he was ready if a "Slob got in my face, running his mouth, calling me out." He eagerly anticipated the opportunity to "bust one of them fuckin' slob heads," he said.

Although Slim never showed me his weapon, the main corridor office apprehended a partner of Slim's who was carrying a sharpened staff of brass stuck up his sleeve. That weapon is shown in Figure 5.1. Slim said he liked this weapon "'cause it goes in real easy."

An August 1985 inmate-on-inmate assault in Lompoc's gymnasium iron-pile was fueled by Crip-Piru hatred and "disrespect." Slim describes the scene:

> He's [the victim] juice-mouthing and disrespecting. He rolled down there [to the gym] with that Piru mentality, then he went back down to his house and came back with two red rags hanging out of his pocket. He said something over the iron. He kept on juice-mouthin', and his friends said, "You can't be fuckin' with those people." Pretty soon a bar came down on back of his head and weights on the front of his head. And it was pretty decent! Some bar, that tri-bar; that'll do a decent job. He got his head peeled open decent too; peeled back to the fat.

I asked Slim how he felt about the attack. He said: "The guy brought it on hisself. That's the only way to think about a situation like that. He can't be all intuned upstairs to bring it on himself. A fool don't live in a penitentiary too long."

Adding to the Piru-victim's behavior in the gym, Slim said the Piru had been walking around his cellblock acting like a "tough guy, raising hell in the TV room," and also trying to organize other Pirus "to roll on" (attack) vulnerable inmates. Slim called this "getting up a slob car." The

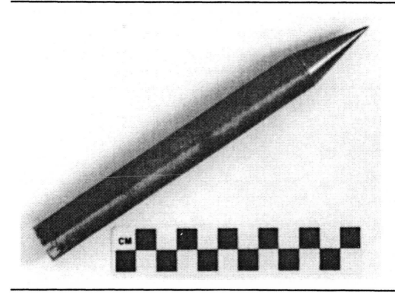

Figure 5.1 Brass Weapon (Similar to the One Carried by Slim The Pimp)

convicts who hit the Piru, Slim said, were "related to the Crips, like Pathfinders. Their tip and Crips are associated, but theirs was a little bit earlier before Crips. They have kinfolk who were Crips."

It isn't uncommon to find Crips like Slim housed in the same cellblock with Pirus. Mixing competing street gangs sets the stage for cellblock violence, but something has to set it off—a pool game or maybe a debt and enthusiastic agitation from bystanders.

Having low numbers of street gang members in each cellblock mitigates the effect of housing competing street gangs together. Slim and other black inmates estimate that there are about 12 Crips and 4 Bloods at Lompoc. When competing sets ready themselves for a fight, an imbalance in set membership frequently stops a fight before it begins: "You can't ride against 'em if you don't have soldiers," says Slim.

Now, at age 33, Slim still lives by a favorite expression: "Live fast, die young, and have a good-looking corpse." When he's on the street, Slim isn't an active Crip, but his emotional ties to the Crips have remained strong.

> Collective violence, yeah. Guys take that real serious. They'll put it on the set [oath of truth], that says you can basically tell if they tell the truth. It's like a religious thing. If a person says it's on the set, he's real sincere about what he's talking about. Then there are collective movements [gangs]. They'll sacrifice their lives for collective ideals. When you under a

constitution and you're called upon to do something, you do it or you jeopardize you' own life or go into pc [protective custody].

Dr. Paul Hofer, a USP-Lompoc psychotherapist, suggests that emotional cohesion binding members to their gangs is analogous in strength and intensity to emotions bonding children to their parents.

EDDIE

Eddie had been in USP-Lompoc for a little more than a year when we met.

I went straight for four years after I got out of [San] Quentin. I did almost nine years in there. One afternoon I was sitting in a San Francisco bar drinking beer and decided to rob an armored truck—just for kicks. I climbed on my Harley, pulled up to the bank [which he had already cased] and waited for the armored truck. It showed up right on time. I stood there watching them unload bags of money and pile them on a dolly. Some ol' fucker was pushing that dolly stacked with money bags. I came up behind him, stuck a gun in ribs and took a bag of cash. I didn't know there was a sending device and money dye in the bag. Then I rode back to the bar, got a beer, and started drinking again. Shit, the San Francisco cops had me in twenty minutes.

I was curious about something. "Eddie, what do you say when you stick a gun in a guy's ribs, as you're robbing him," I asked. Eddie smiled: "Give me your money, or I'll blow your fucking head off. They always hand it over." He laughed.

Eddie is now doing a 20-year sentence:

There are a few people here who are righteously institutionalized. I'm not; well, maybe I am. The streets are geared for failure for a person like me. It scares me to sit in prison and watch the moral decay outside. Things are sophisticated and yet they're very primitive. It's vicious to see what they do to each other in those business offices. I listen to my wife when I'm home, and its appalling to hear what those women do to each other. I'm crazy. I have tattoos. I'm a biker and I look like one. People on the street say, "Here, Eddie, take some grass or coke." Shit, I take it all! It's too easy on the streets. I could outwork any motherfucker. I'm strong, aggressive; I take charge, but you got to learn self-control.

When Eddie was a little drunk, or a little stoned on grass, or a little of both, he was a terrific storyteller. But he wasn't just a little drunk or a little stoned too often (see Irwin, 1980: 19-20). I'd go to his cell in the evening to sit and chat with him and others who came by when they saw me, and I'd often find him so stoned that he couldn't lift his head off his pillow: "Hi, I'm OK," he'd slur, as he was barely able to lift one arm slightly off his bed, "I'll talk to you tomorrow."

Once I found Eddie lying on his bed at 6:30 in the morning, drinking homebrew wine out of a plastic bottle, which he stashed under his bed, and talking to a friend. Eddie wasn't a cellblock troublemaker, so hacks didn't go out of their way to shake down his cell. "If you're a decent dude, they'll leave 'ya alone," he said.

There was a faint smell of grass in his cell, and I saw two roaches squashed in an ashtray on top of his footlocker. Roaches are a clear indication of grass smoking, so Eddie often used his footlocker's padlock as a grass pipe.

"I started drinking last night and I'm so hungover now, there's no point in stopping. Grass helps with the headache, you know. Fuck it, I'll make it to work. If not I'll come back home and go to sleep later. What are they going to do, fire me! Fuck 'em."

Eddie fancied himself as a maker of fine prison wine.

I brew the finest mead you ever tasted. No shit, man, honey mead. I got a lot of recipes, and my best stuff is mead. It's real mellow, but it takes longer to cook than the others, but it's worth the wait. I can get some other homebrew that's ready in two or three days, if I stash it in a warm spot. The best place for cooking it is in the kitchen. There are so many places to hide wine in there, the cops never find it all. And they never really look for it either, unless something happened behind drinking. Then they bring in the serious search-boys who go through everything. It's an ego thing with them, "bust them fucking convicts." You know how they are. Last Saturday morning about quarter to nine, most of the food service inmates were in the back [of the kitchen area], sitting around, drinking and talking bullshit. Some guys were smashed on their asses. A new guy [a food service steward] came in, just looked at us, turned and walked out. He didn't know what the fuck to do.

I visited Eddie in his cell on a Wednesday night in September 1986. He, Cowboy, and several other inmates were busy collecting money to make a special commissary purchase that evening. Eddie was sitting on his plywood toilet-bowl cover, counting money that Cowboy was gathering from inmates along the cell-range. They were all getting excited about going to the commissary. Eddie said he was buying four six-packs of canned orange juice which he, as a self-proclaimed master prison winemaker, was going to ferment into a "delicious sweet, orange wine tonight," he said, "for a Friday night blowout."

Buying a case of orange juice and carrying it into the cellblock in full view of the officer, would, I thought, make them nervous. If the unit officer knew who had the orange juice, he might shake down the convict's cell in a day or two and find the homebrew.

But Eddie wasn't worried. There was a rookie hack working the unit, and a rookie might not think of wine making even if he saw the orange juice. Anyway, Eddie said, a companion would find out where the new hack was located before they walked into the cellblock with the orange juice, hoping the officer wouldn't see them or the juice.

Eddie cleverly thought he wouldn't put the orange juice in his cell at first, but in someone else's cell. Then, later that evening when it was darker and when the officer was walking the ranges, shaking down cells, sniffing the air for signs of marijuana, and fermenting homebrew, he would transfer the orange juice to his cell and begin making his wine. Eddie and the others were certain they could beat the rookie cop at their game of making homebrew. That night, they did.

Wine and grass were two of Eddie's three passions. His tattoos were the third. One midweek evening at about 7:30, I headed to Eddie's cell. Walking down the flats, I saw convict Jake "jiggering" (a jigger is a lookout) at Eddie's cell door. As I approached him, I saw Jake turn his head and say, "Staff's coming," but his warning was a little too late. I walked in as Eddie's tattooist was working on him. When he saw me, Eddie's face relaxed, but the tattooist didn't know me, and looked startled. "Don't sweat it. He's all right," said Eddie to the tattooist; he looked at me to be sure of that. "I won't say anything," I said.

"Hey, you want to see it, the tattoo machine?," he asked. "Of course," I said. Eddie explained:

> I keep it wrapped in plastic bags and stick it in the outlet pipe of the toilet. They never look in there when they shake down. I tie a thin wire to it and hook it under the toilet rim. The rookie cops they send around don't want to stick their hands in my toilet, so it's safe. Otherwise, I keep it in this tin can and shove it under my bed. They never look inside this either.

"Ink," as Eddie called tattoos, cover his arms and chest. His latest (the one I walked in on) was a foot-long .45-caliber revolver tattooed on the right side of his stomach, and positioned so that the barrel stuck under the right side of his wrinkled green army fatigues. Eddie claims that "ink scares new pigs. They think the more ink you have, the longer you been in the joint, and the badder you are. It works. I walk by the office at night with my shirt off when a fish is working, and I can tell he's scared. If new fish cops are scared, they leave us alone."

A small "SQ" (San Quentin) tattoo appears on the inner surface of his left wrist. "I'm proud of this one. I've lived through Quentin. You find a lot of guys with this one on their wrist or pecs [chest muscle]." His ink, his swagger, and his little green hat with its small, upturned brim (I called it his "Alcatraz" hat) made Eddie look as though he had popped out of an Edward G. Robinson prison movie. His image was all-important.

Eddie told great stories. I sat with him and Frankie one morning in the mess hall at about 10:30; Eddie liked Frankie, even though Frankie was black. Frankie and I listened as Eddie told us about an electric chair he made for zapping field mice, which he took from mouse traps set in food storage rooms. Eddie's job gave him access to metal, wire, and similar materials, so for a while I almost believed this.

I took some thin strips of metal, drilled holes at the corners and wired them together into a chair. I even put a back on it, so I could sit those little fuckers straight up. I wrap 'em in place with string around their chest. They sit in there looking like little mouse-convicts. I rigged the chair to an extension cord I made, and I even put in a switch. I got a bunch of mice from the traps in the back and threw them in a bucket of water. I tied up some of them, and lined them up on the floor next to the chair. I take a big one, one that looks guilty, sit him in the chair, tie his little ass up, and then ask him the big question: "Did you commit that crime?" When he doesn't answer, I hit the juice. His little-bitty eyes start bugging out, and he starts to shake. Fried. Then I'd get another one, strap him in, and ask him: "Did you commit that crime?" I never juiced any pregnant ones, though.

Frankie laughed so hard his head dropped to the table top. When he regained control, Frankie looked at Eddie and asked: "Did electrocuting them mice deter any of them others from crime?" With a straight face, Eddie answered him: "Fuck no. These are some bad motherfucking mice!" We roared again, and Eddie smiled and readjusted the brim of his Alcatraz hat. Although he promised to give me the mouse electric chair as a going home gift when I left, Eddie never even showed it to me, even though I asked over and over.

The stakes in keeping rapport can be high. Eddie once asked me to help him and several of his cellblock buddies. His plan was this: I was to withdraw $200 from his savings account in a Lompoc bank, wire $175 to a street person, and keep $25 for myself. Eddie said he was helping friends who had accumulated gambling debts. The debt "was due yesterday and if ain't paid, there's going to be something serious behind it," he told me.

"The warden would hang me out to dry if he found out," I said. Eddie said there was no chance of getting caught. The money, he said, was in his account in a downtown Lompoc bank, and by his writing a letter to the bank, explaining the situation, no one would question the transaction.

"What if the bank teller is an inmate's wife," I said, "and, after using my Bureau ID to make this illegal financial transaction, she told her husband, some convict in here, who then tried to blackmail me into doing other things for him and his friends? What then?"

"It can't happen. Will you do it?" asked Eddie. I said, "I can't." He backed off, apologized for approaching me with his problem, and said: "You'll never hear about this again. I hope this hasn't ruined our relationship." That was at the end of May 1986. Several weeks later, early on an evening watch, convict Mayes was "ambushed" in L-unit, said Eddie. "They hit him on the stairs near C-range. He knew it was coming, so he was packed [carrying a weapon], but they hit him real good. One in the front, one in the back. They opened the back of his arm from his shoulder all the way down to his elbow. I never saw a cut that bad."

Eddie said the attack was my fault, because I hadn't wired the money. With that remark, my patience went out the window, and I told him that paying off Mayes's and others' gambling debts wasn't my responsibility, and that Mayes should have thought about debt repayment long before he lost his money. The issue was then closed, and I never heard another word about it, but it wasn't the last problem I had with Eddie.

Eddie had changed jobs, and now he was the diet cook, preparing bland food for inmates on special no-salt, no-spice diets. I ran into him one morning in the mess hall just before lunch. His eyes were bloodshot and his breath smelled of homebrew wine, but he wasn't drunk enough to arouse anyone's attention.

He took his post behind steamtable three, on the far right of the mess hall. He talked about a visit he had recently with his mother, whom he hadn't seen in almost seven years, and grandmother who visited him because, Eddie said, "she thinks she'd be dead before I get out of here." As we talked, Carl Lowen, a black unit manager, who was supervising the dietline, caught my attention and motioned for me to walk over to him. I did.

He and I talked, and as we did, I looked over at Eddie, but he was noticeably angry and never looked back at me. Lighting Camel after Camel, he paced around his work station, and, after several quick puffs on each one, he threw the half-smoked butt to the floor. Eventually, he just walked away from the diet line, leaving his post to someone else.

As the meal was drawing to an end, I left the diet line and walked toward the exit doors. Eddie was standing near the dishroom, at the back of dining hall. I walked up to him: "What's going on?" He said nothing and just glared at me. "What's the problem?" I asked. "You," he growled. "You were talking to that fucking nigger, and I hate fucking niggers. You left me to talk to that fucking nigger!" As his raving continued, it got louder and louder.

We were standing near the seating area where black inmates

customarily sit. I was getting nervous, as many of them stopped eating and turned toward us. I tried to calm him by saying that Carl was my friend. Eddie didn't want to listen.

As his anger grew, he edged closer and closer to me, until we were almost touching, chest to chest. I thought that he was going to take my head off or that black inmates, who had heard Eddie's racist remarks, were going to start a brawl, and that I would end up in the middle of it.

While Eddie was haranguing me, a food-service staffer in the kitchen got into a scuffle with a Mariel-Cuban inmate who, after refusing to be shaken down, grabbed a four-foot-long, wooden stirring pad and threatened to smack the staffer with it. Another kitchen staffer at the scene radioed for help. I saw Lt. Guy Baker running through the mess hall toward the kitchen, so I turned and joined him and others following behind him. That fight gave me a legitimate and macho way out of my problem.

I avoided Eddie for a week. I met him again in the dining hall. "I scared you, didn't I!" he laughed. "You're damn right. I thought you were going to clobber me," I replied. "I pissed off a lot of people that day. I said some things to a few blacks that I shouldn't have said. We'll see if I have to pay for it!" Eddie's light attitude was his way of apologizing.

THOM

My rockiest relationship developed with Thom, who lived on D-range in L-unit. Thom was black, and for that and other reasons Eddie despised him. Thom, like Eddie, was usually drunk or stoned on weed. Thom was a belligerent drunk, though, and he was always ready to fight when he was drinking or drinking and smoking grass. I can't remember a single day when his eyes weren't glazed by drugs or wine.

I met Thom early one morning in L-unit. I was chatting with inmate Callahan and a few others who had just come back to the unit after finishing their food service jobs. Thom walked slowly by us. He overheard me tell Callahan that I had grown up in New York. "Where?" Thom piped in. "Just outside the city," I replied. "Are you from the city?" I asked. "Brooklyn," he said. "What's a nice Brooklyn boy like you doing in a place like this?" I joked. "Time. A lot of fucking time," he said.

When the unit quieted down in the early afternoon, Thom was slowly walking around the flats near me, looking as though he wanted to talk. "So how long you been in?" I asked him. "Long enough to know I want to go back to New York," he quipped. "Why are you out here? I thought the

Bureau kept guys close to home," I continued. "Well," Thom said, "I was in Lewisburg, but they transferred me here." "Why?" I asked. "I got into trouble," answered Thom. He walked away.

Thom was cold. "He's dangerous . . . one of the most dangerous men in here, especially when he's been drinking," said Mike Rizo. Thom also worked in food service, mopping up after meals. Early in our relationship, I always made sure to walk by him when he was at work. I'd nod, he'd nod, and we'd start talking. It took many long months before he felt comfortable enough to tell me about himself.

One evening, I took him out of L-unit so we could sit quietly in the research office. This was our first and only interview. All other conversations took place in late afternoon in the mess hall, sitting among other inmates, or in the evening in L-unit, hanging over a tier railing. Thom preferred it that way.

I'm 38 years old and I been in penitentiaries for 23 of them. I was first busted at 12. I pulled a fire alarm box. They sent me to the Warwick Training School when I was 13. I did 13 months there. That's where I got to know rapists and murderers. My father would come to visit and give me some money in an envelope for commissary stuff like candy and gum. People would try to take my candy, but I wouldn't fight. A friend told me I'd better fight back, or he would kick my ass. Violence was necessary in the institution. I began fighting by swinging windmills. When I learned how to fight, I was kicking ass. I got to be the second highest guy in the cottage. I was in D-2. Violence does all the talking.

Thom had "family problems," as he called them, and turned to the streets.

My stepmother was nine years older than me. She had a daughter by my father. A lot of resentment fell my way from the family and my stepmother. I found more satisfaction being away from home. It gave me a sense of independence. I was the warlord of the Chaplins [a Brooklyn street gang]. I was gang-banging when I was 15 to about 17. Man, we fought with the Bishops, Corsairs, Lords, Railroad Boys, Hilltoppers—those last two was white gangs. I learned about drugs from the older guys. I OD'd on heroin when I was 13. My father took me to the hospital. I was a fast young guy on the move, and I thought I could handle this [drugs].

After some time on the street, he went back into juvenile detention.

I got busted for snatching a pocketbook and they sent me to Hampton Farms—that's an advanced training school. They had bars on the windows and it was a little stricter than Warwick. I was more afraid than anything else. I knew you had to be bad to survive. After Farms, I went to Elmira, then to Comstock. I've always been a fighter. The cops broke both my arms up there [Comstock]. I got three years in Comstock for robbery. Today, it's a misdemeanor. One year. If I go to jail, I'm trying to make some money instead of working three or four months to get it.

Then Thom went to prison.

After Comstock in 1970, I got busted for armed robbery and got shot up by the police. When I rob somebody, I want to rob them by my motherfucking self. Police shot me in the leg and back, but I was still under the influence. I was using drugs, real fast. I got three years in Sing Sing, then Greenhaven . . . it's near Poughkeepsie. I was becoming a problem there so they shipped me to Dannamora.

After this stint in prison, he committed murder.

Then I got out [in 1974], I got involved with [George]. It was his time. I owed him money, and he performed. He pulled out a gun and twirled it around his finger like some fucking cowboy. His friends were around. I went home that night, a Friday night. I sat down and told my girl about it: "I got a major problem." See, I took her from her ol' man and I knew that'd be trouble, so I told her, "Go back to your husband." I went down there to deal with George. He had a pool room and candy store. It was the threat of life. I made up my mind before I got there. I was lying in bed with my girl and I made up my mind. George embarrassed me to where I had to kill him. He disrespected me to the extreme where there was no other outlet. The motherfucker declared war on me! I went to kill him. "OK, motherfucker, I'm back," and shot in the air. The others I put in him. I grew up knowing that if you got a beef, you take care of it. I knew he had a couple of kids, we were reasonable close too. I thought about his old lady. I thought about it a bit. It bothered me a bit.

Thom was transferred to USP-Lompoc, from USP-Lewisburg. "I got stabbed up in Lewisburg. I got stabbed five times. A guy's pissed 'cause he's imprisoned. The hostility's in there [Thom pounded his chest]. He basically goes for it. If a person got to die, he got to die. I want to be sure I'm not one of them."

Thom and I talked, on and off, all year. The day I left USP-Lompoc in September 1986, Thom had been tossed in I-unit again, for drunkenness and fighting. Just before I left the institution at 4:00 that afternoon, an I-unit officer told me about him. "We had to go into his cell and pull him off his cellie. He was sitting on the guy's chest and punching him. What an asshole." (There was double celling [putting two inmates in one cell] in administration detention then, because of cellblock renovations.)

When I returned to USP-Lompoc in May 1987, I passed through lower-I on my way to upper-I. As I did, I noticed Thom's name listed on the small roster-board, showing the names and cell numbers of all lower-I convicts. At first, I thought there was another convict with the same name. But I was wrong.

I asked Lt. Howie Brooks, a GS-9 lieutenant, if Thom was in lower-I. "Yeah, what an asshole!" he remarked. "I thought he had been transferred last fall," I said. "He was, but now he's back," Brooks said. "Why?" I asked. "Somebody tried to kill him. They did a real good number on him. They wanted him even before he got off the bus," said Brooks.

Just after Thom returned to USP-Lompoc, Brooks said, "he got smashed. We had him in here [lieutenant's office], and he was yelling and screaming, and he picked up the coffee pot and it looked like he was going to throw it. Guys saw that and ran out of here and into the corridor."

In the middle of this scene, Barry Jeunesse walked in. "That stupid shit was standing there, yelling and holding the fucking coffee pot, threatening to throw it at Lt. Graddick. I told him, 'Put that fucking coffee pot down and stop this shit.' He did. Then he started crying like a fucking baby."

At about 8:00 the next evening, Brooks and I went into lower I-unit to see Thom. He was left alone for a day to sober up and calm down. Brooks interviewed Thom, asking for "his side of the story." Thom was cited for drinking and for threatening staff; he was really worried about his future.

> Look, Lt. Brooks, you've known me for a long time now, and I'm not such a bad guy. I never did nothing to you. Look, man, I was drunk. I don't get that way too often. I was real upset about coming back in here again. I didn't mean to hurt no one, you know that. Maybe you could talk to the captain for me, man. I could use your help with this one. Help me out with this one. I won't do it again.

Thom paced back and forth in his cell, nervously rubbing his hands together. He was as contrite as he possibly could be. He asked Lt. Brooks for a few aspirin, since he still had a splitting headache from yesterday's homebrew.

Thom said softly, "That shit's [homebrew wine] bad for you, Mark, I got to quit this time. What are you doing back here, Mark. Didn't get enough last year, huh? You can't stay away, can you. Look, man, will you talk to Brooks for me, will you?"

I replied, "I'll see what I can do. But from what I heard, you raised some serious hell and scared the shit out of people with that pot of hot coffee."

Thom responded, "I was drunk, man, I didn't know what I was doing."

I asked, "What are you doing back, Thom? The last I heard, you were being transferred."

Thom replied, "Yeah, they sent me back to Lewisburg, and some boys there tried to kill, man. They beat me real bad."

"Why?"

Thom lowered his head and said quietly, "I'll tell some other time." Then after a brief pause, he perked up, "You still working on the book? Is it done yet? Now don't forget me, when you get rich!"

RED HOG

Dannie Martin was a wonderful storyteller and he was always sober. I also met him in the mess hall, as he was working as a food server on a steamline, pouring spoonsful of heavily buttered cooked corn into small plastic serving dishes. Red Hog became my friend and a reliable source of information about prison goings-on.

I was born on July 28, 1939. My father was an alcoholic. My mother was a Christian woman who never smoked or tasted alcohol. I am the oldest of four brothers. My earliest memory in life is standing by a coal oil heater in a wooden shack, trying to get warm. I was six years old. My mother came walking out of the small bedroom. One of her eyes was blue and swollen shut. She left the house and came walking back in with a rub board she used to scrub clothes. She went back in the bedroom and beat my dad half to death with it. Someone helped him out of the house that day and he never lived with us again.

In 1949, we moved to Pinedale, California; it's about seven miles north of Fresno. We were a very poor but very happy family. In 1953, I cut school with an older chum, stole a car, and got picked up for joyriding. I got probation after spending some time in juvenile hall. In 1955, I stole another car and was sentenced to Camp Owens, an honor camp near Bakersfield. I escaped, the first or second day there. I was caught and got a year in reform school in Paso Robles. That was one of the meanest places I've ever done time. I had three fights in my first week. The staff were brutal. I've always hated violence, but I try to answer it with the same determination as my mother. It wasn't too long before they left me alone. When I came home to Clovis [near Fresno] High, I was a senior. I thought I was cool. This was the time of James Dean, Elvis, and the Platters. In 1956, I broke into a wine cellar in a nearby suburb and took most of the liquor. I was caught and sent to Tracy, which was a prison for young adults and grown men. I was released in 1958.

I joined my father near Beaumont, Texas. He had quit drinking and married a nice Mormon lady. I met and married a beautiful, quiet girl from Louisiana. We moved to Houston. I met George Hines there. He was the best con man that ever came out of Texas. He is legendary in the Texas underworld. My wife had a baby girl in 1960. About that time, George and I buncoed a Dallas nightclub owner out of $18,000. We knew he was connected, but he was better connected than we thought. I moved back to Fresno. Before 1960, I used grass and benzedrine, occasionally. I know I am intelligent, but I am very naive and silly about drugs. I got hooked on paregoric, too. On our way back to Fresno, I robbed a drugstore. The man behind the counter put his hands up before I even pulled my gun. I began burglarizing drugstores in Fresno, taking only the drugs. In February 1962, I got one-to-ten in Soledad. I went to San Quentin in 1963 during a race riot at Soledad. I got out of Folsom in 1966. I knew the men who started the Mexican Mafia in 1958 and the Aryan Brotherhood in 1967. George Jackson and all that crew. When I was released, I jumped parole and hit the road. My wife had left me and married a hillbilly musician. In July 1968, I was convicted in Fresno of burglarizing a drug supply house. I did three years in Folsom Prison for that. I jumped parole, again, when I got out, and moved to Seattle and bought a ten-acre farm in Arlington.

Between 1971 and 1974, I was smuggling huge amounts of drugs across the border at San Diego. Seventeen of us were indicted in San Diego in 1975 for smuggling. The October 1977 *Penthouse* ran a thirty-page article about us. I was found guilty and sentenced to federal prison for ten years. We went to McNeil, but first I went back to Folsom for a couple of years to do my violation. During this time, I won two trials: kidnapping and robbery, and drug sales. I was released in February 1980. In May 1980, I robbed the Silverdale [Washington] branch of SeaFirst Bank of $105,383. A trusted friend put the FBI on my trail, after I loaned him $40,000. On September 10, 1980, I tried to rob a bank in Cle Elum [Washington]. I got eighteen years for that one, and fifteen years for the Silverdale job.

—6—

LIFE INSIDE

STREET LIFE, PRISON LIFE

> Judges, lawyers, newspaper reporters, and criminologists should not, by imagining themselves in the place of inmates in a high-security prison, conclude that the inmates will be psychologically damaged by the experience. The inmates of high-security prisons are experienced and better prepared to do time than the judges and citizens [Ward, 1986: 31-32].

Lompoc inmates take pride in calling themselves "gangsters," and they say that they enjoy a gangster lifestyle, even though it often leads them to prison. Lompoc's inmate culture has been "imported" from their former street gangster way of life (Irwin and Cressey, 1962; see also Irwin, 1970, 1980; Jacobs, 1974a; Minor and Couriander, 1979; cf. Clemmer, 1958; Reimer, 1937; Sykes, 1958). "Doing time," living in prison for years, sitting idly in jail for months while awaiting trial—all are inevitable parts of a gangster lifestyle. Inmates know it and accept it.

Lompoc inmates, who grew up living by rules of street culture, find prison life easy, because inmate culture is built on social and expressive patterns that come from the street. Prison life doesn't damage these inmates, instead it strengthens their social identities as convicts and as street gangsters. "A stand-up dude reputation," says convict Frankie, "carries from the street to the joint to the street."

Lompoc inmates claim that doing time isn't punishment. They hasten to add that when they're released to the street the high risk of returning to federal or state prison by committing new crimes will not prevent them from doing so. For these high-risk criminals, crime is a way of life and going to prison isn't a burden. Of course, they never say that to Federal Parole Commissioners. Many inmates say, too, that daily life in Lompoc, and in other prisons where they have done time, is easier, less frustrating, and more secure than life on the street. For many of them, in fact, prison has become their preferred lifestyle. They never say that to Federal Parole Commissioners either.

When Lompoc's inmates, most of whom are recidivists, had been released from other prisons, they weren't successful at staying on the street for too long. But those inmates don't take their return to prison as a personal failure. Rather, they are proud of being strong enough to survive in a maximum-security prison, of being able to cope with the strains of prison life, and of being thought of by outsiders as potentially violent men. (Irwin [1970: 137-138] found similar attitudes among California state penitentiary inmates.)

To the inmates, prison is an attractive alternative to the uncertainties of street life. Usually, outsiders fail to believe that long-time felons, in spite of what they say, even in the most sincere and earnest tones, may not wish to be on the street; that street life may be threatening to ostensibly independent and violent men; and that these men are incapable of accepting the responsibility of a "straight," or noncriminal, lifestyle.

Campbell (1986) paints a poignant picture of life on the street in America's poorest urban neighborhoods, the very neighborhoods where American convicts spent their formative years (see also Ferdinand, 1987; Harris, 1981: 125-126; Irwin, 1970: 29-32; Irwin and Austin, 1987: 13-14; Piliavin et al., 1986; Thornberry, 1987; Wilson and Herrnstein, 1985; Wolfgang and Ferracuti, 1982).

> Young males in these neighborhoods are likely to undergo their socialization chiefly on the streets. . . . Overcrowding in the home and the boy's desire to associate with his peer group will naturally draw him there. It is on the street that he gains exposure to adult role models and seeks to demonstrate his masculinity. His mother's attitude to his street life is often highly ambivalent, as Curtis [1975: 31-32] notes: "In addition, the female head and other women in the family may suggest in an undertone that some overt masculine expressions are necessary coping devices, despite their ostensible enmity to such behavior. Worse than a no-good man is a sissy." Street-corner life for most of these men involves staving off the boredom of poverty and unemployment. It is in this context that talk takes on a central role. It provides the main source of entertainment, and its expressive function allows the men to control and monitor their self-image. . . . A second concern among this all-male group is the demonstration of sexual prowess. This happens chiefly in the world of talk. . . . Another important aspect of manhood is the ability to drink large quantities of alcohol. . . . As the day continues, the level of drunkenness goes up, tending to increase the vehemence of the verbal battles.
>
> Coolness . . . autonomy . . . commanding respect . . . machismo are also central to the preoccupations of the men. . . .
>
> There is no starting- and finishing-time for street life. It is an ongoing party that changes its character constantly as individuals join and leave in the course of the day. . . . The street . . . represents an area that is "up for grabs" in terms of control and territorial rights. The police often represent the main rivals for ownership of the neighborhood, and . . . ethnographic

accounts [show] that men deeply resent the harassment they suffer while simply hanging out on their own "turf." The public nature of the street also ensures the almost continuous presence of an audience. The demonstration of valued personal qualities requires a public arena [Campbell, 1986: 118-121].

Prison life is all this and more. Hassle-free, Lompoc's inmates—its "thieves," "hustlers," "dope fiends," "heads," "disorganized criminals," "state-raised youths," and "low-class men" (Irwin, 1970: 7-32, 61-85)— receive material necessities and social services, which they probably weren't enjoying on the street (Davidson, 1974: 58 challenges Irwin's classification). There are also familiar expressive styles of social and verbal interaction. Coolness. Bravado. Machismo. Rivalries. Hassles with the "cops." Beating the "man." Verbal combat. Public shows of strength and machismo. Fighting for territory. Fighting for respect. Fighting over "ladies." Drinking. Drinking and fighting.

DAILY ROUTINE

Two time structures never vary in inmates' daily routine: watch and institution-count schedules. Inmates pursue their work and social activities within shift schedules and around institution counts. Inmates' employment and social activities schedules are fitted to three, eight-hour watches. Social activities occurring within each shift vary depending on the day: All work days are structured by one time schedule, and all nonwork days are structured by a different schedule.

Cross-cutting the watch schedule are institution counts: Six times a day, every day, all inmates are required to be locked in their cells for the count, when inmates in every cellblock are visibly identified and counted by correctional staff.

During institution counts, cellblocks are absolutely quiet except for the reverberating sounds of cell doors clanging shut and the jingling of correctional officers' keys, fastened to their leather belts by strands of heavy dog-leash chain.

Every inmate, without exception, must be located; and, too, when a correctional staffer counts an inmate, he is also certifying that the inmate is a living, breathing human being, not a skillfully manufactured mannikin. (A list of inmates' names, called an "out count," identifies inmates who must be accounted for outside of their cellblocks—in the hospital, in administrative detention, or in food service, for example.)

Three institution counts occur in the evening watch, three in the morning watch. The 4 p.m. count is the first evening watch count and is especially important.

From 5 a.m., the last morning watch count, to 3:50 p.m., when inmates are recalled from work, there is a great deal of inmate movement. Breakfast begins at 6 a.m. and lasts for 30 to 45 minutes, after which inmates return to their cellblocks. At 7:40 a.m., inmates get their work call and move to their place of employment, to the education department, to the yard, or to vocational training; by 7:50 a.m. they are expected to have arrived.

At 11 a.m. lunch is called, and at 12:15 p.m. inmates are called back to work. "Work recall" is heard broadcast through the institution's public address system: "WORK RECALL, WORK RECALL, INMATES CLEAR THE MAIN CORRIDOR, CLEAR THE MAIN CORRIDOR!"

At 3:50 p.m., inmates are recalled from mechanical services work crews, Unicor factories, general education classes, the general library and the law library, and vocational training (in dental prosthesis, welding, electrical work, computer work, and barbering), and they are expected to return to their cellblocks and to their cells in time for the 4 p.m. count.

Although inmates' supervisors must account for the presence of their assigned inmates during each shift, the 4 p.m. count always creates a slightly nervous peak of anticipation among correctional supervisors, who stand around the main corridor near central control until the final tally is compiled by the central control officer from inmate counts telephoned in from cellblock officers.

Accounting for all inmates at 4 p.m. is treated differently than the other evening and morning watch counts, conducted at 6:30 p.m., 10 p.m., 12 midnight, 3 a.m., and 5 a.m. The 4 p.m. count is a "stand-up" count. When a cellblock officer walks passed inmates' cells, looking through the small window in each steel cell door, each inmate must be standing, and the officer must make eye contact with each one. This security requirement is highly stressed.

With inmate movement during the day, inside and outside the facility, inmates may try to initiate an escape. After placing a dummy in his bed just before a count, an inmate may hide somewhere in the rear compound and try to escape over the perimeter fences when it's dark.

Lompoc's Inmate Accountability policy statement (Federal Bureau of Prisons, Lom 5511.2, Inmate Accountability, 1984) specifically addresses this contingency: "Counting Officers should be positive that they see flesh and breathing pulsations of each inmate counted. When making night counts, flashlights should be used judiciously, but enough light should be reflected on the inmate to leave no doubt as to whether or not a dummy is being counted."

Figure 6.1 shows a dummy head fashioned out of plaster-like material, painted flesh color, with human hair used on the head and for the mustache. This was used in an escape attempted from K-unit in spring 1986; the dummy now lies in a bed in the new staff training room (called the "reality" or "hot" room, by staff).

Shift watches and counts are unalterable, and all social activities rotate around them. The weekday schedule focuses on work, school, and vocational training for inmates. Some inmates work full time in a Unicor factory; others work half days in mechanical services and attend a vocational training or education program the other half day; still others work full time and attend a college class in the evening. But the weekend and holiday schedule is devoted to recreational activities.

In spite of inmates' individual workday activities, every Monday to Friday work day begins with a quick 6 a.m. breakfast, unlike the longer weekend and holiday 10 a.m. brunch. On work days, 800 to 1,000 inmates file into the dining hall for breakfast: hot and cold cereal, toast, scrambled eggs, and fried bologna or Spam is a common menu.

Returning to their cellblocks after breakfast, men shoot pool, watch early morning television, lie in their cells, or stand around talking. Around 7:30 a.m., anticipating the 7:40 a.m. work call, they begin to congregate around the cellblock door; all inmates' beds must be made by 8 a.m.

At 7:40 a.m., seconds after the central control room officer pulls the work call whistle, the cellblocks open and hundreds of inmates fill the main corridor, most walking to work. Some inmates who are on vacation or who have the day off walk quickly down the gym corridor to the big yard with its running track, tennis and handball courts, and "iron pile" (the outdoor, weight lifting area in the rear compound). Food service inmates, who were at work by 5 a.m. preparing breakfast, walk slowly back to their cellblocks.

Hundreds of inmates walking to the east end of the main corridor turn down the work corridor, which opens to the sunshine of the east side of the rear compound, on their way to mechanical services and Unicor shops. The California coast location often brings heavy fog over the institution, which can make visibility near zero. On mornings like these, the operations' lieutenant calls, "Fog Line." Inmates aren't permitted to walk freely in the rear compound on their way to Unicor and mechanical services, but must take the underground work tunnel, whose entrance is half-way down the work corridor, to their work locations.

At 7:50 a.m., the peacefulness of the main corridor is again restored, as the control officer announces: "ATTENTION IN MAIN

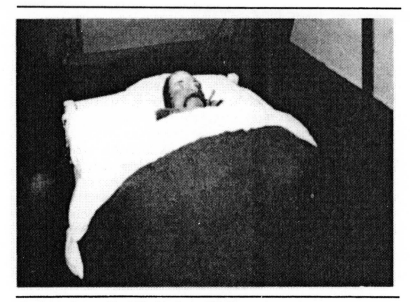

Figure 6.1   Dummy Head (Used in Spring 1986 Escape Attempt)

CORRIDOR, MOVEMENT IS NOW OVER, MOVEMENT IS NOW OVER. CELLBLOCK OFFICERS SECURE YOUR DOORS FOR ONE-WAY TRAFFIC ONLY!"

At 8:50 a.m., the peace is broken inside as an activities movement call is heard: "ACTIVITIES MOVEMENT, ACTIVITIES MOVEMENT." Also at this time, inmates who have been on the yard since 7:50 a.m. are now recalled inside: "ATTENTION IN THE YARD, ATTENTION IN THE YARD, ACTIVITIES RECALL, ACTIVITIES RECALL!"

After about ten minutes, the activities movement is ended: "ATTENTION IN MAIN CORRIDOR, ACTIVITIES MOVEMENT IS NOW OVER, ACTIVITIES MOVEMENT IS NOW OVER. CELLBLOCK OFFICERS SECURE YOUR DOORS FOR ONE-WAY TRAFFIC ONLY!"

When lunch is announced at 11 a.m., Unicor inmates are called inside and each cellblock is phoned in a specific order by the operations' lieutenant, who leaves his desk in the lieutenant's office and is now stationed at the rear of the dining hall. Cellblock order is determined by their respective "weekly sanitation score." (Each cellblock is inspected weekly, by a three-man staff team, which includes John Sams, and is given a numerical score—100 is perfect, and 90 meets the minimum institution standard.)

The midday meal, as every meal, is served from one of three stainless steel steamtables, manned by inmates wearing white aprons, clear plastic gloves, and white hair nets. Food-service workers, both inmates and staffers, make sure that each line is well stocked with quickly diminishing items. It's important that food be served quickly, especially at midday, since inmates must return to work at 12:15 p.m. Recurring delays in food service bring Unicor production delays and generally increase staff stress levels as a meal drags on.

At the midday and evening meals, inmates may choose not to eat the hot meal, preferring to prepare a salad from the salad bar and accompany it with hot soup or chili from the soup bar. The salad bar is a popular item; in this agricultural area of southern California, fresh produce is readily available to inmates.

Religious and dietary meal requirements also are met at each meal. With an authorization card, inmates receive their meals from a special diet line or from a "commonfare" line. Diet-line inmates usually eat the same "mainline meal" (the standard meal), but prepared without salt and seasonings by an inmate diet-line cook.

Commonfare meals meet religious requirements of Jewish and Black Muslim inmates who require special diets. These men eat especially prepared platters of fresh produce, fruits, and some type of protein such as a 6.5-ounce can of tuna fish or sardines.

Other religious requirements are met, too. In May 1987, for example, during the Muslim Ramadan festival, food-service workers prepared bag lunches for Black Muslim inmates. These lunches included a sandwich, cookies, and fresh fruit. The meal was consumed in the dining hall, after sunset.

Following the midday meal and work recall, the main corridor quiets down again. Activities movements are called at 1:30 p.m. and 2:30 p.m., with yard recall at 3:20 p.m. Work recall is sounded at 3:50 p.m. On special occasions, such as Christmas and New Year's Eve, early work recall ends the work day for staff and inmates at 2:50 p.m.

By 3:55 p.m. cellblock doors are shut and locked and the institution is completely silent as correctional staff are busy in each cellblock racking inmates in their cells, cell-range by cell-range, in preparation for the 4 p.m. stand-up count. After the hustle of daily activities, especially during the work week, the 4 p.m. count provides inmates with 15 to 20 minutes in their own cells, alone and away from the game playing and stylized social interactions characteristic of mainline inmates.

As I walked down cell-ranges and peered in cells, inmates stood up if they were sitting or lying on their bed, or they continued to read or listen to music. Some men would already be up, brushing their teeth, combing their hair, changing clothes, or staring out of the cell window. Inmates rarely said anything, changed their facial expressions, or even made eye contact.

The evening meal begins shortly after the stand-up count, at approximately 4:45 p.m. The commissary also opens at this time, so inmates hustle from the dining hall to the commissary, or vice versa.

The evening meal offers a wide variety of hot foods in addition to the salad and soup bar. Fried T-bone or rib steaks, pork chops, fried chicken, and Mexican food are among inmate favorites.

After this meal, the evening watch routine centers on regular activity movements and institution counts. In addition to recreation activities in the yard and in the gymnasium, the education department's general and law libraries are open, and instructors from local colleges teach two-year and four-year college courses.

The inmates' general activities center also is open for scheduled meetings of, for example, the Toastmasters or Alcoholics Anonymous. On the first Friday of each month, the Tribe of Five Feathers has a traditional dance in the visiting room, attended by community members. Other inmate groups, too, such as the weight lifters' club, occasionally meet with community visitors in the visiting room in the evening.

Cellblock doors stay locked after the 10 p.m. count, though inmates are free to wander in their cellblock as they please, watching television or playing pool, until they are racked in for the night at 11:30 p.m. By asking the unit officer, an inmate can rack in and have his cell door locked at any time in the evening. All inmates remain in their cells until after the 5 a.m. count, when they are racked out for breakfast, and the beginning of the next work day.

Weekends are broken by frequent activities movements and brunch. Saturday, for example, begins at 7 a.m. with a coffee hour in the dining hall. Inmates are served sweet rolls baked by inmates on Friday morning; all breads, rolls, cookies, and pies are baked in the institution, and they are delicious.

Two activity movements follow the coffee hour, with brunch served at approximately 10:15 a.m. Unlike the quick and already prepared workday breakfast, weekend and holiday brunches are leisurely, often including a menu of fried eggs cooked to order, freshly cooked french toast or fresh pancakes, sausage or bacon, fried potatoes, hot toast, and fruit juice; the salad bar is also available. Following brunch there are four activity movements before dinner and several others after the dinner meal.

Weekend and weekday evening activities feature basketball or softball tournaments, popular action movies such as Escape from

Alcatraz and Rambo, and occasional outside comedians, bands, or a prison-theater group. The Geese Theatre, which plays in maximum-security prisons around the United States, performed in early 1986; there were about 150 inmates at the start of their performance, but when the "moral lessons" were broadcast to Lompoc's convicts, in staged words and deeds, inmates laughed, smirked, groaned, and all but a small handful walked out. I enjoyed it, though.

HOLIDAY TIME

Major holidays are special times. As America gears up for Thanksgiving, Christmas, and New Year's Eve and Day, so does the penitentiary. The commissary stocks a variety of Christmas and general holiday cards; gift packages of meat and cheese are available to inmates who wish to send family gifts. Holiday pictures can be arranged during family visiting, which is extended to seven days from five days a week and to two weeks at Christmas.

To accommodate increased phone use, living unit telephones operate 12 hours instead of 8 hours a day. To meet visiting needs, each inmate receives 60 visiting points during December instead of his monthly 40-point allotment (points are used at a rate of one each hour on week days and two each hour on weekends and holidays). To expand gift-purchasing opportunities, each inmates' commissary spending is increased to $130 for December from the regular monthly $95 allotment.

Special meals are served for each major holiday. Thanksgiving dinner, served at midday, is a veritable feast: fresh turkeys, hams, several types of potatoes and vegetables, fresh rolls, and "store-bought" mincemeat and apple pies.

Food service inmates decorate each steamtable with colorful, festive gourds and tiny turkeys fashioned from crepe paper and cardboard. Even the mood among inmates and between inmates and staff was festive during my time at USP-Lompoc at Christmas 1985.

On Christmas there was another special meal: stuffed Cornish hens, baked potatoes, corn on the cob, fresh biscuits, apple pie, more decorations, and, of course, holiday entertainment.

Warden Christensen and Captain Collins were present for the Christmas dinner, as they were for the Thanksgiving and the New Year's dinners. During the Christmas meal, the captain stood in the entry door of the dining hall, and the warden and I stood inside the dining hall. The warden made several trips around the dining hall (including to the steam lines), examining the food and chatting with inmates. The meal went on for almost an hour and a half. On their way in or out of the dining hall, inmates stopped to shake hands with the warden and captain and to wish them "Merry Christmas." New Year's Day brought another special meal of grilled T-bone steak, boiled potatoes, mushroom gravy, peas and carrots, and apple pie.

On both Christmas and New Year's weekends, there were tournaments in handball, tennis, racquetball, volleyball, horseshoes, bridge, basketball free-throw, and bingo. Winners and losers were awarded sodas, winners got 12 and losers 6. Entertainment included two movies, Code of Silence (1985) (with karate king Chuck Norris) on Christmas, and Prizzi's Honor (1985) (a drama dealing with organized crime and contract killers) on New Year's Day. There was also an outside rock group on New Year's weekend.

Christmas Eve and New Year's Eve were treated as special community-wide events. Early work recall at 2 p.m., brought all inmates into the institution and back into their cellblocks.

On Christmas Eve, staffers from education, administrative systems, communications, Unicor, hospital, recreation and correctional services were assigned by John Sams and Gene Gill to distribute to each inmate a Unicor Christmas gift box of cheeses, meats, and sweets. Unit management teams were also present in their respective cellblocks; some inmates and staff shook hands, but most nodded and silently acknowledged the occasion as staffers went from cell to cell handing a Unicor gift to each inmate. After each inmate had received his Unicor gift, hot chocolate and cookies were available for inmates in each unit.

Jim Finley used the Christmas Eve holiday in a special way: He greeted each of his inmates, one by one, shaking their hand, and wishing them "Merry Christmas and Happy New Year." Finley said he wanted to bring each inmate an honest sense of friendliness and community.

On New Year's Eve, too, there is early work recall. This time, rather than receiving a gift and refreshments, inmates are served freshly baked cinnamon rolls and eggnog.

I was in K-unit with a staff psychologist and two mechanical service staffers. A food service staffer delivered several large pans of freshly baked cinnamon rolls and several cases of eggnog. We set up a table on the flats to hold the plates, cups, and trays of cinnamon rolls and eggnog. Some inmates, hanging around the table, were chatting with staff as the food was being arranged; others shot pool or stood around talking, giving the appearance they didn't know we were there. Above, inmates were leaning over tier rails, peering down at the food and drink.

When everything was ready, the unit counselor standing on the flats yelled that food was being served. Inmates congregated, waiting in line. One staff server offered each inmate a warm cinnamon roll and another staffer poured cups of eggnog. When the cinnamon rolls were gone, inmates returned for seconds and thirds of eggnog; some men made off with quarts of eggnog when they thought we weren't looking. This is the only occasion during Lompoc's yearly calendar of events when staff actually serve inmates. Over 100 inmates were served, and friendly chatter was exchanged. *small #*

Festive inmate meals, gift and food distributions, and shared personal sentiments by staffers are institutional attempts to control staff-inmate social relations at sensitive times of the year.

GOING TO WORK

In contrast to the conventional portrayal of inmates as reacting to "the pains of imprisonment" by becoming assimilated into the inmate subculture, evidence . . . [suggests] that some prison inmates minimize these "pains" by attempting to maximize the legitimate gratification obtainable in prison while not being motivated to obtain a speedy release. . . . The preference of institutionalized inmates for recreational over treatment activities suggests that they select enjoyable pursuits rather than activities which may potentially help them to . . . succeed after release [Goodstein, 1979: 257].

Eddie says that pleasure, above anything else, motivates inmates: "These fuckers don't give a shit about anything but what's going to happen in the next 30 minutes. The only things they worry about are where they're going to get their next joint, a glass of wine, or a piece of ass. They just don't give a fuck about anything else. They don't think about tomorrow."

One way of guaranteeing legitimate pleasures while serving time is by earning spending money. Gambling, making loans of cash and property, buying sex, "keeping a homosexual," buying drugs, and even contract killing depend on a convict's cash position.

Inmates go to work every working day. Some divide their days between a paying job and a VT, but no one is permitted to "lay up" all day. It is a moot point whether an inmate enjoys his job or VT, or whether his job or VT is rehabilitative. "Refusing to work or refusing to accept a program assignment" is a prohibited act, and an offending inmate will be sent to I-unit. In 1985, of 1,741 incident reports, 9.4%

(164) were written for refusing to work and .06% (1) were for malingering. In 1986, of 2,049 incident reports, 9.7% (198) were written for refusing to work; no incident reports were issued for malingering.

Inmates can work for the institution (in food service, in the hospital, as an orderly, in mechanical services, or on the inside-grounds crew) or for Unicor. The institution and Unicor each have their own wage scale; Unicor wages are higher. Accordingly, Unicor jobs are the prison's best jobs, according to inmates who are concerned about making money.

There are five grades of income for Unicor inmates: $.22, $.44, $.66, $.88, and $1.10 per hour, respectively. After eighteen months, inmates receive a longevity increase of $.10 per hour, and, based on the quality of their work, inmates' supervisors may issue an additional $.5 per hour as premium, or bonus, pay.

The hourly rates for institution inmate-employees is scaled into four grades, with hourly incomes of $.11, $.16, $.27, and $.38. Here supervisors may issue their inmate employees a 50% quality-work bonus for each two-week pay period.

Depending on their job, pay-grade, and longevity, an inmate working at pay-grade 1, the highest in Unicor, receiving additional longevity and premium pay, may earn more than $200 a month. Some Unicor inmates told me they made as much as $500 to $600 a month (see Fleisher and McCarthy, 1988).

Institution jobs, such as food and orderly services, are low-paying, low energy-level jobs; production levels and quality control are much looser here than in high-revenue Unicor factories. Some inmates, such as Red Hog, prefer these jobs to Unicor. "I would rather not work for the government that put me here," he said. "Anyway, if you work in Unicor, you have to work all day." When Red Hog was serving cooked vegetables twice a day, he seemed quite happy, although he did complain occasionally about having too little recreation time. I thought his light work schedule gave him plenty of time to play racquetball in the afternoon sun (which he thoroughly enjoyed) with inmate Fritz, who was serving a long sentence for conspiring to overthrow the U.S. government. After a few months of serving cooked vegetables, Red Hog began an orderly job, mopping the main corridor a few times day. "This doesn't take as much time as serving corn," he said.

From his institution savings account, an inmate may request that funds be sent to street relations (but recipients must be approved institution visitors; these people can deposit money into an inmate's account) and he may request a transfer of funds, depositing his money into a private bank account.

WEAPONS

Inmate alliances are stimulated in the work place. Work-crew, factory-crew, and food-service ties can be positive, but these inmate networks can be used for getting drugs; for manufacturing, buying, and smuggling weapons; or for plotting escapes. Inmates on work crews (the plumbing crew, for example) have access to hacksaw blades (which are carefully watched and counted daily by work-crew supervisors), and to metal and plastic used to make shanks, pipe-bludgeons, and other killing weapons. Figure 6.2 shows a senior lieutenant holding a convict-made "battle-axe" found in an inmate's cell; surely this didn't come through a metal detector, nor did the convict walk down the main corridor holding it. A snitch quietly told the SIS who had it.

Social links among crew members are needed to smuggle weapons from a shop where they are made, into a cellblock where they are used. "How does a guy get a shank from a factory in Unicor into the cellblock?" I asked Big Brother. He smiled and shook his head in disbelief, showing disgust with my naivete.

> Ain't you learned nothing yet? You mean you don't know? All you got to do is smuggle it out of a shop when the boss ain't around or ain't looking; that's most of the time. You give it to a guy on the inside-grounds crew. He takes it to where you want and drops it off. It'll cost you, though.

Figure 6.3 shows "shanks" (knives) made by inmates in Unicor and in mechanical services shops. They had been transported to living units in the low-rent district and were found outside cellblocks, hanging from cell windows. The largest shank, the one with electrical tape around its handle, was found stashed in a garbage can in the dishroom in the mess hall. The shank next to it, with two holes in the handle, was a lawnmower blade.

Plastic shanks, inmates say, escape detection in metal detectors. Figure 6.4 shows a variety of these.

SMALL PLEASURES

With a regular, tax-free, overhead-free income, an inmate can make his prison life more comfortable by purchasing luxury food and personal items from the well-stocked prison commissary. Wage-earning levels, purchasing power, advancement in pay grades, getting the good

Figure 6.2 Staffer with Battle-Axe

job in prison industries, and getting along with the boss are just as important as they are to workers in the outside business world.

Acquiring the accoutrements of the prison "middle class" is strictly limited by the community's regulations, defining what may and may not

Figure 6.3 Shanks

exactly

be possessed—this is a maximum-security prison, after all. Many items are not sold in the prison's commissary, because they may either be fashioned into weapons or used for escapes.

Then, too, the commissary's inventory has its limits, as would any retail store. The rules of supply and demand operate; inmate requests are satisfied as the commissary's inventory keeps expanding and changing with demand. Inmates' purchases are also limited by the "spending policy," which caps individual spending at $95 a month, except at Christmas time, when it is expanded to $130.

Shopping at the commissary is the highlight of the evening watch and is an eagerly anticipated event. Access to the commissary is regulated by the last two digits of each inmate's register number; different number patterns are served each evening watch, and movement to the commissary follows the order by which cellblocks are called for meals.

On the tiers, up and down each cell-range, inmates who shop that evening are getting their shopping lists prepared. "Man, just get the fuck out of my way, when that door opens," says inmate Jack to his partner, as they wait together for their cellblock door to open. When it does, some inmates break into a near gallop, as they head toward the commissary. "Slow down, stop running," shouts a main corridor officer.

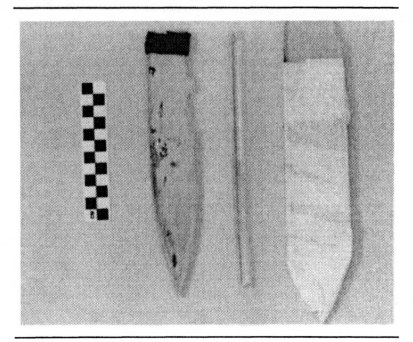

Figure 6.4 Plastic Shanks

Tens of inmates "tear ass" in front of him, trying to beat most of the others to the beginning of the commissary line. The central control officer slows speeding traffic by partially closing the corridor-wide grill at the east and west ends, permitting only one man to squeeze through at a time. "Racing in the corridor," as hacks call it, ends.

Some men prefer to go to the commissary before eating dinner, and some miss dinner while waiting in line. But that doesn't matter, because they'll leave with bags of "goodies" and junk food.

The prison commissary stocks food and personal items. In the following list, I've included items in each category. Prices are as of April 3, 1986. Note that they are competitive with the free market. As of May 1987, the commissary was computerized and each inmate's purchases are now tracked as they are made, with costs deducted from his account automatically. In FY '86, commissary sales reached $1,476,500, or about $1,265 per inmate.

> *Stamps/coins/photo tokens.* Inmates can purchase up to ten dollars a
> week in coins, quarters or dimes, for use in their cellblock vending
> machines and in the visiting room, where they also use the photo tokens.
> (An inmate who wants a family picture buys a token at the commissary to
> cover the cost of the Polaroid photograph; he gives the token to the

inmate photographer in the visiting room, who records his work in a log, monitored by the visiting room officer.)

Health foods. Carob-coated peanuts ($1.45), granola bars ($.35 each), kosher dill/hot pickles ($.40); candy/sugar, sugar cubes, 2 lbs. ($1.50), Hershey bar with almonds ($1.55).

Body care. Mennen's Afta Shave ($1.70), Ban Roll-On ($2.70), Copper-tone Tanning Lotion ($3.75), baby oil ($1.60); hair care, Brylcream ($3.40), Curl Activator ($2.50), Proline hair food ($3.30); dental care, Poly Grip ($2.20), Pearl Drops ($2.55); soap, Neutragena ($2.00), Zest, ($.70), laundry powder ($1.30).

Batteries. 9-volt ($2.25), watch ($1.00).

Soup. Chicken, garden vegetable, shrimp ($.50).

Miscellaneous. Headphones ($9.95), combination lock ($3.95), 2-sided safety mirror ($4.50), molded shower shoes ($2.80).

Stationery/dictionary/almanac. Photo album ($11.25-large), pens ($.20).

Clothing/sports. Red/blue bandanas ($1.15), weightlifting gloves ($14.40), handball gloves ($17.30).

Snacks. Mixed nuts ($2.35), Cheezits ($1.75).

Special purpose orders. Sony headphone radio [no price listed], Sony Walkman SRF-10 [no price listed], Timex watch #58347 [no price listed], #32717, sweatsuit set ($30.35).

Beverages. Taster's Choice ($5.15), orange juice ($.55), Taster's Choice Decaf ($6.70).

Tobacco. Camels/Kool/Marlboro ($.80), Pall Mall ($.85), Bugler can ($2.20), Big Red ($.85).

Fresh fruit. Apples, grapefruit, oranges, lemons, avocados (price varies).

Pastries. Apple strudel ($2.00), bear claws ($.45).

Ice cream. Dreyer's vanilla, chocolate, chocolate chip, strawberry, neapolitan, black walnut ($.90), Oreo ice cream sandwich ($.70).

Leaving the commissary with shopping bags full of edibles such as snack crackers and potato chips, cartons of "ready-mades" (street cigarettes), or cigarette papers and Bugler (an inexpensive smoking tobacco), canned fruit juice, and pieces of fresh fruit, inmates wander back to their cells. I have seen inmates literally staggering down the main corridor, balancing all their purchases in their arms. The main corridor officer never offers to lend a hand.

In early evening after a trip to the commissary, many inmates walk and talk with companions in the main corridor during activities movements as they eat pints of Dreyer's ice cream. As pleasant as this activity sounds, commissary items can also be used in a variety of violations.

DEBTS

Most of the action in prison revolves around opening up the system. Getting more food, better clothes, pornography. . . . Whatever criminals enjoy outside and are denied inside they attempt, when in prison, to obtain illegally. . . . Who is going to be the bookmaker inside? Who is going to smuggle in "grass," hashish, and LSD "tabs"? Who is going to corrupt warders, in order to arrange illicit channels for mail and money? . . . Who is going to run the rackets? . . . And don't let us pretend, along with all the other prison researchers who have held their hand up in horror at what they saw in prison, that the rest of the prisoners don't get any benefit from this arrangement. . . . They can buy dope, they can get uncensored messages outside—because there are prisoners running rackets [McVicar, 1982: 209-210].

Rackets can't run without "money" (see Gleason, 1978; Williams and Fish, 1974: 39-94). Money can be cigarettes, "weed," heroin, personal favors, but most often it is cash (sometimes called "white" or "white money" by former state convicts).

Although inmates can't directly transfer funds between their own accounts, these transactions do occur, using an intermediary on the street. A Lompoc inmate's wife, girlfriend, or mother, for instance, who receives money from an inmate, can deposit it in another inmate's account, or in an account of an inmate in another prison.

Street drugs are purchased this way by Lompoc inmates, using their street connections. Big Brother says,

If an inmate in Unicor wants to buy street drugs, he'll send money to a street connection, his wife, say, or his girl. She'll buy the drugs from her dealer, step on them [cut the drugs], take hers and then walk his in [the inmate's drugs] through the visiting room. Buying drugs or a contract killing, happens the same way. You can do this anywhere in the country.

In trying to curtail this activity, all funds credited to inmate accounts by street people, or debited from inmates' accounts and mailed to street people, are carefully monitored by the institution.

There are frequent rumors of large quantities of cash circulating among inmates. But, asked Big Brother cynically, "Do you think that if a convict had $1,000 in cash, and other convicts knew about it, he would have it very long?"

At Lompoc, as in all major prisons, money is a medium of exchange, along with drugs and commissary items, all of which can be used to settle debts. As inmates get themselves into cash or commodity debt, by overspending at illegal cellblock stores or by gambling, debtor-creditor problems begin.

So-called "2-for-1 stores" operate in cellblocks to supply inmates with cigarettes, for example, when they are short of money; when an inmate customer takes one pack of cigarettes, he returns two packs. Storekeepers rely on receiving the money owed them on time, unless an inmate builds a large debt and then loses his job. For the most part, though, inmate-to-storekeeper exchanges are small, with inmates paying their debts. Large, unpaid debts may lead to trouble.

Hundreds of unpaid dollars are closely linked to macho images. The creditor feels like the debtor is taking advantage of him personally. Frankie says, "It's not the money, it's the principle. What am I a penitentiary punk, that this guy can disregard me? He can't disregard me!" When a creditor interprets a debtor's long-term indebtedness as his own personal failure, or as a sign of weakness, as an indication that he can't collect the debt, violence may result.

A cellblock loanshark, and companion to Slim, told me that in his business,

It's cash or your ass. They [debtors] give up something as collateral or square it with a sweat suit. One guy was in debt to me and I shifted it. I told him he had to go to the 2-for-1 store [to get a loan to pay the loanshark]. [The debtor] had to pay double for what he owed me, to the guy over there. Some guys get three for two.

Red Hog explains further:

Some guys loan cigarettes for interest. If you loan a guy a carton, you may want it returned on Monday. On Monday, there's no payment. This guys says, "Fuck you, I don't have to return the cigarettes." Then you get your knife and cut his head off, or knock him in the head. They knew the rules before they borrowed the cigarettes. Violence lets others know to pay. He robbed you, took your money, disrespected you, he seriously undervalued you. Honor to us, that's the most important thing in life; we don't have contracts. A guy who doesn't pay is no good. He is no good to society because he's here, and now he's no good to us. He's beyond the pale of both worlds. Even if the store owner is small, like you, he's not thinking about fist fights; he'll get a blade and that'll make them even. He's [debtor] worthless; he deserves to be killed.

Maintaining respect among mainline inmates, building prestige, and protecting one's self-image apply to prison rackets, too. The simplicity of violence and its link to prestige and honor are explained by Red Hog.

Most violent convicts don't commit a violent act to increase their prestige. They did the violence for another reason, and the prestige followed. They got some prestige from killing a few cons, so they went ahead and killed a few more. They like the prestige. There are times when you have only two choices. Either kill him or be a spit-on punk.

There can also be a nonviolent resolution to debtor inmates. Big Brother, who says he ran a cellblock store, told me that he took a businesslike approach: "I have accounts for write-offs. You set a certain amount aside, take the loss, and the dude can't come back. He's more hurt than you! You got to be crazy to kill some dude for cigarettes. Getting another 25 years over a carton of cigarettes is crazy."

GAMBLING

"Convicts will bet on anything." says Slim. "One guy in here was really strained up behind football. He owed something like six or seven guys about a couple hundred."

Betting on football, basketball, boxing, the World Series, the Super Bowl, poker games, dominoes, and inmate softball tournaments, is common. But it is difficult to spot and stop.

When officers conduct cell shakedowns and come across betting slips identifying who owes what to whom, the slips are confiscated, and the inmate is cited for gambling. However, in 1985 and 1986 only 2.6% (48) of 3,790 incident reports were filed on inmates for gambling, possession of gambling paraphernalia, and conducting gambling pools.

I saw a punch-board, found during a cell shakedown in September 1986, which had several dozen tiny holes punched in a thick piece of cardboard, each hole covered by thin paper. Within each hole, was a tiny slip of paper with a football score written on it. For $1 an inmate bought the right to choose a hole and a score. The winner was to have won a new Timex quartz watch, which was confiscated along with the punch-board.

COLLECTING DEBTS

Failure to pay gambling debts (or any debts, for that matter) can have serious consequences. Slim, who claims to have street experience as a debt "collector," and who now busies himself offering cellblock loans, provides his view of prison debts.

I try to be "business" in my dealings. In business, I have so much understanding, and once it gets past that point, business is business, and bullshit is bullshit. It's stupid to get into debt in a prison environment, knowing you can't pay a debt, to get into debt. If I let you get off without paying me, how are the other people going to think about it. If there's small debts and he's procrastinating, he gets an arm broke or leg broke. Just because a little blood was shed doesn't mean the debt's paid. Then you tag interest on the debt. If a guy's lacking and slacking in payments, you put a little force into the squeeze play. I used to collect for a bookie, do a little muscling for him; that was a good business, too. I used to feel sorrow for some of them; they had no way of paying their debts; they'd get deeper and deeper in debt. Now I'm gonna do my job. Some people had special ways; they broke arms, legs, or busted him up good; some even burn his car or bust his windshield. If he ain't got nothing of value, the last alternative is to get stuck. He might not be hit to get killed; he be hit to get stuck. If they can't pay, most guys will "pc-up" [put themselves in protective custody]. They know some drama come of it. Some guys if they can't pay their debts, will get into a guard's face, and lock up. That's not a violent move, that's a cowardly move, because he can't deal with problems he created.

"RUNNING A STORE"

"If I don't steal something every day, I feel bad," said Callahan, after he walked into L-unit with pockets full of food stolen from the kitchen. Food is stolen from the prison kitchen every day, despite regular shakedowns at the mess hall door. When Eddie was diet cook, he and Cowboy, for instance, missed mess hall dinner three or four nights a week, preferring to eat freshly prepared hamburger burritos or grilled hamburgers in Eddie's cell, where they could drink homemade wine with their dinner and smoke a joint afterward.

Stolen food is either traded (for more desirable types of food, alcohol, or drugs) or sold to inmates or to two-for-one, cellblock storekeepers. Cellblock stores can be a source of regular cash income if a storekeeper can obtain a sufficient inventory of stolen items at low prices. But it's difficult to steal large quantities of food from food service.

Food thefts aren't of sufficient quantity to operate a store with a high enough sales volume to yield high levels of profit. The prison commissary, however, supplies storekeepers with sufficient inventories, at reasonable prices.

Big Brother describes how some storekeepers get around the $95 limit on commissary purchases.

You got a guy who works in Unicor, and runs a store. He makes a good living out there, but he wants more than just a little taste. So here's what he does. A convict sends $700 to someone on the street, who takes that money and sends $100 [each] to seven other convicts. They kept $25 for their trouble, and spend $75 at the commissary. Then they turn around and give the stuff to the storekeeper. It's easy.

Cellblock stores, stocked with varieties of food commodities, are popular sources of late-night snacks. Unopened packages of Saltine crackers; sardines; six-and-a-half-ounce cans of tuna fish; hard-boiled eggs; whole and sliced onions; a variety of sandwiches such as hamburger burritos, ham and cheese, cheeseburgers and hamburgers; and, on weekends, large and delicious freshly baked cinnamon rolls are available for sale.

Sales are cash, credit, or "return-like-goods with interest." Cigarettes are exchanged two-for-one on payday, or when inmates receive money from the street. Sardines and tunafish are highly prized commodities, bringing a premium price. A six-and-a-half-ounce can of tuna or a small can of sardines sells for about $3.50, depending on supply and demand.

Line hacks and convicts alike say that convicts run stores in every cellblock. In 1985 and 1986, despite custodial supervisors' insistence on regular cell shakedowns, .4% (9) of 3,790 incident reports were filed on inmates for conducting a business.

Homemade wine, prepared in multigallon quantities by a cellblock wine maker, also may be added to a storekeeper's inventory; more commonly, though, wine makers operate independently. Drugs, too, such as marijuana joints, are for sale by drug merchants. Joints are sold thin at about $1.50, or thick at about $3.50, depending on the availability and quality of marijuana.

Operating a well-stocked store takes skill and a dependable inmate network of food-service thieves. Some food-service inmates, who aren't interested in operating a store, try to gather goods for sale or trade their inventory for drugs, usually marijuana. Once in possession of drugs, they can use some, trade some, and sell some. Cash from sales is used to buy more expensive drugs.

Limiting the sale and distribution of stolen food and the consumption of homemade wine is a full-time 18-hour-a-day job for cellblock hacks. In every cellblock, on the day and evening watch, unit officers are required to shake down at least five cells and to conduct searches for wine concealed in public areas of the living unit, such as behind the television or above the hot water heater in the unit's janitorial clean-up room.

When hacks find stolen food (hamburgers, burritos, or cinnamon rolls, for instance) in cell searches or inmate shakedowns in the main corridor, they sometimes discard it. Sometimes it is saved and given to the lieutenants' and main corridor officer's orderlies, to use later as rewards. Canned foods (tuna fish and sardines) are returned to the kitchen.

ALCOHOL AND DRUGS

Red Hog writes that,

Federal prisons are more relaxed these days than state prisons. The prisoners are of a more cosmopolitan type, and there is very little racial tension. A convict can also get a shot of dope or a drink of booze now and then. Not enough for a habit, but enough to take the edge off a bit [*San Francisco Chronicle*, October 18, 1987].

The basic ingredients of homebrew are water and sugar; fruit, jam, or anything fermentable, oranges, for example; and, if convicts can get it, yeast. Yeast is carefully guarded. "Possessing yeast is a capital crime around here," said a senior lieutenant. "You know the best prison bakers are always the best wine makers." If they can't get yeast, then a piece of uncooked bread dough also works to encourage fermentation. Eddie claims to use "a starter compound, like sour-dough starter," but I never saw it.

Homebrew is cooked in any sort of container which permits gases to escape. An ideal container is the empty milk bag from the mess hall's milk machines. The cleverest brewing technique I saw was discovered in K-unit. A milk bag was full of water and pieces of fresh, sliced oranges. It was wrapped in an army blanket to keep in the heat, and stuffed into an inmate's wastepaper basket. Since venting gases have a distinctive "sweet" smell, the bag's vent tube was stuck into a can of Pine Sol and water, which was taped to the side of the wastepaper basket. The cell smelled like the great outdoors.

The kitchen is a popular place for cooking homebrew because it can be concealed in any of dozens of warm hiding places. Eddie said that he once cut through four bolts that secured a 2,000-pound capacity loading-dock scale, and, with the help of several companions, slid it aside, to hide a multigallon milk bag full of fermenting homebrew beneath it.

Drinking homebrew in the cool, dingy storerooms of food service is safer than trying to smuggle it out of the mess hall. Smuggling is best done at the end of a meal, when the shakedown officer has already shaken down tens of convicts; when his attention has been diverted by some other task, such as the need to yell at convicts to "move along, keep moving, get off the wall"; or when rookie hacks are practicing shakedowns. Wine is smuggled in small plastic containers, hidden in a convict's baggy fatigue jacket, in the rear waist-band of his pants, or in his socks, just above the top of his steel-toed, black work boots.

Homebrew, says convict Ford, "really fucks you up. It eats at your insides and really fucks up your stomach and kidneys." A lieutenant told me that, "Convicts piss in their pants and shit all over themselves when you have to fight with them when they're drunk. When you get 'em in the I-unit trap and strip them, they are embarrassed, after they have shit in their pants."

When homebrew is found in a cell search or during an inmate shakedown, it is dumped and the container is taken to the lieutenant's office, where the contents are tested for alcohol. All confiscated drugs and drug paraphernalia are taken there, too, for testing and identification of drug compounds.

Homebrew is the easiest and cheapest drug to get; a dollar will buy a quart of "good stuff," according to Eddie. Heroin, cocaine, crank (speed), PCP, LSD, and black-tar heroin, which were rumored to be on the mainline, have to be smuggled in through the visiting room. High risk means high cost. Some inmates and most line hacks and lieutenants said that few of these hard drugs were on the mainline. At least, few of them were found.

Slim had thoughts on this, too.

> Weed, heroin, and crank are most common in here. There's death behind drugs, there ain't no question about it. If a guy makes a drug deal and doesn't come through [with money], he know his ass is in a sling. You got guys in here who are supporting heroin habits. You got crank-heads . . . speed freaks. Guys got to have it. There are guys supporting families on drug dealing in here. At [maximum-security state prison], guards realize cons are hooked. A couple of hundred dollars comes in handy. When a cop can put $300, $400, or $500 in his pocket three or four weeks before his pay check comes, he can bank it and pay those little bills around the house. I don't fault a man for that. Shit, in here he'd probably get $400 or $500 an ounce for heroin. This much heroin [the quantity of a matchhead] would cost you about $50 in here, $10 on the street.

Because of close personal and electronic surveillance, a video camera that records the visiting scene, and an extensive federal information network on the street, marijuana and narcotics (usually heroin) are difficult to smuggle to inmates through the visiting room.

Dave Nero, a GS-8, and a GS-7 colleague, said they made a "major visiting room drug bust" in January 1987. "It's the biggest drug bust in Lompoc history, at least the biggest anyone remembers," said Nero.

We got this old lady, a grandma type, who was visiting some sleaze. She had 62 balloons of grass stuck away in the cups of her bra. She had big sagging tits, so the balloons weren't visible. The guy in back was watching on the camera all along. When we took 'em, her old man had swallowed eleven fucking balloons. We stuck him in a dry-cell, and waited for him to shit 'em out.

Dry-cells are stripped of everything but a bed. A sequestered inmate who is suspected of swallowing smuggled drugs can spend up to seventy-two hours in a hospital dry-cell. He lives in his underwear and is watched twenty-four hours a day, by an officer sitting in front of the doorway. Bowel movements are collected in a bedpan, and the feces are inspected for balloons or condoms packed with drugs, such as marijuana, by breaking them apart with a stick or by squeezing them with a gloved hand. Watching a dry-celled convict is overtime work!

Of 1985's 1,741 incident reports, 17.63% (307) were written for narcotics offenses and 12.98% (226) were written for intoxicant violations. In 1986, there were 2,049 incident reports: 13.61% (279) were written for narcotics offenses, and 13.46% (276) were written for intoxicant violations.

Several common factors affect nonreporting. Work-crew supervisors may not report one, or more, mildly drunk inmates on their crews, because supervisors may feel the need to get work done. When a rookie hack is working the evening watch in a cell block, drunk inmates may go undetected unless one of them causes a problem. A few days after finishing his OJT, a rookie, working in K-unit, told me: "I don't want to know what's going on in here. I just want to finish my shift and get the fuck out of here alive."

—7—

SEX

MAINLINE HOMOSEXUALS

In the joints of America, many terms are used to designate effeminate homosexuals (female role players): "skull-buster," "bitch," "punk," "homo," "kid," "queen," "ol' lady," "broad," "faggot," "fruiter," and "fag." They are also commonly referred to, by convicts and line staff alike, as "she." (At Lompoc, I never heard the terms "jocker" or "pitcher," for the male role player, or "catcher," for the female role player, though I've heard these terms used commonly in the Washington State Penitentiary [Wooden and Parker, 1982: 3, also cite these terms as being used at a California state prison].)

Of all the sex-role terms, "punk" is both the most ambiguous and the most highly charged, because its meaning overlaps with notions of low machismo. "Punk" commonly designates a noneffeminate, female-role-playing homosexual, but effeminate homosexuals can also be called punks, although fag is a preferred designation for effeminate homosexuals.

Punk also connotes inner weakness, as well as possible sexual orientation: All wimps are punks; not all punks are homosexuals; and not all homosexuals are punks. Punks simply don't cut the penitentiary mustard as real men: they are weak, they lack inner conviction and strength, they give in to the demands of others too easily; and they are easily manipulated. "A man can be a homosexual," Frankie said, "but not a weak punk." Big Brother claims that "punks get beat up and fucked because they are weak, not because they are queer. A punk is a man without no balls at all."

A punk doesn't have the respect of either inmates or staffers and is easy prey. Correctional staffers tend to agree with convicts: Punks are wimps and snivelers.

At USP-Lompoc, there are four dominant categories of homosexuals: "fags," "fuck-boys," "straights," and "turn-outs," said Big Brother. He explains:

> Here you got fags—them are the queens, and fuck-boys, they fuck the queens. They are like closet homosexuals, you know. They're both fucking homosexuals, man. All them other words are street talk. In

prison, you got fags and fuck-boys. [Queen, ol' lady, ol' man and punk, among others, are also heard on occasion, and are used more often by well-seasoned former state prisoners.]

"Sometimes," adds Big Brother, "fuck-boys come out of the closet and walk with the fags." Fags and fuck-boys, according to him, and other convicts, think of themselves as homosexuals, and are considered as homosexuals by convicts.

"Straights" and "turn-outs," both male sex-role players, don't think of themselves as homosexuals, even though they have sex with men. Other inmates don't think of them as homosexuals, either. Straights and turn-outs are often married. On the street, straights and turn-outs say they never get involved in male-male sex. Straights are sometimes referred to as "regular" convicts, but this is ambiguous. A regular can also be a convict who isn't involved in male-male sex.

FAGS AND FUCK-BOYS

You can always tell an ol' time convict when you strip search 'em. When he bends over and spreads 'em, if you can see up his asshole and right out his mouth, you know he's been here a while [a veteran line hack, during my OJT].

Boozer, Crazy, Magic, Slim, Red Hog, Jimmy-John, and Big Brother helped me determine the number of homosexuals on the mainline. In his east-end unit, Boozer said "there are three fags; one with an ol' man and two freelancing. Freelancers have seven or eight inmates who mess with them regular." Inmates who were known to engage in sex in his unit, according to Boozer, made up about 14% of its population in May 1987.

Slim suggests "on this end here [west end], you have maybe about 10 with lovers. Maybe 20. On the other [east] end, especially in H-unit, about the same. They balanced about the same at both ends." After trying to make sense of their unit-by-unit "educated guesses," I determined that about 10%, or approximately 120 mainline inmates, were actively engaged in sex in 1987.

This is a very conservative estimate, based only on reported data that I was able to confirm. Sex is a sensitive issue; inmates don't easily divulge details of their own sexual behavior, nor will they snitch on others. I learned to be suspicious of inmates who too readily offered sexual information about themselves or others. Many inmates who are sexually active are married, said these convicts, so their identities

required protection, lest information leaks cause needless embarrassment for wives on the outside.

Sexual relations are usually between members of the same racial/
ethnic group, though cross racial sex does occur. In May 1987, there
were at least five mixed couples on the mainline, according to Big
Brother. There was one dominant-black/submissive-Hispanic couple;
three or four dominant-black/submissive-white couples; and one
dominant-white/submissive-black couple.

Some convicts have mixed opinions about homosexuals. According
to Eddie, "Homosexuals can't be trusted. Violence happens behind
homosexuality, but not who gets to fuck the punk, but the shit the punk
gets into. It's a very insecure lady who shaves every morning. If you're
weak enough to suck dick, you're weak enough to snitch!"

Red Hog claims "regular" convicts can't trust homosexuals, especially
in doing business. "They're emotionally all fucked up. They were abused
kids, you know."

There's another viewpoint, too. Jimmy-John, who has a history of
sexual assault in prison, said that "[homosexuality] gets to be a habit, it's
hard to break. It's like having a monkey on your back. For homosexuals,
he gets used to taking a man inside either orally or anally; that's hard to
get off." "Some guys get so turned on to butt fuckers," said Slim, "that
there's nothing in the world like it to them."

Fags are often distinguishable by their gait and dress. Fuck-boys are
not distinguishable by clothing, facial cosmetics or hair-do, gait, or
speech.

Bureau policy permits only authorized clothing to be worn: prison-
issue olive-drab for work, and brown khaki for the visiting room, with
black, steel-toed shoes. During the evening, when dress rules are
relaxed, inmates wear leisure suits, sneakers, sweat suits, and sweat
shirts with their olive-drab pants. However, facial make-up, hair
barrettes, and articles of women's clothing are forbidden.

On occasion, though, a Lompoc fag sneaks a barrette, fashioned in
the prison hobby shop, into a fresh coiffure, or "she" tries to wear blue
pool-cue chalk as eye shadow. Barrettes are confiscated when seen, and
fags wearing facial make-up are ordered to wash. Confiscating barrettes
usually provides a good laugh among correctional staffers, behind the
closed door of the lieutenant's office.

One weekday morning in September 1986, when men were hanging
around a cellblock door awaiting work call, a unit staffer walked in and
spotted a fag dressed in a skin-tight, powder-blue jump suit. "Take that
off before you go to work. We don't go to work in jump suits in federal
penitentiaries," he told her. She was upset, but listened anyway. That
day at lunch, however, I saw her in the mess hall wearing the jump suit.

Fags make themselves visible. In May 1987, there was a cadre of four white fags walking the mainline together, one of whom had just come out of the closet.

Two fags, who got a lot of attention on the mainline, were Hispanic. One wore a carefully controlled hairdo and light blue pool-cue chalk as eye make-up. The Hispanic fag wore very tight sweatpants showing a "panty line," created by her bikini underwear, and on top, she wore a tight, brightly colored, short-sleeve T-shirt.

Billie, as she called herself, was among this group, and had been a "hot number" on the mainline, during my research. Billie never wore women's clothing, but sported tight-in-the-crotch sweat pants, and displayed herself with a highly exaggerated, rear-end-swaying gait. On occasion, a line hack would order Billie to "stop that ass-swaying shit, and walk like a man!" (Billie had been in the spotlight since the summer of 1986, providing a constant source of humor for inmates and staff alike.)

As he made his 4:00 p.m. stand-up count, the cellblock officer quickly peeked into Billie's cell, making sure that she was present and standing up. Billie was there, alright, but she was lying on her back "jerking off," said the young officer. "She was staring at *Sports Illustrated* pictures of men athletes [he grimaced] that she has taped on her walls."

Later, in the same cellblock, inmates along the flats were temporarily double-bunked, while a cellblock was fitted with new electronic locking devices. Billie moved in with Franco. The cellblock officer said:

> Franco screamed like hell about it. I told him he better shut or I'd shoot him for refusing programs. So he shut up. One morning, a couple a days after Billie moved in with him, just after breakfast call, Franco stormed up. He was fucking hot. He was screaming about Billie, again. I said, "Calm down, what happened?" He said, "I woke up this morning and that fucking queer was jerking on my tool."

Billie often propositioned inmates in her cell block. Inmate Joey, who lives on the flats near Billie, is friendly with inmate Eric. Joey said Eric received a note from Billie, scrawled in pencil on the face of a white, legal-size envelope: "Cum in this envelope, I want to taste you, Love, Billie." Eric was flattered, Joey said, and had a good chuckle. Inmates along the flats laughed about this for weeks afterward.

However, on one occasion, before I arrived at Lompoc, Billie did get herself in potential trouble. According to a staff source, Billie was getting up early each morning, before the majority of inmates were awake, squatting on the end of her bunk and loudly crowing like a rooster. Billie didn't do this just once or twice; her crowing became a regular and annoying part of the early morning. After a few days of crowing, inmates began to grumble, but after weeks of crowing, someone threatened Billie's life. A staffer said that a convict told him this: "I'll kill her fucking ass, if she don't cut that shit out. This is a fucking prison, not a goddamn barnyard. I don't want to hear any fucking chicken, or donkeys or fucking cows, either. I'll cut her [Billie's] fucking head off." At that point, Billie was placed in protective custody, and early morning peace was restored. When I left Lompoc in May 1987, Billie was walking the mainline, safe and sound.

"Good homosexuals," like Billie, seem to engender more convict patience than nonhomosexuals may enjoy. Inmates says that homosexuals are different, and that getting along with them requires patience and a sense of humor.

Another popular homosexual, in a different unit, was annoying inmates by playing her radio too loudly and refusing repeated requests to lower the sound. Several inmates solved the problem in their inimical way. A unit staffer told me: "Someone shit two long turds on the fag's bed sheet, and then rolled them up and down, and left them there for her to find." The sound was turned down and remained that way.

Fags seem to have their day in the sun. When a good homosexual arrives on the mainline, she may move into a prominent social position, catching lots of flirting glances, overly friendly gestures, and offers for a quick liaison. I was "hit on" once, one evening in September 1987. I returned to the penitentiary at about 6:30, wearing blue jeans, a blue hooded sweat shirt, and sneakers. (During the day watch, staffers never dress this way.) I checked out my keys from control, and clipped them on my belt. As I walked down the corridor, I pushed them behind me, near my right rear pocket; they weren't clearly visible from the front. I was approaching the east-end grill, when a convict walked out of M-unit. As he came closer, he checked me out carefully, scanning my body up and down. He smiled: "Hi, how'ya doing," he said coquettishly. This isn't the way convicts greet staff. I pulled my keys forward, letting them bounce and jiggle on the front of my pants. I never wore jeans and a sweat shirt inside the penitentiary again.

"Getting with a homosexual," Big Brother says, "is easy. It's like on the street. It's easy to meet ladies at work." Big Brother explains:

> A new one comes on the mainline, and may find a job as an orderly in food service. On her first day on the job, she may ask you if she can borrow your mop. That's where a conversation starts. Then you ask, "Who you with?" If she is free, and even if she isn't, you may give her cigarettes, but mostly offer friendship. That's the friendly way. Another way is to "gorilla it out of him." First, you don't let the homosexual use your mop or bucket: "Keep away from that motherfucking bucket, bitch," you say. "Don't you touch nothing. You understand." Then the homosexual knows what's happening. If she doesn't put out, she'll lose her job. Most

dudes use the "I promise you" tip: I promise you this or that. You can do it with finesse or rough.

Thom adds:

If one looks good, you walk up to her, "you look very good!" "Well," she thinks, "my man think I look very good, too." You keep that going, and you got her. It holds a lot of mental effect. I see a guy who looks kind of soft, "Hey, man, you look kind of good." After three or four months, they start to believe it. The dudes I'm involved with are on a dominant-factor type situation about that. A person clings to the fact that a guy wants someone. It gets your nuts out of the sand; you got to get this thing off.

In addition to pleasure, there are serious risks, say Slim and Big Brother. Slim:

Trouble starts when some guy picks at homosexuals who aren't interested. They are trouble. Couple weeks ago some dude came to me, and asked if I'd talk to this dude, a white dude, and tell 'em to stop pressuring his ol' lady. I went to him and told him that I knew "his people" [his friends] and they want him to lay off. He said he wasn't doing nothing, just talking to her. I told him to stop talking to her.

Big Brother:

A fag may tease guys, thinking that his man will protect him. Then you get trouble between them [the ol' man and potential suitors]. You got to remember that these good-looking homosexuals are a breed of individual not made up mentally correctly.

A convict may want a homosexual who already has an ol' man. Rather than directly confronting him, said Big Brother, the suitor "drops a cop-out [a snitch note] on the guy for locker-knockering to get him in I-unit, so he can get at the homosexual. Then when the guy gets out, he'll run down the dude."

Slim adds another variation:

Around here with homosexuals, say this homo want to get together with this guy, but she got an old man, she been with a long time. She knows that getting together with that guy is going to bring conflict. Well, she pays some dude to bust up her ol' man to get him off the mainline. Once the guy get busted up, they going to get him off the mainline. They they're free to get together.

There's still another twist. Slim:

You got guys who get their rocks off, turning a date, you know, turning a trick. Some guys in [inmate-inmate] marriages, don't mind a trick for drugs, cash, or commissary. The husband automatically gets an issue off of that. The guy who's turning the date [the "john'] gets his rocks off, the homo gets paid, and the husband got the homosexual. Them is just freaks, guys who fuck and suck for drugs, cash, and commissary. Maybe about half the population in here is tricking.

More serious is the case of an inmate raping another's fag. Big Brother says:

Somebody rape your homosexual. Let's say it's a friend who raped your homosexual. You don't want to kill nobody over a fag. It's a bad labor to have on you to be governing them guys. [It's emotionally difficult to be deeply involved with a fag.] You got to have the extra capacity to uphold on them boys. [You have to be tough, if you keep fags.]

At this point, Big Brother talked about the emotional side of inmate-inmate sex.

Homosexuals, by and large, take the place of women. The same principles apply, but they are a little more raw. The only thing they can't have is a baby. Most dudes with homosexuals are married [to them], and don't let them go out fooling around. AIDS stops dudes who have homos from going out. It all depends on you whether you're going to pamper him yourself or put him on the street to get money. Some homosexuals are very expensive to keep. If their tastes aren't satisfied, they begin looking for a new ol' man who'll take care of them.

The case of Queenie and Paulie was the hottest (and most potentially dangerous) homosexual affair, that occurred during my research. A popular American Indian homosexual, Queenie, was new on the mainline. A staffer said that even before Queenie got through

A & O [admission and orientation] guys were hitting on her and trying to get dates. Some of those horny cons were licking their chops; they were waiting for a piece of that sweet ass. Man, she didn't even get off the bus yet, when cons were hanging hard-ons out their cell windows and screaming for that young, tight ass!

According to Big Brother,

several blacks took him hard, real hard, and he didn't like that, so he wanted back with his people, but they couldn't support his habits. He was a very expensive individual. You couldn't miss him. You ever hear that saying? You couldn't miss him with wine, reefer, drugs, he wants it all. He found a white man to support him.

Slim, who lived in Queenie's unit:

She's a $1,500 whore. That's how much he [Paulie, Queenie's white lover] paid for her. I'm glad it happened. I know this guy who was in the shower while they were doing it—that's disrespect for you. Take your knife up in there, and run 'em out, naked and all. They was in there when the

[handwritten margin notes: "interesting", "How it is the married convicts who engage in homosex rel more so then unmarried convict"]

lieutenant was making his rounds. Queenie got caught with three bottles of weed. The police was walking around and no one was keeping point. They got 'em. Queenie was out the next day. Some dude got paid to take the fall for the weed. Paulie paid $1,500 to the Indians to leave them [Paulie and Queenie] alone. I don't know call girls or righteous female hookers who cost $1,500. Paulie thinks Queenie's a woman. Does he got a pussy like the pussy God created for man? They [the American Indians] was going to burn him [Queenie], anyway. They was going to get Queenie off the mainline; they already got the money. There's a jealousy thing there, too. Since they got their money, they say, "fuck him." Some of them liked him [Queenie], too. They'll [the Indians] pump it like a racial thing. [Grey Feather] told him [Queenie] he wasn't to fuck with no blacks, Mexicans, or whites. Then Paulie fell in love with him and paid for him. Then they started plotting how to get him out of there.

After they were caught having sex in a shower, Queenie and Paulie were locked away in I-unit, in separate cells. Both were despondent. Queenie attempted suicide. "It was bullshit," said an I-unit officer. "She tied her sheet around her neck and tied the sheet to the grill. But she had her fucking feet on the deck the whole time. Fucking fags can't even kill themselves the right way."

Paulie didn't try to commit suicide. Paulie was always well groomed and clean shaven, but when I saw him in I-unit, he had stopped grooming himself: He had a multiday, scraggly beard, and his hair was uncombed. I watched him spend his days pacing back and forth in his cell.

"They're actually in love. They have an intense, emotional attachment like heterosexual love; they love each other like a married couple," said a staff psychologist. Paulie's wife was doing time in another federal prison.

STRAIGHTS

Straights "use" fags and punks. They don't bother turning-out inmates. It is possible for neither to be considered homosexual by other inmates, nor do they consider their own behavior to be homosexual. Some straights develop lasting relationships with other straights, with one playing the dominant role, the other the submissive role. There tends to be a strong sense of privacy among straights who have developed long-term sexual relationships. *[handwritten: hmm.]*

Thom is a straight. He said, "sex is sex," and it doesn't matter how or from whom he gets it: "I don't care who's sucking my cock, a man or woman. I just close my eyes and imagine whoever I want. Shit, we're in California, 90% of the motherfuckers here are gay anyway. If you get the dick, you always on the dick; these motherfucking homos love takin' the hammer."

Late one morning, around 10:50, inmate Maury came to work in the dining hall, with his breath reeking of homebrew, his eyes blood-shot, and wearing a silly grin. We stood together, chatting. I soaked up his continuous stream of convict stories about the men coming through the chow line. After about 30 minutes, he turned, leaned over toward me and quietly said, "Hey, don't say nothing, but, see that guy—about fifth in line, over there—that's my ol' lady."

This caught me by surprise. Maury had already told me, on many occasions, about his wife and girlfriends, and that he would never "fuck with homos; they're bad luck." He denied ever having had male-male sex in any prison before, and claimed never to have engaged in male-male sex on the street. If fact, he always enjoyed telling me that "beautiful women think my tattoos are sexy. Yeah, they love to rub 'em, if you know what I mean."

I looked down the line and didn't pick out anyone in particular. "Who?" I asked. "There, over there," he said, "that old dude right there." Now I paused.

His ol' lady looked fifty-five to sixty years old, and every bit the stereotype of a graying convict. After I spotted him, Maury, who is in his thirties, turned to me: "Do you think he's too old for me?" What could I say? "No, he looks like a decent guy."

From that time on, whenever I spent time in Maury's cellblock, with him, with another convict, or with the unit hack, I carefully watched who Maury talked to, who walked into his cell, and who stopped to chat with him at his cell door. His "lover" lived only a few cells away from his. During many observations, I saw his lover walk into his cell more often than other inmates; I noticed the older convict smiling at Maury whenever they were together; I heard a deferential style of speech between Maury and his lover, with Maury being dominant and in control of speech situations, and with his lover deferring to him when decisions were made, particularly about commissary purchases.

The sex life of straights has been disrupted recently, according to Big Brother. A new trend ("fag-on-fag," he called it) in prison sex emerged about 1982-83, he said, and it is now causing problems for straights.

> The basic penitentiary law was, no homosexuals can have sex with other homosexuals. Regular guys can't compete with homosexuals. A regular convict may slap him trying to stop it. Homos can get relief with another [one], but not with a straight. Homos on homos get into sixty-nining, rimming, and sadomasochism. We can't deal with that. That's tough to compete with that.

TURN-OUTS

Turn-outs seduce inmates with promises of commissary items, wine, and friendship and kindness. Their strategy of seduction is passive, as opposed to "gorilla tactics," as Big Brother calls more aggressive "moves." Eddie said that,

> Turn-outs get a guy drunk and he's lying down. There are a lot of guys who want to [have sex], but won't until they're drunk. There are a lot of guys on the pipe, and you wouldn't guess who they are. Movies have you believe that men fight over queers, but it's a small percentage. It's a big toss-up between what's real and not real in here; usually men don't confront other men about a homo.

Inmates who are turned out may become fags, punks, or fuck-boys. Usually, though, a turned-out inmate is considered a punk, not because he engages in female-role sex, but because he didn't have "the balls," as Eddie says, to resist a turn-out's advances. Before being turned-out, he was a wimp, now he's a wimp and a homosexual punk or a "spit-on punk," as Red Hog calls them.

Straights and turn-outs sometimes use "sex-things" (as I call them). These inmates deal sex for free or for a few commissary items. They are sometimes crazies who are used for sex, and little else. They have few social connections on the mainline. Sex with a sex-thing was described to me as "throwing him down on a bunk, tossing a fuck-book over the back of his head, and humpin' away. A hole is a hole."

RAPE

Late one morning, just as lunch was called, Slim wandered into the research office. Magic, a 31-year-old convict doing time for kidnapping and murder, wandered by and peeked in the door. When he saw Slim, he, too, came in and sat down. Then Crazy passed by. He saw Slim and Magic, so he also joined us. Now in his late 20s, Crazy said he was finishing a long sentence for conspiring to kill prominent elected officials: "I wanted to be the first black man to assassinate a [powerful government dude]," he said.

Crazy was a homosexual and a "cutter" (when he was frustrated, he would slash his forearms with a single-edged razor; both forearms were covered by thick layers of criss-crossed razor scars). Crazy was becoming anxious about his impending release. "Is there any homosexuals in Sacramento?" he asked me. "Why?" I asked. "I'm going up there, when I get paroled," he explained. "I guess so. There are homosexuals all over California," I joked. Magic and Slim were bursting with laughter.

I talked to Slim, Magic, and Crazy about their experiences with sexual violence in institutions. I also wanted to know why they believed rape isn't more common at USP-Lompoc.

Magic said he was introduced to institution living at about age eight, and to homosexuality not long after that. He was housed in a juvenile home in Maryland; today, he said, his ten-year-old son lives in the same juvenile home, having been committed there by his son's mother.

Magic explains how he was introduced to sex.

> You don't get letters or calls, your momma don't come to visit. You need something, so you go to somebody, then that guy wants to sleep with you. A counselor put me in the hole, because I wouldn't let him suck my dick, and I stayed there until I let him. Counselors brought me and some others booze and dope for sex. We had to blow them, and they wanted us to fuck them. If we didn't cooperate, we went to the hole.

Crazy said he killed a sexually aggressive convict when he was 17 while serving time in a Louisiana state penitentiary, before he came into the FPS. His nickname was earned in this incident, he said.

> [He came up to me saying] I like you, you're a cute young boy. This guy was big. Then one day I was standing by the cell block door and he came up. He grabbed me by the shirt and threw me up against the locker. I came off it and hit him in the belly and hit him and hit him again. He went down and my buddy came up and started stabbing him in the head. We killed him, and I got one year running with my other sentence.

One incident of sexual aggression occurred during my research. I was sitting in the lieutenant's office, drinking a cup of coffee at about 7:15 in the morning. A lieutenant walked up and handed me a stack of Polaroid color photographs. "Ever seen an asshole like that one?" he asked. The top photo was a close-up of a highly swollen, bright-red perianal region, that looked as though it had been turned inside out. An eye-opening sight, first thing in the morning.

The morning before at about 7:30, a cellblock officer had called a senior lieutenant, asking for help. "I walked into the unit," said the lieutenant, "and these two guys were faced off. One had a chair up in the air, and the other one was holding a pool cue." According to the investigation, these two middle-age inmates were "long-time lovers," and, on that morning, their sexual intercourse became violent. "Shit," commented a GS-8, "they just had a little lovers spat, ain't nothing."

I read the medical report. Both men had multiple black-and-blue bruises and abrasions (inflicted by punches). One inmate had a nasty bite on his left trapezius muscle, and the other had numerous and shallow, knife-inflicted punctures in the outside of one thigh.

I mentioned this case to a staff psychologist. Inmate sex is often sadomasochistic, and this type of incident isn't surprising or unusual (Wooden and Parker 1982: 14, also note the sadomasochistic nature of prison sex).

Why were there so few reported incidents like that one? I consulted a few experts. "Here," said Magic,

> Freelancing homosexuals, yeah, fags, keep down rapes. It keeps down rapes, and a whole lot of other things too! If there's enough homosexuals, he [new inmate] won't get turned out. If there's enough homosexuals, he [an attractive inmate] don't have to worry when he sees two dudes like us [pointing to Slim] looking at him. Some dude looking at me that way, and I put my knife in him. There be people in here who suck on those things and take those things up the ass; they go out there and kiss their wives and play with their kids. How can they do that. They don't have no conscience.

"He's right," said Slim. "If there's enough homos, there's no rapes. Rapes are on cons who aren't homosexuals." Magic looked at Crazy: "Ain't that right, Crazy?" "Yep!" he said, with a little grin on his face.

Magic continued. "You know what else, man? The feds will ship your ass if they catch you fucking some dude. They likely to send you to [USP] Lewisburg. I'd rather jerk off every day than go to Lewisburg."

Slim said, "I like pussy too much to fuck assholes. Anyway, some dudes is real serious about their ol' ladies. If you don't want no drama, then you better fuck fifi, and leave them ladies alone. All you got to do is hold a fuck-book and hump fifi. You get off, and stay out of trouble." Magic, Slim, and Crazy almost laughed themselves off their chairs. (A fifi bag is a plastic bag filled with either rags or liver, stolen from the kitchen, and heated by warm tap water in a cell sink. An inmate either holds the top or ties it off, and inserts his penis.)

HOMICIDE

Serious sex-related violence is infrequent at USP-Lompoc, but it happens.

> Under the guard of U.S. Marshals armed with sawed-off shotguns to prevent a possible mass escape attempt, a half-dozen of the most

dangerous men in the U.S. prison system were brought to Los Angeles last week to testify as witnesses in a prison murder case.

The courtroom security was the heaviest seen at the U.S. Courthouse in years, and the story told by the convicts assembled from prisons throughout the nation was every bit as rough as the reputations of the witnesses themselves.

There was an undercurrent of danger in the courtroom as the witnesses spoke about the prison killing and described the pattern of violence in which it was set.

Among the convicts themselves, however, there was an almost lighthearted mood as they took turns describing such prison realities as homosexual prostitution, heroin use, and easy access to weapons.

Willie Crusco Free, 35, was charged with fatally stabbing his prison boyfriend 67 times with a sharpened dinner knife in the recreation yard at Lompoc Federal Penitentiary on Sept. 18, 1983. Free smiled at times as the testimony unfolded last week and yawned occasionally as his defense lawyer pleaded with the jury to acquit him. . . .

Testimony revealed that Codianni, 33, a "punk" nicknamed Lady Claudine by other Lompoc prisoners, had initially agreed to provide sex to Free as often as three times a day in exchange for protection and a steady supply of heroin.

Just three weeks after arriving at Lompoc and establishing his relationship with Free, however, Codianni found a new drug supplier [*Los Angeles Times*, January 26, 1986; a photograph of Willie Free, with his arm around the neck of Louis Codianni, also appears there].

A convict who claims familiarity with this case told me his story.

Codianni was freelancing. She [Codianni] was selling blow jobs in the TV room of her unit. Some guys in the unit told Free about it. They laughed and told Willie: "Hey, you can't hold your ol' lady, huh?" Willie told her to cut the shit, but she didn't listen. So Willie did her on the yard.

He also said he witnessed the killing:

I was out there. Guys were playing racquetball and tennis, some blacks were shooting hoops. When Free hit her, everybody on the yard stopped, and nobody moved. He kept stabbing and stabbing, and didn't stop even when the pigs rolled up. I was out there the next day, and there was pieces of dried flesh stuck to the concrete.

In February 1986, an experienced custody staffer gave me his eyewitness account of the killing. This was his story.

I wasn't the first one out there. The rec yard officer was there, but no where around it. He saw it and called for help. He was new; I couldn't blame him—what can you do? I wasn't gonna jump in the middle of it. Willie turned [Codianni] into hamburger; he was dead when I got there. I was standing from here to there [about 6 feet]. I knew Willie, we got along OK. I said, "Willie, put the knife down, he's dead." He just looked at [Codianni]; he didn't listen, and stabbed him seven, eight, nine, ten more times. Then a pack of guys came up behind me and got him going again. [Willie] stood up holding a bloody knife and looked at me. I said, "come on now, Willie, take it easy." Willie was so angry, he wanted to pick up the body and throw it over the fence. He wouldn't even put his knife down, and we weren't gonna try to take it from him. We walked him in to the institution, and he was still holding the knife. When we got to I-unit, he dropped it.

Staffers said that Free's weapon was a sharpened, stainless steel dinner knife, hidden in the institution since it was an FCI. Figure 7.1 shows a shank made from such a dinner knife. These knives aren't used in the penitentiary any longer.

There was another sex-related killing in 1984. A staff eyewitness:

I was first on the scene. I stood in [the victim's cell doorway] and watched. [A staffer] came up right after me. We stood there. What can you do? We yelled at [him], "Drop the knife, put it down," but he just kept stabbing [him]. Blood was everywhere, splattered on the walls, and it was running over the floor. He kept stabbing him until his arm got too tired to stab anymore. Then he dropped the shank.

AIDS

Red Hog tells an interesting story:

In the latter months of 1985, one of the most voracious homosexuals in the federal prison system violated parole in Florida and was returned to the men's maximum-security prison at Lompoc to finish his sentence. This one was so predatory that the cons had long ago nicknamed him "Honey Bear." Honey Bear was known to shoot a load of "crank" and go walking down a tier advertising favors at every cell he passed; he would enter at the beck and call of anyone who was interested. If there happened to be two men in the cell, appropriate adjustments could be made. The Honey Bear was an accommodating soul. No one seemed to notice the little sores on the back of Honey Bear's neck, although quite a few of his "clients" had an intimate view of them. Early in 1986, the sores got out of hand, and he was having other health problems. Honey Bear went to the doctor and was soon diagnosed as having AIDS [*San Francisco Chronicle,* August 3, 1986].

Figure 7.1 Sharpened Dining-Hall Knife

These days, when the topic of discussion turns to inmate sex, it also turns to AIDS. "Now," said Thom, "you have to know who's blowing you and who he blew before."

Verified AIDS cases were top-secret information at USP-Lompoc. Administrators didn't want to add to the circulating rumors and sense of panic which some correctional staffers and inmates were already feeling; making public a list of AIDS inmates would have been putting AIDS victims on a hit list.

is this wise?

Staff and inmates felt that the dreaded disease was a genuine threat to their safety. Correctional officers who may have to touch inmates' blood, or were likely, as they are in I-unit, to have urine and feces thrown at them, were particularly worried. As a precaution, rubber gloves and disposal instructions are available to staffers in each department, for cleaning blood and body fluids.

Anticipating staffers' anxiety about AIDS, USP-Lompoc received a Bureau training film and authorization for a physician's assistant to discuss AIDS and answer staffers' questions during annual training, beginning in fall 1985.

Those hacks who were working in close contact with inmates felt that the Bureau's efforts were insufficient. At several early recalls, Warden

Christensen addressed AIDS scares and rumors, and briefed staff on additional measures taken by the Bureau to decrease the probability of staff and inmate infection.

Despite this, staff anxiety was high. "If one of these thugs is on a range dying," said a hack, "I ain't gonna be the one to give him mouth to mouth. Fuck him . . . it's him or me. I got a family."

Inmates were alarmed also, and they adjusted their sexual behavior. According to Big Brother, sexual promiscuity rapidly decreased after numerous and "righteous" AIDS rumors began percolating in the cellblocks.

Inmates reported that the old days of grand-scale sex are not likely to reoccur as long as there is AIDS. A Lompoc old-timer reminisced about past years, in the days of FCI-Lompoc.

Things was different before AIDS. I remember a group suck off in [a] TV room. There was this queen here then, she sucked off 79 guys straight. Some guys even got seconds. Guys was standing in line, laughing and having a good time. The last dude in line, he was a big black buck, he wanted more. He been through the line a couple times. She was down on her knees and took that big black pecker in, and started sucking. Then she got tired—can you image sucking that many convict-cocks, and stopped sucking and dropped it out of her mouth. That queen looked up at that buck and said, "I can't do it no more, my jaw's too tired." He didn't want to hear that shit. He looked down at her and smacked her across the face, a good one, too. He said, "Suck, you fucking bitch, suck." That was the cock-sucking Olympics, all right.

When I left USP-Lompoc at the end of September 1986, fags weren't having too much trouble finding partners. By March 1987, though, Lompoc's spotlighted Hispanic queen, who had been a favorite of many inmates since September 1986, was finding it difficult to get a date. She began "main-corridor cruising," an activity designed to pick up men. A staffer told me that, "[She] has been trolling in front of the lunch room, sucking her thumb. Every day she's out there, up and down, sucking that thumb, looking for a man."

Early in the spring of 1986, rumors circulated that an inmate, suspected of having AIDS, was transferred to the Medical Facility for Federal Prisons at Springfield, Missouri. Everyone was very tight lipped about this, for good reason. Penitentiaries are, in the best of times, hard to live in and to manage. An AIDS scare, based on a rumors and misinformation, could have further increased AIDS anxiety.

I couldn't find out anything, from anyone, about this purported AIDS victim. All of my best sources either didn't know anything themselves or weren't talking. Every day, I commuted with Jerry, the hospital administrator. More than once I asked him about AIDS and, he would just drag on his cigarette and stare at me. I quit asking.

Rumors and gossip can spread through USP-Lompoc very quickly, but sensitive information rarely leaves the narrowly circumscribed channels for which it is intended. I wasn't privy to top secrets, but in May 1987, the Bureau reported seventy-five diagnosed cases of AIDS. Nineteen inmates had died and twelve others had been released with AIDS to the street, according to staff sources (see United States Department of Justice, 1986).

MANAGING SEXUAL AGGRESSION

Homosexuals raise tension levels in cellblocks, especially if they are getting attention from more than one suitor. I've seen problems arise between a fag and her suitors: She may be harassed or her clothes burned by a spurned lover, or she may be continually hit-on by a small army of aggressive inmates. Under these conditions, she may be transferred to another unit. Alternatively, the unit manager, counselor, or unit officer can confront her suitors, ordering them to back off.

A homosexual may develop a short-term relationship with one man in the same living unit. As long as this temporary union stays in the background and doesn't cause any disruption, the couple may be left alone by unit staff. But if a homosexual relationship becomes troublesome, causing even minor cellblock disruptions, then she and her lover will most assuredly be placed in separate cellblocks.

Some inmates claim that separating a fag and her guy never works. "They got to put a queen and her ol' man in the same cell in I-unit or they'll drive the cops crazy," said Red Hog.

If neither party finds their separation fair or just, a common response from one member of the couple, said a counselor, usually the fuck-boy, is to request a BP-9, claiming the actions of the institution unjust and violating inmates' rights. Red Hog claims to know homosexuals who have done this; he laughed about it and shook his head in disgust.

The adjustment of younger and vulnerable inmates, though few of them are assigned to Lompoc, is an important concern for correctional supervisors who recognize that aggressive advances may quickly turn into a fist-fight or shanking between competing aggressive suitors. These inmates tend to be interested more in the domination and aggressiveness of their conquest than in the sexual satisfaction and temporary emotional closeness it permits.

If a situation in a cellblock looks as though it may get out of hand, a younger inmate may either be placed in protective custody, or may ask to "pc up" (state-prisoner talk for putting yourself in pc) until either the tumult diminishes, his aggressive suitors are dealt with, or he is placed in another cellblock.

Access to freelancing homosexuals, Bureau discipline, and potential retaliation by a jilted lover seem to be the key internal social control mechanisms keeping the lid on sex-based violence. Of 1985's 1,741 incident reports, .7% (12) were for engaging in sex, and .1% (1) was for making sexual proposals or threats. In 1986, there were 2,049 incident reports: .4% (8) were for engaging in sex, and .2% (3) were for making sexual proposals or threats.

8

SCENES OF DISCIPLINE

VERBAL CONTROL

My staff role at Lompoc, like Marquart's "outside-insider" research (1986a: 16)—he worked as a correctional officer in a Texas state maximum-security prison (see *Newsweek,* October 6, 1986)—allowed me to gain a close and vivid look at scenes of discipline and of violence in which I was able to hear conversations between staffers and inmates. These opportunities provide data that are unavailable to "outsiders."

Talking to inmates played a significant role in inmate discipline. At Lompoc, correctional officers' physical or verbal abuse was not tolerated by the administration, the senior correctional staff, the Federal Bureau of Prisons, or the inmates. Instead, numerous styles of talking to inmates have emerged as hacks', and other line-staffers', primary means of social control. That contrasts sharply with Marquart's findings (1986a: 355): "Informal norms of the guard staff justified violence. . . . The use of unofficial force was so common in the institution . . . that the guards viewed it as an everyday operating procedure and legitimized its use."

A Lompoc staffer's only offensive or defensive "weapon" is his ability to elude trouble with talk. A skilled staff-talker can usually get himself, other staffers, or inmates out of a "tight spot." The mark of a good staff-talker is getting an inmate, even an aggressive one, to do as the staffer wishes. An inexperienced staff-talker or an overly aggressive one might find one or both of his eyes swelling and turning black.

Lompoc's line-talk was also a verbal mechanism used mainly by correctional officers in many ways to bolster their prestige and status. In this prison society, staffers' and inmates' talk is inextricably bound to their public social images.

TAKING CONTROL

Mike Rizo, who sometimes acts as chairman of IDC, and I were standing in front of the mess hall after lunch on a Wednesday afternoon in September 1987. A couple of bakery convicts had given me a bagful of my favorite black walnut cookies. We were eating them and talking about inmate discipline and the role of UDC and IDC in regulating inmate behavior.

> You got to treat these guys right. When you say you're going to do something, you have to do it. They remember staff who shine them on or who don't do what they said they would do. We try to be sure that there's no problem like that here. Open communication is what it takes. Then, we have single cells, so guys can get some privacy, and they don't have to put on a show for staff and other convicts. The weather is important, too. If they screw up too many times, we'll ship them to Leavenworth or Lewisburg. They know it, and they don't like it.

Rizo also suggests that convicts respect each other's violent dispositions.

> On the street, these guys walk around knowing they're bad. They can stand on a sidewalk somewhere, look around, and know they're meaner than anybody they see. They'll come after you and think, "What's he going to do about it?" They'll cut your head off, and it won't bother them. But in here, if a guy thinks he's bad, all he's got to do is stop and look around. It's not like the street. For every bad guy, there's a 100 guys who are worse. Anyone of these guys can cut your head off. That keeps them in line.

I asked Lt. Rudy Marks the same question.

> I think it has a lot to do with the weather. This is the garden spot of the Federal Prison System. Good weather, yard recreation all year, and single cells are hard to give up. Single cells are really important. They allow them to get away by themselves, to vent alone without a roommate there. When there's a roommate in there, a guy can never get away. It's important for them to get away for a while, vent their emotions by themselves and get control. Lompoc inmates have gotten away from a violence mentality that you find at other institutions.

Lt. Lee Galland, formerly of USP-Marion, said that controlling a disruptive convict's behavior sometimes depends on clever manipulation:

> If you get some white, neo-Nazi convict or an AB who's been fucking up and giving you problems, and he won't listen, all you got to do is tell me: "Listen, partner, any more of this shit and you're going to Lewisburg." Lewisburg is the home of the Washington, D.C. blacks; they don't care for Nazis and ABs. And those Nazis and ABs don't want anything to do with those blacks. Those blacks will take their heads off.

Inmates don't talk about single cells, sunny weather, or good rapport with staff, as factors controlling violence. But they do talk about the threat of a disciplinary transfer as something to keep in mind. Most say that "picking up a new beef" (a new criminal charge) and the certainty of "getting more federal time," keeps them from committing serious acts of violence. Big Brother has been in the FPS for almost fifteen years, spending almost half that time in penitentiaries:

> Convicts who resort to violence aren't intelligent people. It's stupid to kill somebody over something trivial like an argument over something that doesn't matter. The best strategy is to take it to him, and talk to him, but not right away. You got to wait until after he's played four or five games of basketball and been running up and down the gym. He's all sweating and too tired to fight; then you go talk to him and get it all worked out. I don't want to do no 25 years for killing a stupid motherfucker over something stupid.

Eddie has a strong opinion, too.

> This place is like neutral ground. There's something stifling around here. I'll tell you why I'm not violent. I don't want any more time. In state joints, they don't prosecute. There's no deterrent to killing another inmate in the California state system. Around here, people who kill are people who don't give a fuck. The fed's give 300 and 400 years for that shit. In the state, you get a life sentence, you do 10 years and go to the [parole] board. You get a life sentence from the feds, you got to bring [do] 20 [years] to the board [Federal Parole Commission]. I knew two dudes in [San] Quentin who took a claw hammer and dug out a man's chest and shattered his heart with the hammer. They didn't get no time for it. They went home within a year. They were nice dudes, too; they'd talk to you. You'd never know they were vicious dudes. They're maniacs. They're the crazy bastards who were strangling puppies when they were six years old. San Quentin appalled me at the time. I couldn't believe that things like that could happen. Places like San Quentin and Folsom and Attica manufacture violence. I have enough fucking foresight to realize the trouble that it will cause me. There are two kinds of people in prison. Inmates who suck the man's ass, and guys who say "fuck you, I ain't doing shit for you, I'm gonna kill you." That's the guy in San Quentin. I won't suck their asses. I make my bed, I wear clean clothes and say "yes" and "no" . . . that's all they get. They have control. I know it.

Thom offers similar thoughts about lifers and violence which run contrary to conventional "state-prison" folklore that "lifers don't have anything to lose." Thom said that

> lifers commit suicide by setting themselves up for getting killed. It's gotten to the point around here, where a man's got to do another man's thinking for him. Cons will create situations so they will get killed. Killing them ain't worth it. Feds don't fuck around. A guy would get 25 extra years and 3 to 4 years locked down at [USP] Marion.

Staff try to establish control from the very beginning of an inmate's sentence, according to UDC and IDC members. In relatively minor incidents, "taking [an inmate's] good time" is often a serious enough sanction to let an inmate know who's boss. Schafer (1982: 148) suggests that there's "no empirical evidence that good time serves as an incentive for orderly behavior or that the power to take away good time helps staff control [prisoner] behavior." However, at Lompoc, when good time is removed, reearning it can be a strong incentive to obey the rules. "Once we take it, we [IDC] can hang it out there like a carrot in front of a horse, and they go after it," said Rizo. Taking good time is taking control. This UDC case illustrates it. The UM presided and I was the second member of the UDC hearing team.

Jerome, a black inmate in his mid-twenties, had recently arrived from a Texas state prison and had spent a short time in a Texas FCI. At the FCI, he told his unit team that he was interested in welding VT, he said. He claims, too, that his FCI unit team told him that because he was being transferred very soon, he would have to arrange for welding VT at USP-Lompoc.

Jerome told this story to his unit team at his USP-Lompoc "intake" session, according to his UM. Unfortunately, welding VT was full at that time, and openings weren't anticipated for several months. His unit team assigned him to a school program, and also gave Jerome an opportunity to choose another VT program, according to his UM. Jerome was angry about not getting welding VT, and he refused to attend school; one midweek morning, he didn't leave his cell at early work call and was reported missing by education staff. Jerome was cited by his counselor for refusing programs, a 300-level violation. Jerome also made sure that other inmates knew that he was protesting that day, as he made a loud scene in his unit. He was sent to I-unit.

The three of us were standing near the upper-I conference room. Jerome wore handcuffs and a belly chain. The UM read the charges against him, and, for the hearing record, Jerome was asked why he didn't accept an offer to attend school or to enroll in another VT program. "They [his FCI unit team] told me [in Texas] that when I got here, I'd get welding. Now you tell me I can't," growled Jerome. The UM calmly responded. "Let me explain it to you again. . . ." Each time Jerome heard that welding VT was full, he got angrier and his voice got louder. Finally, Jerome was really upset. "Fuck this shit," he yelled, "I'm not going to do nothing 'til I get welding. I ain't going to your school. I ain't doing shit. Fuck you and this fuck this place. I want to go back to Texas . . . now. Let me out of here, I want to go back to my unit."

The UM responded, "Oh no, you can't do that. Are you sure you don't want to accept school or another VT until welding has a spot for you?" "Fuck no, now let me out," demanded Jerome. "This is your last chance. We can do this the easy way or the hard way," said the UM. "Well fuck you, too," asserted Jerome to the UM. "OK," said the UM, "I'm going to refer this to IDC, and I'm recommending that all of your good time be removed." Jerome was stunned: "You can't do that." The UM responded: "Oh, really! I just did it. Now, let's put you back in your cell, and you can think about that."

About 30 minutes later, I walked past Jerome's cell and heard him talking to his cellie. "They took all my good time. They can't do that. Shit." Later, the UM said, "That young man just didn't want to learn, now did he? But I think he got the idea that we run this show."

"I'M GOING TO SHOOT THE BASTARD"

In a state prison, they don't sweat your time. When you get drunk in a state prison, eight out of ten times a guard will tell you to go sleep it off. In a federal pen, they sweat your time. Here, they want to send you to the hole, write a shot, take your good time. Feds sweat your time [Slim].

The formal discipline system begins by writing an incident report, known in hack slang as a "shot." Citing an inmate is "shooting" him. I heard a GS-8 line hack use this expression on my first day. He had just finished a heated interaction with a convict: "I'm going shoot the bastard," he promised. I was taken aback. In 1985, staffers shot an average of 145 inmates a month, and, in 1986 they shot a monthly average of 171 inmates.

Lieutenants oversee the shooting of inmates. They keep the incident report log, investigate shots, and lock away disruptive convicts in I-unit. Only lieutenants can lock up convicts. At an initial shot-investigation hearing, a watch's shot-lieutenant may decide to resolve minor (400-level) shots informally, if the inmate also agrees to the conditions of the resolution. A lieutenant also has the discretionary authority to "expunge" (squash) minor shots (UDC can do this, too).

The shot-lieutenant may also choose, in cases of nonviolent or nonalcohol- and nondrug-related offenses, to send the shot to UDC, but to "let the convict walk," that is, not to put him in I-unit. But, of course, this depends on the inmate's offense and whether he passes the "attitude test." A convict's politeness and contrition are now very important. If a convict can sweet-talk his way out of trouble, he has insulated himself from discipline. This verbal strategy also applies to informal disciplinary situations. A convict may, indeed, sweet-talk his way out of trouble with a new hack. And if sweet talk doesn't work with a new hack, a convict often tries an aggressive approach. Some convicts don't bother with sweet talk when they face off against a new hack, they're just aggressive. But when a convict faces a lieutenant, either with sweet or aggressive talk, the convict almost always loses. And so the verbal game continues.

The initial shot-investigation hearing usually doesn't involve too many hassles. But if there is going to be trouble anywhere in the formal disciplinary proceeding, it often happens here, and is triggered by a minor act or an aggressively uttered word which is interpreted as a challenge by either a convict or lieutenant. Emotions now elevate quickly, as this situation easily gets out of control. "I jumped in his shit with both feet" is a line-hack expression often used to characterize this or another highly emotional convict scene.

AT THE SCENE

Toch (1977: 21-22) suggests that by "seeing violence-precipitation as an intersection between violence-prone personal dispositions and the situational stimuli that invoked these dispositions . . . a prison incident could result . . . given a perceived affront to an inmate who is oversensitive to such affronts."

In this prison world of carefully cultivated, social images, "if you can get a loud mouth away from other convicts, you can usually talk sense to him. But when he's around other convicts, like in mess hall, he'll put on a show for everybody," said Lt. Merchant. When doing "attitude adjustment," particularly in high visibility settings like the mess hall or the main corridor, damaging a convict's image can be dangerous. "You have to give them an honorable way out, and leave it up to them," says Lt. Galland.

In cases of informal (face-to-face) discipline, and in every other verbal encounter with convicts, a hack's or any other staffer's speech can promote, elude, escalate, or alleviate violence. Sometimes a rookie hack learns this lesson the "black-and-blue" way. After about one year on the job, a hack was punched out one evening by a convict. The punch was thrown about 30 feet from central control, and in full view of tens of inmates waiting in the commissary line. I didn't see the incident, but I asked Eddie about it the next day. A friend of his, then in I-unit, threw the punch. "He's a fucking punk and deserved it. He talks down to us, and treats use like we're not human. Fuck him, he got what he deserved.

The pig opened his mouth and Marvin had enough of his shit. You know that punk piece-of-shit even pissed [in] his pants. I'm surprised he didn't shit [in] his pants."

Scenes of discipline always test the fragility of a convict's brittle image. But treating a convict with respect, by not openly challenging his mainline tough-guy image irrespective of his behavior, is a challenge to a line staffer whose own mainline image is also subject to the same social pressures that affect an inmate's. Some staffers say, "Let 'em fucking scream. If they don't disrespect me or lay a hand on me, I'll usually let 'em scream. You got to cut 'em some slack sometimes."

Being patient can be tough, though. Early one morning, before 8, Mike Rizo and I were sitting in my office. Convict Smitty spotted Rizo. He stormed in and howled: "I got this paperwork in, man, and got back nothing but some bullshit. This is fucking bullshit, man." He thought his "time structure" (the time he'll serve and his estimated release date) had been incorrectly computed by someone in administrative systems. "I'm tired of this bullshit, man. Why can't those dumb motherfuckers do it right? I told 'em and told 'em, and nobody listens. This is my motherfucker time they fucking with!" Smitty yelled. Up to this point, Rizo had said nothing. He asked for Smitty's paperwork. He read it, picked up the desk phone, and resolved the problem. Smitty was right about the mistake.

Daily, the warden, the captain, and the AWs set the tone for informal inmate problem solving and discipline. An example of this took place one day at the mess hall's exit door. A hack is posted there after meals to shake down inmates, looking for pilfered food and homebrew. Not every inmate is shaken down—one hack can't shake down hundreds of inmates. Each hack has his own shakedown strategy, though. Some stop every third, fourth, or fifth inmate; other hacks who see a group of three or four inmates walking out, one in front of the other, stop the middle inmate or the last one. (When inmates are trying to leave with stolen food or homebrew, they often walk out, two or three at time, with one of them trying to look guilty—he's the decoy.) Hacks also look for telltale signs of food smuggling, such as bulges around the ankles or waist, or a gait that looks too studied to be natural; this is often a giveaway that the inmate has cans of stolen sardines lining his socks or stuck under his pant's waistband.

That day's shakedown officer, a one-year veteran, shook down every fourth or fifth inmate as they filed out after lunch. A white inmate in his early thirties came walking out alone, and didn't make eye contract with the shakedown officer. The convict acted as if the officer weren't there. The hack called to him: "Come here, partner, I want to shake you down." The convict didn't stop. The officer moved toward him, again asking him to stop for a shakedown: "Yo, come here!" The convict kept moving. The officer now walked up behind the convict and put his right hand on the top of the inmate's right shoulder.

Quickly reacting to this, the convict stopped, turned around and went nose to nose with the hack: "Don't you ever put a hand on me, you hear? Don't ever touch me!" he growled in a loud voice.

The officer, taken aback, quickly explained: "You didn't stop, partner. I want to shake you down." At that point, the warden, who had been watching and listening to the entire scene, stepped away from the corridor wall and walked toward the center of the corridor, moving closer to the convict. He stopped when he saw Lt. Merchant walking toward him. Merchant also saw the event, and he wasn't pleased with the convict's attitude.

"Lieutenant, talk to that gentleman!" said the warden, as he pointed at the convict. "I'll take care of it," said Merchant. He got the inmate aside, outside the flow of corridor traffic. Merchant stood between the wall and the convict who faced the wall with his back to passing inmate traffic. Standing almost chest to chest, Merchant stuck his right index finger in the convict's face. Quietly, but very forcefully, Merchant said: "You're a convict and around here convicts do what they're told. Don't you ever talk that way to an officer, again. You understand me?" The convict replied: "But I didn't know the officer was talking to me." "Bullshit, you heard him. Don't play that shit with me!" exclaimed Merchant.

The inmate then stood silently, not moving a muscle. When Merchant finished giving his lesson in "Lompoc etiquette," the inmate walked over to the officer and stood quietly for his shakedown. Five seconds later when the hack finished, the convict turned away and walked away. But that wasn't the end of the story.

Christensen then asked Collins, who also watched the event, if he knew that troublesome convict. "I think he just drove up," said the captain. "But I'll find out who he is, and what unit he's in. We'll keep an eye on him." Collins has considerable personal influence among inmates, as chairman of IDC and captain. Captain Collins is father-confessor and personal counselor to many inmates, and for all inmates who appear in front of the IDC he is judge and jury. Despite his power, inmates say they have respect for him as a "man."

Convict Geraldo, a middle-aged Mexican Mafia hit-man, alcoholic, and heroin addict, with a long history of in-prison violence and repeated alcohol-related offenses, was a regular in front of the IDC. Geraldo's jacket was as thick as Webster's unabridged dictionary, but he had a pleasant way about him and a good sense of humor. Most of all, Geraldo knew how to be contrite. I listened to him as he sat before the IDC, just about two months before his parole, charged for insolence to staff and for being drunk.

"When are you going to learn, Geraldo?" queried Collins. "I know, boss," said Geraldo quietly, with his head hung low: "I try, but you know how things go when I start drinking a little. I'm sorry, boss. Let me out and I promise, no more wine before I go home." Collins retorted, "That's what you told me last time and the time before that. What I ought to do is just leave you in here until the day you hit the street." At that point, Geraldo almost began whimpering like a puppy. "But I'm not letting you out today, either," said Collins. "We got to keep you out of trouble. I'm going to keep you in here until a week before you go home. Then I'll see to it you get out. You can say good-bye to all your homeboys and see everyone before you go." At this point, Geraldo smiled, "Thanks boss, I understand."

Inmates say they can trust Collins. "When he says he'll do something, he does it. But don't fuck with him," says convict Wilbur.

Every day without fail, convicts approached Captain Collins at the mess hall, as he stood at the entrance door. A convict wanting a private conversation, pulled him aside and they talked against the main corridor wall. Others were content to stand between Collins and the stream of convicts entering the mess hall.

I saw a clear indication of close rapport between Collins and an inmate during the 1985 National League Championship Series between the St. Louis Cardinals and Los Angeles Dodgers. Collins is an avid Cardinals fan, and convicts know it. I was in my office, when I heard inmates' screams and yells, coming from the west end of the main corridor. I stepped into the main corridor, just as the lieutenant's office door burst open. Lt. Baker and another lieutenant walked out. "What the fuck is going on out here?" questioned Baker. "It's the ball game, Baker," I said. "Crazy bastards," said Baker, as he shook his head and walked back inside his office.

The noise was coming from the C-unit television room. I went up there to watch the game. The room was packed, and convicts didn't pay attention to me as I leaned against the main corridor wall, peering in through the room's glass windows. Captain Collins also heard the noise, and left his office to join me, just a few minutes later. We stood together watching the game.

It was late in the game, and Collins' team was losing. When a Dodger player hit a home run, adding insult to injury, Collins walked away, looking rather dejected. As he walked down the main corridor, puffing on a cigarette, an inmate walked up next to him. The inmate was laughing and was, apparently, a Dodger fan.

I was still standing at the television room window, but now I watched Collins and the inmate, walking shoulder to shoulder. The inmate said something to Collins and then laughed, but Collins shook his head from side to side. At this point, the inmate reached around Collins's shoulders with his left arm and embraced Collins, pulling him toward him slightly, and just for a second. They walked together for a moment longer, and then Collins entered his office. This was the only time, during my research, that I saw an inmate touch an upper-echelon administrator.

Convicts are less polite, less friendly, and far more acrimonious when dealing with line hacks and some lieutenants, than they are with the warden and the captain. At about 9:20 on a midweek evening watch, I was working with GS-7 Norm Vanny in F-unit; Vanny had several years' experience. Lt. Brant called Vanny and told him to find an extra mattress for an inmate who had just been released from I-unit.

We went from cell to cell, from A-range to B-range to C-range to D-range, and on E-range we found a bed with two mattress. Vanny removed inmate Wood's mattress, neatly remade the bed and then confiscated some pilfered food—about a half-pound of sliced American cheese wrapped in plastic wrap; an onion, sliced and wrapped in plastic wrap; a hard-boiled egg; and several fresh jalapeno peppers—that was sitting on Wood's footlocker.

Wood had been watching television, and when he returned to his cell about thirty minutes later, finding his food and mattress missing, he stormed down to the flats to see Vanny. "Man, why did you shake down my cell?" Wood asked. "I took your extra mattress," Vanny replied.

"I don't have no contraband in there. Leave my house alone," asserted Wood. Vanny retorted, "I'll shakedown your cell whenever I think it's necessary." Wood asked, "Why did you take my food?" Vanny told Wood that "food should be eaten in food service." Wood argued, "Not necessarily!" Vanny insisted, "Yes, necessarily!"

"Oh, man, I give up. You got me," exclaimed Wood, who turned away and walked back to the television room.

Sometimes a convict's most serious protests are made silently. Convict Jose, according to his supervisor, arrived for work in the kitchen wearing sneakers. His supervisor, Mr. Cummingham, told him to return to his cell and put on the regulation steel-toed safety shoes. This item of dress is a requirement imposed on every inmate, even inmate office workers. Jose refused.

Cummingham then ordered Jose to put on safety shoes. Jose became angry and shook his fist in Cummingham's face: "You'll be talking to

God if you don't stop this shit," threatened Jose. With this, Cummingham called Lt. Hammer, the operations lieutenant, and requested immediate assistance.

Cummingham shot Jose for "threatening a staff member," the more serious of Jose's two offenses ("disobeying an order" is the other violation). Jose was escorted into the lieutenant's office by three correctional officers. I was already there when Jose and Cummingham came in, and I listened as Cummingham explained to Lt. Hammer what happened.

Two big correctional workers joined the three hacks already there. Everyone stood within ten feet of Jose, who was seated in the orange vinyl chair. Lt. Hammer asked Jose: "Why did you refuse to wear safety shoes?" No answer. "Did you shake your fist at Mr. Cummingham?" No answer.

Jose stared at the floor, not saying a word. After several minutes of this, Jose, who was holding a small piece of paper, threw it on the floor, not lifting his eyes as he did it.

Loudly, Lt. Hammer ordered, "Pick it up!" Jose sat passively, staring at the floor and not moving a muscle. Lt. Hammer barked at the line hacks: "Put some iron [handcuffs] on him, and leg irons. And put him in lower-I, so we don't have to gas [antipersonnel gas] him later to get him out of his cell." Lt. Hammer looked at me, smiling curiously. "He's trouble," said Hammer. "Listen," he said to a line hack, "I want you to go down to his unit and shake down his cell. Do a real good job. Do it now." The officer returned shortly with a two-foot long, one-inch diameter, ten-pound iron bar.

That evening at about 8:00, I went with Lt. Brooks to I-unit, to process Jose's shot. We walked to Jose's cell on lower-I, and found him lying on his bunk in the dark. He spoke politely and quietly, answering each of Lt. Brooks's questions.

Lt. Brooks told him that he was being charged with possession of a weapon, and then asked, "Why did you have an iron bar in your footlocker?" Jose replied, "There's no shelf in my footlocker. I used it for a shelf. It's not a weapon. I hang my underwear on it." Brooks listened quietly and wrote down Jose's comments.

Convicts, especially when they get in trouble, try to play on their relationships with lieutenants. Many knew one or more lieutenants in other federal institutions; in some cases, their acquaintanceships go back several decades. (Warden Christensen told me there were a lot of inmates at USP-Lompoc whom he first met at USP-McNeil Island, 20 years earlier.)

On a midweek evening watching, K-unit's rookie hack called Lt. Bob Houser, the operations lieutenant, and asked for assistance with a convict. According to the lieutenant's interview with the convict and from the statement of the unit officer, the problem began after an activities movement had ended. The K-unit officer wanted to lock the main corridor door, but convict Franco (who recently transferred in from USP-Marion's control unit) refused to stop talking to another inmate, just outside the K-unit door. Officer Johnson told Franco several times to get inside the unit, and each time Franco refused, according to Johnson. After telling him, several times, to come inside, Franco yelled: "Don't you tell me what to do. I'll be there when I'm done," according to Johnson. At this point, Johnson called for help.

I accompanied two officers to K-unit, escorting Franco back to the lieutenant's office. This was uneventful. Once inside, Franco sat in the orange vinyl chair. Lt. Houser asked Franco why he yelled at Johnson. Franco was appropriately contrite: "Listen, boss, I didn't mean to disrespect the officer . . . I didn't mean to yell at him, it just happened. I got a loud voice anyway, boss. You know." Lt. Houser told Franco that "at Lompoc, convicts don't yell at staff." At this, Franco quickly brought up his alleged acquaintanceship with Lt. Baker, using him as a character reference. With his hands folded and in a quiet voice, Franco reported: "I'm not hostile . . . I knew Baker at Marion, he'll tell you. It was a mistake, it won't happen again." Lt. Houser replied: "All right. But next time, you're going to I-unit."

When they're among lieutenants, inmates become fawning and usually don't "disrespect" them to their faces. Rather, they'll usually listen to lieutenants' orders, carrying them out quietly. Firsthand experience has shown inmates that if they get into a "pissing contest" (a hot verbal interaction, as they're called by staff and inmates) with a lieutenant, they'll quickly lose any special favors which might have come their way.

Lieutenants exert critical informal control over new and often unruly inmates. USP-Lompoc received approximately 68 inmates on disciplinary transfers from other federal institutions in 1985. Among these and other newly committed inmates, there are some who sought to enhance their mainline reps by raising hell.

A new Lompoc convict, acting out aggressively, always comes face to face with a lieutenant who takes the convict's "positive adjustment" as his personal responsibility. Hacks call this process, "getting the young man's attention."

Lesson One takes place in the orange vinyl chair, when the inmate first gets into trouble. He is now expected to listen quietly as "his" lieutenant, accompanied by three or four staffers, spells out the rules of proper behavior and outlines the repercussions of continued hell-raising.

Perching half on and half off a large wooden desk near the front of the orange chair, the lieutenant leans far forward, coming almost nose to nose with the convict as he delivers his message from above. If the inmates passes this attitude test by not talking back, not smiling, not throwing paper on the floor, not spitting, and not doing anything disrespectful, he usually walks. But there are exceptions.

Some young convicts in their late teens and early twenties (often calling themselves "soldiers"), openly announce their hatred of cops. This proclamation is guaranteed to generate a lot of tension, as staff bystanders anticipate a fight.

I was standing with Gary Charles, the GS-8 evening-watch main corridor officer, on an otherwise quiet Tuesday night in September 1986. We were leaning against the corridor wall near central control and talking, as the central control officer announced an activities movement, over the P.A. system. Most inmates were sauntering by, but Henry, a black 19-year-old newly arrived convict, ran past us. "Slow down, stop running," yelled Charles, who then turned to me: "I told that stupid motherfucker to stop running during the last [activities] movement."

Henry slowed down, turned his head slightly and muttered a few words at Charles, as he kept up his half-walk, half-trot down the corridor. Charles chased him down and brought him to the lieutenant's office.

"Sit down right there," ordered Charles. Henry reluctantly sat down in the orange vinyl chair. Anger oozed from Henry's face: his jaw muscles were tense; his eyes were wide open; his neck muscles were straining tightly; and he started to sweat. He leaned forward, resting his forearms on his thighs; his fists were clenched; and his head hung down slightly. Henry refused to look at Charles, who was sitting in front of him, on the edge of the wooden desk.

Calmly and sternly, Charles recited Lompoc's litany of do's and don'ts: You don't run in the corridor; you don't "give lip" to officers; you don't argue with staff; and you don't raise your voice to staff.

I was watching and listening, as were Lt. Houser, the evening-watch operations lieutenant, and Lt. Rudy Marks. Everyone stared intently at Henry, just waiting for him to take a swing at Charles. But he didn't.

After the first lesson ended, Henry was permitted to return to J-unit. About 30 minutes later, J-unit's rookie hack called central control, requesting assistance with a "loud convict," he said. Lt. Houser, Charles, a GS-7 hack, and I went to J-unit. As we arrived, the rookie officer opened the cellblock door. Standing there, looking angrier and more agitated than he did about 30 minutes earlier, was Henry. Apparently, according to the hack, Henry became furious while playing pool and threw down his pool cue, and began a screaming tirade about Charles.

Lt. Houser handled the situation; he listened patiently as Henry raved about Charles. Now Charles was getting hotter: His face tightened and fists clinched. Lt. Houser told him to keep quiet and stay well out in the corridor. Henry yelled that "he's [Charles] always on my back . . . he picks on me." His comments were mixed with declarations of his manhood and demands to be treated like a man.

A few minutes had passed since we arrived, and the cellblock door was still open; no J-unit inmates had gathered around to watch and listen. To remove Henry from the J-unit, Lt. Houser cleverly challenged him. "If you're a man," Houser said to Henry, "you'll walk like a man down to the lieutenant's office." Henry accepted that challenge.

As we walked down the main corridor, Henry was flanked by Lt. Houser to his left, the GS-7 to his right, Charles was in the rear to Henry's left, and I was in the rear to his right. As we walked, I noticed that Charles didn't take his hand off his long, steel-cased, four-battery Mag Light, the unofficial weapon of the line hack.

Sitting again in the orange vinyl chair, this time with Lt. Houser directly in front of him, Henry aggressively recited his violent history and his intent to fight and kill hacks, if necessary: "I'm a soldier. . . . I'm nineteen years old and I've killed a man. . . . I'm not afraid of any fucking hack and I'll kill any one of you. . . . I'm not afraid of going to Marion. . . . I'll go one-on-one with any hack."

Lt. Houser listened without saying a word, and when Henry finished, he quietly said that Henry must spend at least one night in I-unit. "For what?" asked Henry. "Because loud and aggressive behavior is not permitted in the penitentiary," said Lt. Houser. "Tomorrow," Lt. Houser assured him, "your team will see you."

Lt. Houser then told Henry exactly what was about to happen: "I want you to stand up, you'll be cuffed and taken to I-unit for at least one night." As Henry stood up, he stared at Charles, who was standing across the room, and said: "I don't want him to touch me. He ain't going to have the honor of cuffing me." Henry and Charles stood motionless for a moment, glaring at each other.

"O.K.," said Lt. Houser, "I'll put the cuffs on." Henry turned around and was handcuffed, and off we went to I-unit. About halfway there, Henry slowed his pace, lowered his voice and said with an audible cracking anxiety: "Am I getting out in the morning?" Lt. Houser responded, "That's not up to me, you'll talk to your team tomorrow."

Henry picked up his pace again, and then initiated more macho talk: "I am a soldier. . . . I'm not afraid of Marion. . . . I ain't afraid of you motherfuckers. . . . I'd kill a hundred cops if I have to and it won't bother me . . . fuck all of you." When we arrived at I-unit, he stopped talking.

Henry was escorted into the I-unit trap. Lt. Houser told Charles to stay in the corridor. Henry didn't know that he was going to be strip searched; he strongly resisted the idea of standing naked in front of us.

Henry stood with his back against the left side wall of the trap. Lt. Houser was standing directly in front of him. Quietly and repeatedly, Lt. Houser explained that all inmates were strip searched here, that he was not being singled out, and that staffers weren't trying to harass him. Henry breathed deeply and remained quiet. Lt. Houser explained and reexplained the procedure to him for 15 to 20 minutes, before Henry began to unbutton his shirt.

As he slowly removed his shirt, shoes, socks and pants, Henry's facial and verbal expressions began changing from anxiety to anger. Seeing this change, Lt. Houser moved forward slightly, getting a little closer to him.

Henry took off his T-shirt and held it in his right hand. Now, except for his army-green boxer shorts, Henry was naked. With his left fist clenched, Henry tossed his T-shirt in the direction of a GS-7 hack who was standing in front of Henry and slightly to his right.

With this movement, Lt. Houser pushed his body into Henry's, holding him firmly against the trap wall; Henry's arms were pushed up against the trap-wall and held there tightly by the GS-7 officer and a lower-I hack, who came into the trap for the strip search.

From a nose-to-nose position, Lt. Houser looked squarely into Henry's eyes. "Are you O.K.?" he said. "Yeah," Henry responded, as he averted his eyes slightly to the left. "We'll let you go, but don't make any movements unless I tell you to," Lt. Houser instructed in a calm and fatherly tone. From this point on, Henry cooperated.

Henry's behavior in I-unit became increasingly disruptive, and he remained there for more than a month. After I left the penitentiary, Henry "went-off," as hacks say about convicts who suddenly become violent. A staffer told me what happened. While taking a shower, Henry ripped the water pipes from their containing brackets on the shower wall. Six to eight hacks, including Charles, went into the upper-I, A-range shower to get Henry, who was screaming and armed with a shaft of water-pipe. Despite the odds, Henry didn't go easily. Several hacks were banged up and bruised, and Henry was dragged, fighting all the way, down to a lower-I cell.

"TEACHING 'EM WHO'S BOSS"

On occasion, convicts do something so outrageous that pressure is exerted, by the custody department on an entire cellblock or on a Unicor or mechanical services shop, to restore and reaffirm control.

In retaliation for "busting their homebrew," several convicts shoved epoxy glue (which they got in the hobby shop) into the keyhole of the unit's office door. It isn't uncommon for a new hack, as in this case, to take his shakedown responsibilities very seriously, and, in response, it isn't uncommon for convicts to retaliate. Said an avid convict drinker:

> Fish police can make their rep by busting brew, but they got to leave some for us. That's only right, man. You all can go drink on the street; we got to do it right here and not get busted for it. Man, that fish police was tearing that place apart from the minute he got in the unit. He was looking everywhere and even got a ladder to check high spots. He looked behind locked panels, on top of the soda machine, and in back of the TV. He found the shit, too. The dudes didn't like him finding their brew, so they hit back.

One office door lock was glued and feces were smeared on office door handles several times, during my research. In a more serious case, also in retaliation for finding too much homebrew, convicts smashed a cellblock office window and tossed lighted matches through it, trying to ignite the office chair. Gluing locks and wiping feces on surfaces (which staffers are likely to touch unsuspectingly) aren't unusual styles of convict retaliation, though they occur infrequently, for good reason. "Let's teach 'em who's boss," said an upper-echelon official, as he ordered a shakedown in L-unit after convicts wiped feces on the unit-officer's door handle and caused some minor physical damage. I observed two full-unit shakedowns (one in D-unit, one in E-unit), and I was a member of this shake-crew in L-unit. Each unit proceeded in the same way.

A shakedown team composed of 10 to 15 hacks, including as many rookies as could be found, one or two lieutenants, and GS-7s and GS-8s (off-duty GS-8s sometimes went along just for fun) made their way to L-unit, wheeling along several huge plastic garbage dumpsters. L-unit's UM and other team members hung around watching.

Inmates know what's about to happen, since they weren't allowed to go to work at early work call. The unit remains locked down all day, so inmates lose pay and personal property.

Each new hack learns the policies concerning inmate property. They are instructed to remove from each cell all property which is not within policy specifications. Thus, if policy specifies three pairs of underwear and the inmate has four, the officer takes the fourth pair. And so it goes for every nonauthorized object. Figure 8.1 shows two commonly found and discarded inmate-made gadgets; one is a "stinger" (a water-heating device) and the other is an "extension" cord.

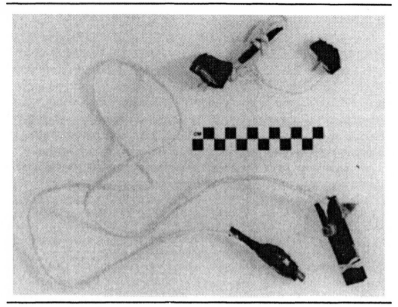

Figure 8.1 "Stinger" and Extension Cord

In a shakedown, nooks and crannies are combed in every cell. Hacks check inside every cardboard box; look inside, under and behind every footlocker; open every book; inspect and feel every article of clothing; check inside toilets; and so on, searching out "hot," or "hard," and "soft" contraband. Hot contraband can be used as weapons or in escapes; shanks, rope ladders and hacksaw blades are hot. Soft contraband is everything else not permitted by policy.

Up to now, the institution had informally permitted inmates to accumulate and possess soft contraband. These objects include the small niceties of an inmate's cell: a plywood toilet cover, sometimes painted or decorated; a plywood mattress board, used legitimately only with medical authorization; extra (usually overdue) library books; extra handballs; extra paper and envelopes; unauthorized photographs, etc. But now, all of it is taken away. Underwear, handballs, pornography, toilet covers, stolen food, and other unauthorized things drop from everywhere, falling to the flats. As time passes, the pile of stuff grows, eventually covering the flats. Inmates stand quietly outside their cells watching.

"You got to clean house every now and then, and the convicts give us the excuse to do it," said a unit management team member. Shanks and other weapons are always dangerous, but soft contraband can also bring trouble. Weapons and drugs are hidden in extra everyday things, such as the waistbands of underwear or in the tips of dirty socks, things which usually go unsearched, according to convicts. Even a mundane object like a thick Polaroid photograph, has been known to conceal drugs, and can conceal explosive chemicals, according to staff sources.

Figure 8.2 shows a six-inch-thick stack of innocent-looking legal documents that were mailed to a convict in a cardboard box; the legal-length pages were glued together at the top, producing a solid paper area of about four inches. The glued pages were separated, revealing a deep, rectangular compartment. An SIS investigation uncovered a plan to mail dynamite sticks to a convict in the near future, if this box went uninspected.

After a shakedown, hacks and unit team members always talk about inmate retaliation on those convicts whose behavior instigated the shakedown. Following the D-unit shakedown, one officer said to another: "We'll find whoever did it, dead in the morning in front of the office door. They'll take care of it themselves." This was just talk, it didn't happen.

Precautionary shakedowns occur in the weeks before major holidays and sporting events. Instead of taking unauthorized property, officers search for homebrew wine. Just days before Thanksgiving 1985, a shakedown officer told me they had taken between 40 and 60 gallons of homebrew wine from units in the low-rent district.

A third type of control shakedown occurred once during my research. After lunch at about 2, a triple deuce came in from the cable factory, about a half mile from central control.

As we went running out there, we passed tens of inmates working out on the iron pile, in the warm afternoon sun. I heard a few convict-quipsters hollering, "Go get 'em," "Here comes the cavalry," "Man, look at that fat one." Figure 8.3 shows the iron pile, from my perspective, as we ran by it.

A brief and minor drunken fistfight had already been controlled by Unicor staffers by the time we arrived. Though the event seemed inconsequential, I heard staffers talk about a shank that one of the fighters passed to a partner of his during the fight. According to the rumor, the fighter's partner, who walked out of the shop as we were coming in, had tossed the shank over the compound fence, landing near the iron pile. Several of us were asked to search the shop, looking for a body that might have been shoved in a corner or stuck under something after being stabbed. After making a thorough search of the factory, we returned inside.

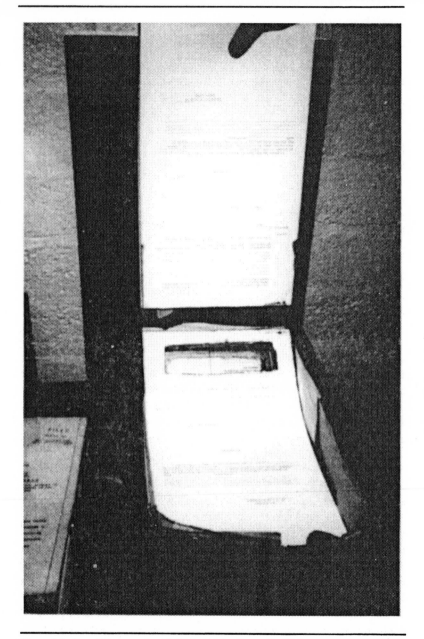

Figure 8.2   Legal Documents with Hole Cut for Dynamite Sticks

Figure 8.3   Iron Pile, Rear Compound

There, in the main corridor, near central control, about 25 staffers had gathered where the gym and main corridors join. Some men were buzzing about the incident, while others, who didn't make the run to the cable factory, were asking if the rumor they heard was true: that a staffer had been shanked in the stomach at the scene.

Rumors started flying. Staffers wanted to know who was stabbed, and which convict did it. Others asked what had happened to the shank. Still others asked if the shank, which had been thrown over the rear compound fence, had been found yet. As a precaution, an officer was sent to comb the grassy area adjacent to the fence near the iron pile.

I still didn't know why these staffers, from many different departments, were standing in the corridor. After an emergency staffers normally return to their offices without much hesitation. This situation was obviously different. Before too long, the central control officer called yard-recall, bringing in inmates from yard. As they walked down the gym corridor, all inmates were stopped at the metal detector.

Rather than clearing it quickly and walking on, as usually occurred, each convict was thoroughly shaken down by line-staff and unit-team staff, standing in the main corridor in full view of senior administrators.

This, too, was a quiet event. Inmates didn't ask any questions or voice complaints or dare to gripe, even though the group shakedown took about 30 minutes. Radios, jackets, books, notepads, hats, handball gloves, and everything else they had with them was carefully searched. Convict by convict, each one was patted down before they were permitted to return to their cellblocks for a shower.

As it turned out, a staffer in Unicor had broadcast an erroneous radio transmission to central control, mentioning the possibility of a shank and an alleged shanking of a staffer. When the rumor was pinned to this transmission, an upper-echelon official asked the control official: "Who called in?" The officer replied: "I don't know, boss. It all happened pretty fast." The official responded: "Find him."

The shakedown was intended, in small part, to search for a rumored weapon. But later a senior staffer told me that an upper-level official was upset at inmates' "cat calls" from the iron pile. I had run past the iron pile many time before, in responding to emergency calls from Unicor, but iron-pile inmates had always stayed quiet. No one, not even Slim, had an explanation for today's cat calls.

THE SNITCH

Convicts have the snitch system. Prison administrators regularly point to the great number of active snitches as proof of failure of integrity in the convict society. A popular folktale . . . tells about the warden of a midwestern institution who was unexpectedly presented with a mess hall riot. . . . Negotiations got nowhere. Finally, the warden got on the P.A. and announced that if the mess hall wasn't emptied immediately, he would throw into the room a bag with all the "snitch-kites" (informing letters and messages) he had received in the past week. . . . There was silence for a moment; then everyone silently got up and left the mess hall [Jackson, 1984: 254-255].

"If it weren't for the snitches and the snitches who snitch on snitches, this prison wouldn't be able to run," said Lt. Baker. Despite what convicts say about killing snitches, snitching is common, and snitches aren't killed. Snitches are vital information links between mainline inmates and correctional staff. A big carrot hangs in front of a reliable snitch: staff support at his parole hearing. I saw this happen in 1985, but staff support was perfunctory and had no effect whatsoever on the parole commissioners. There were several of these cases during three, eight-hour days of parole hearings. In each of these cases, the convict's sentence wasn't shortened by even one day. In one case, when the staffer representative and his convict later met, the staffer said, "Well, we tried."

Figure 8.4 Marielito Shank, Snitched-Off

USP-Lompoc inmates cooperate with staff. A surprising feature of inmate-staff cooperation is that inmates rely on staff to solve inmate problems. A senior lieutenant said, "I get snitches' notes all the time, from inmates who have personal items stolen from their cells. They want me to investigate it, rather than resort to violence. These inmates put up with line-jumping, and even open, friendly relations between convicts and staff. This is really unusual for a maximum-security penitentiary."

The SIS receives snitch-notes "giving up" (identifying) other inmates who have committed offenses or who have hidden away weapons. This snitch-note (copied verbatim) was given to an SIS by a black inmate, snitching off a Mariel-Cuban's shank. The Cuban's weapon is shown in Figure 8.4.

Liutenent,

I write you because
do you hive this Cuba God
a hive problem to this black person
so this Cuba a hive knive in
the wall top tha electricity
hollow.
This Cuba name is [inmate x]. This cell [xxx]."

Perhaps the most noteworthy byproduct of Lompoc's passive and self-interested social control system is the degree of tolerance and patience shown by USP-Lompoc's convicts toward other inmates, particularly toward mainline snitches.

Conventional wisdom suggests that snitches are killed. Why aren't these snitches killed? Convicts need snitches, says Big Brother.

> A snitch bailed me out of I-unit. They put me in there on hearsay evidence. But it didn't bother me. I just waited for "inmate investigators" to be put on the case. I knew snitches was going to free me, and they did. They give up perpetrators behind closed doors or drop snitch notes to the lieutenant. A clean-out snitch may be taken out [killed], but it doesn't happen here.

(Convicts at the Washington State Penitentiary distinguished between "snitches" and "dry snitches"; USP-Lompoc convicts didn't make this distinction in their regular speech. A "clean out snitch," as Big Brother called him, doesn't hide his snitching from other convicts, but a "dry snitch" does his snitching quietly, usually writing notes, called "kites" by state prisoners.)

Eddie says that snitches also check violence.

> The number one deterrent [to violence] is informants. If you stab someone or hit someone with a weapon, there would be a hundred guys running to the lieutenant's office. Feds don't have pc [protective custody] units like the [California] state does, with their own yard and commissary. The feds send you to another prison. They put you on inmate monitoring, but what happens if the best friend of the guy [the assaulted inmate] who wants you is in there with you? You're dead.

9

SCENES OF VIOLENCE

PRISON VIOLENCE

There is a great deal of research on the correlates and causes of prison violence. Surveys have been done in state and federal prisons, examining the roles of age (Mabli et al., 1979; MacKenzie, 1987), overcrowding (Ekland-Olson, 1986; Ellis, 1984; Farrington and Nutall, 1980; Gaes and McGuire, 1985; Nacci et al., 1977a, 1977b), boredom and idleness (Sykes, 1958; Sykes and Messinger, 1960), ethnic and racial rivalries (Carroll, 1974; Davidson, 1974; Irwin, 1980; Jacobs, 1977, 1983: 61-79; Jacobs and Kraft, 1978; Sylvester et al., 1977), and sexual jealousy in generating violent behavior among convicts (Cohen, 1976: 53-58; Lockwood, 1980, 1982, 1986; Nacci and Kane, 1982, 1983, 1984; Wooden and Parker, 1982). The presence of rival street gang members or of local prison gangs appears also to contribute to prison violence (Irwin, 1980; Jacobs, 1974a; Park, 1976). And of course, socio-psychological issues have been widely studied as causes of violent behavior (Toch, 1969, 1975, 1977; Toch and Adams, 1986; Toch et al., 1987; Walkey and Gilmour, 1984).

The general conclusions of all this research are that violent convicts commit violent acts; that convicts who feel powerless, mistreated, idle, bored, sexually frustrated, and cramped also commit violent acts; and that for all these reasons, prison violence will continue (Jacobs, 1976: 80). Toch (1978: 21) extends these views:

There are two favored perspectives relating to prison violence. One . . . centers on *violent inmates*. . . . Some inmates are consistently violent persons, who happen to be explosive in prison, but are likely to act out in almost any setting. . . . A second portraiture conceives of inmate violence as at least partly a *prison product*. The most extreme version of this view is that of abolitionist critics who see prison aggression as a natural (and presumably, legitimate) reaction to the frustration of being locked up. Other critics also argue that prison incidents denote lax security, and thus suggest negligence. This view is to some extent shared by prison administrators, who think of controlling violence through perimeter architecture, ingenious hardware and deployment of custodial personnel. This context-centered view is a negative one, because it seeks to prevent violence by reducing the opportunities for aggression, rather than by trying to affect the motives and dispositions of violence participants.

After being personally involved in or seeing violent acts, from fistfights to homicide, and after interviewing perpetrators and victims, I've come to believe that convict violence at USP-Lompoc is at least partly the result of inmates' street culture. Inmate-on-inmate attacks were promoted most often by face-to-face rivalries, retaliation, "machismo," "disrespect," and drunkenness. The motivation for Lompoc's one homicide, during my research, was "political," but all other violent incidents might have occurred just as easily on the street, and for the same reasons.

Convict violence was self-rewarding behavior (see Bowker, 1980). In my experiences with penitentiary violence, assailants often looked and talked as though they had enjoyed committing their violence. Violence reinforces a convict's status and prestige and adds macho-value to his mainline image. In turn, this image is currency with which to buy "social space," power, control, contraband, sex, and so on.

Hacks use violence also, and in ways similar to convicts. But for hacks, prestige accrued in dealing with or meting out violence can be transformed into promotions and pay increases.

VIOLENCE AT LOMPOC

There are three "official" ways of dying in the FPS: either an inmate is killed, commits suicide, or dies of natural causes. From 1981 through 1986, with an average daily population of 1,139 inmates, USP-Lompoc has averaged 1.02 homicides per year.

Assessing the nature of assaults is a more difficult problem. Table 9.1 shows USP-Lompoc's 1985 and 1986 assaultive incident rates; this analysis includes all aggressive acts initiated by an inmate toward another inmate or staffer, as reported in USP-Lompoc incident report logs. These logs record inmate infractions and include the violation code (101, assault; 201, fighting), the inmate's name and unit, and the date on which the incident report was filed. These logs are the grossest level of reporting violations. Incident report logs don't differentiate types of assault or any significant details. Staffers may cite an inmate for fighting if he is just threatening to fight another inmate; or with assaulting staff if he throws a carton of milk, a cup of urine, or urine mixed with feces, or if he tosses a food tray at a hack. Some new hacks cite verbally aggressive convicts with assault. But in the log books, fights are fights and assaults are assaults.

TABLE 9.1
Assaultive Infractions Rate at USP-Lompoc, 1985-86

Infraction Type	(n)	1985 Rate/100 Inmates Per Month	(n)	1986 Rate/100 Inmates Per Month
100-Level				
Killing	(1)	.01	(1)	.01
Assault	(54)	.37	(120)	.86
Possession of a Weapon*	(66)	.46	(65)	.46
200-Level				
Fighting	(59)	.41	(79)	.56
Threatening Staff	(27)	.19	(43)	.31
Total Assaultive Infractions	(n = 207)		(n = 308)	

SOURCE: USP-Lompoc Incident Report Logs, 1985-86.
NOTE: *Possession of a weapon isn't an assaultive "incident," but since it's often directly related to assault, I've included it here.

A closer look at these incident reports reveals that few assaults on staff or inmates resulted in bruises, broken bones, or serious lacerations. Assaults resulting in any degree of injury are reported by each federal institution in their monthly correctional services report. Table 9.2 shows physical assault rates.

During my research two inmate-on-inmate unarmed assaults resulted in severe injuries to the victims, and the others had injuries no more serious than bruises and cuts. In several cases of inmate unarmed assault on line staff, staffers' black eyes, bloody noses, and contusions weren't "injuries," by staffers' definitions, but simply obvious (and proud) signs of "not taking any bullshit from convicts," said a line hack.

Two inmate-on-inmate armed assaults were serious, resulting in multiple shank punctures; two others involved shank lacerations; one resulted in a non-life-threatening shank puncture; another inmate was smashed in the head with a weight lifter's triangular barbell; the other armed assaults caused either no injuries or minor cuts. There was one inmate-on-staff armed assault during my research; this resulted in no injuries, either to the hack or to the inmate.

Figure 9.1 shows several "strap-on" shanks and a short "sticking" weapon, which was made by embedding a galvanized nail into a melted plastic handle (dining hall utensils are plastic). Victims of armed assaults are "stuck" or "shanked," not stabbed, and the events themselves are called "stickings" or "shankings."

TABLE 9.2
Physical Assault Rates at USP-Lompoc, 1983-86
(Per 100 Inmates Per Year)

	1983		1984		1985		1986	
	Rate	(n)	Rate	(n)	Rate	(n)	Rate	(n)
Inmate-on-inmate								
armed	1.62	(17)	1.05	(12)	.66	(8)	1.03	(12)
unarmed	.19	(2)	.09	(1)	.41	(5)	.94	(11)
Inmate-on-staff								
armed	.10	(1)	.17	(2)	.17	(2)	.09	(1)
unarmed	.10	(1)	.26	(3)	.25	(3)	.94	(11)
total		(21)		(18)		(18)		(35)

SOURCE: USP Monthly Report of Assault Data and the Correctional Services Report, July 1986.
NOTE: Average Daily Population, 1983 (1,049), 1984 (1,146), 1985 (1,208), 1986 (1,167).

According to Big Brother, short shanks aren't killing weapons, but are used to "teach loud-mouth motherfuckers some manners." To use a strap-on shank, the attacker ties the strap firmly around his wrist. Ideally, this prevents the attacker from losing his weapon and having it used against him by the victim or by someone else who may jump into the fray. Convicts call this "strapping down with a shank" or "filling your hand." Not all weapons have fastening straps, but, says convict Doyle, "when a guy is hell-bent on killing somebody, he'll tape the shank in his hand with masking tape or electrical tape, or whatever kind of tape he can steal." According to convicts, aluminum shanks such as the one shown in Figure 9.1 with a tightly wound cloth handle and a lace strap can get past the penitentiary's metal detectors.

AT THE SCENE

At the ring of a triple-deuce phone or at the high-pitched squeal of a body alarm, lieutenants look as though an electric current has just passed through them. They react almost involuntarily as they dash out of the office and run to central control, where the control-room officer tells them the location of the emergency situation.

Emergencies are quiet events. The rattle and jingle of security keys, bouncing on hips and echoing in the hollow main corridor, is the only noise. No yelling. No buzzers. No bells. To the sound of keys, men dash

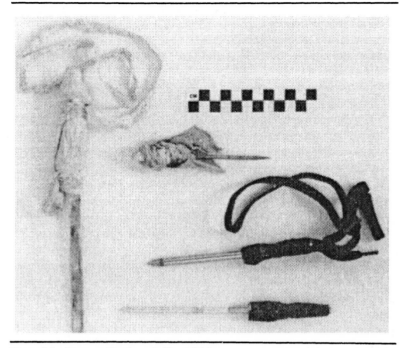

Figure 9.1 Strap-on Shanks and Short Sticker

out of their offices along the main corridor and stand for just a moment
to see the direction in which others are running. All office doors are
locked; corridor grills slam and lock; inmates working in, or walking
along the main and work corridor stop in their tracks to stare at
sprinting and panting staffers.

Up front, a buzzer rings for an instant—a half second, if that long.
When staffers in the personnel and the business office hear it, they, too,
stop whatever they're doing and begin their sprint toward the inside.
These men, clad in business suits, push into the central control sallyport,
waiting for the main corridor grill to slide open. When it does, Gene Gill
or Chuck LaRoe is standing there, directing them to the lieutenant's
office; they are a backup crew. A backup crew is a precaution against
diversionary violence or a false alarm. A call from Unicor, for example,
which is one-quarter mile away from central control, may be a planned
diversion to get staffers away from an incident occurring somewhere else.

A Special Operation Response Team ("riot squad") is prepared to
respond to riot or hostage situations, but there isn't a tactical squad, or
an emergency response team ("goon squad"), which handles routine
emergencies such as fights, stabbings and killing. It is the responsibility

of all male employees to respond to emergencies; women never respond.

On the day watch, 40 to 45 men respond; on the evening watch, 8 to 9; and on the morning watch, about 4. Staffers who are directly supervising inmates don't abandon them to respond to an emergency. Inmate work-crew supervisors, food-service stewards in kitchen, or cellblock correctional officers, for example, will not respond, because doing so will leave inmates unsupervised. Similarly, Unicor staffers will not respond unless they are requested to do so by correctional services.

In my experience at scenes of violence, I found that whatever the degree of an inmate's injuries (from cuts to fatal stabbing), staffers' reactions are fundamentally the same: faces are exemplars of dispassionate concern, expressionless with eyes open wide; they efficiently assist injured inmates; they effectively manage inmates who are hanging around, watching. They never panic, raise their voices, or lose control.

The physical damage inflicted to an inmate during a serious assault is treated as if it were invisible: no one shows visible emotional reactions to pools of blood running on the floor, blood splattered and dripping on the walls, and a writhing, injured person—at least, not at first. Once the initial tension of the scene wanes and control is regained, staffers relax, cigarettes are lit, laughing begins, comments about the event are bantered about among staffers.

In a minor emergency, a loud but not violent inmate-to-inmate confrontation, a lieutenant (usually one who knows one or both inmates) will take charge of the scene. The goal is to handcuff the inmates, to take them off to I-unit, and to begin their investigation. Such an encounter may last only five to ten minutes.

A September 1987 a minor incident in K-unit was controlled by Lt. Hammer. Jesse Jennings, K-unit's counselor, called Lt. Hammer and asked for assistance. I joined in. When we walked into the unit, convict Rulan was hanging from the C-range tier railing, leaning over the flats, and waving a steel mop wringer in one hand and threatening to use it on convicts Jones and Stockie. Jones and Stockie (who are cousins) were standing on the flats. Jones was holding a pool cue tightly in his right hand, and Stockie had both hands full of pool balls. Hammer was talking to Rulan, trying to convince him to put down the mop wringer and to talk about the problem. Meanwhile, Jones and Stockie never took their eyes off of Rulan.

I walked between Jones and Stockie. "Come on, put that shit down, walk out quietly," I suggested to them. "No fucking way, man, not until that fucker puts that wringer down," said Stockie.

Rulan's cell was on D-range at the front of the tier, directly overlooking the pool table. Rulan decided to mop his cell as well as the tier's front end. According to Jones, who was playing pool with Stockie directly below Rulan's mopping, Rulan yelled down to them, "Push the table out of there."

Jennings said that Rulan "didn't want to get water on the table top, as he mopped up the tier." Rulan grumbled at Hammer: "They didn't pay no attention to me. They looked up at me, and didn't pay no attention. So I told them again, "Push that fucking table out of the way so it don't get wet."

Jennings said that "Rulan went down to the flats, grabbed the table and pushed it under C-tier. Jones and Stockie said something to Rulan, Rulan said something back, and then I heard yelling. When I looked, there was Rulan hanging off the tier with a wringer in his hand, and Jones and Stockie had cues and pool balls."

Hammer talked to Rulan for about ten minutes, and finally got him to put down his wringer; only then did Jones and Stockie put down their billiard equipment. Later, a staffer told me that Rulan "was a fag, and he was trying to defend his honor in there. Everyone knows he's a punk." This is the commonest postscript, offered by staff and inmates alike, to most incidents.

In a more serious emergency, a no-weapons fight, the combatants are separated and checked for injuries: if one or both are injured, they are taken immediately to the hospital; if they are able to walk, they do so, or, if one of them is seriously hurt, a physician's assistant and gurney are brought to the scene.

A Sunday evening meal in May 1987 had just began. Lines were forming at each steamtable; there were perhaps 200 inmates in the mess hall. Lts. Brooks, Mahan, and I were shooting the breeze at the mess hall doors, standing just outside them in the main corridor. As we talked, I glanced into the mess hall and saw two inmates pushing and grabbing each other's clothing. Their chowline didn't disperse, but the line bowed, giving them more room to fight; no one else joined in the fracas. I tapped Lt. Brooks on the arm: "There's a fight." He looked in, saw it, and the three of us ran in; the inmates in line moved aside for us. The dining hall then became dead silent.

At the scene, Brooks and Mahan jumped between the fighting convicts, separating them. Brooks grabbed his inmate from behind in a bear hug, pushing him away from his opponent toward a table, where he shook him down and cuffed his hands behind his back. As this happened, Lt. Mahan took his inmate in the opposite direction, out of the mess hall and down to the hospital to have his bloody nose checked.

Within 45 seconds both inmates were removed, the meal lines had reformed, and the noise increased to its normal Super Bowl level.

Brooks asked me to watch the mess hall door, as he tended to his inmate in the main corridor, asking him about any possible injuries. As I stood there, an inmate walked by me, shaking his head from side to side, and said with a laugh: "Fried chicken make men go crazy."

In December 1985, at about 11:50 one morning, I was standing at the entry doors to the dining hall with a lieutenant and Captain Collins. The main corridor was filled with inmates going to lunch, coming from lunch, and sauntering up and down the corridor before work recall.

A call came over the lieutenant's radio from central control: "Body alarm in K-unit!" The dining hall doors were slammed closed and locked by the main corridor officer. The operations lieutenant yelled to the captain, who was next to me: "Body alarm in K-unit!" We turned and started running. As we ran, Captain Collins yelled repeatedly, "Get out of the way," to inmates who, in the noise of hundreds of inmates in the corridor, didn't hear us coming.

As we entered K-unit's open door, the counselor, standing expression-less just inside the door, said: "It's upstairs, TV room." His tone of voice and look in his eyes told me it was the "real thing."

The captain, who was one step ahead of me, hurtled the six flights of steel stairs two at a time. Up we went, into the TV room. As we entered the room, I saw Carl Lowen kneeling over inmate Ralston who was rolling from side to side in pain. Carl, who ran upstairs after hearing the rumbling of fighting inmates from his office three floors below on the flats, had Ralston wrapped in an army blanket, knees slightly elevated. He was holding Ralston's head on his forearm, keeping it off the concrete floor, and telling him, "They're going to be here in just a minute. The PA is coming, they'll take good care of you."

Lying in an expanding pool of blood coming from a badly lacerated forehead and smashed face, Ralston moaned, rocking back and forth in pain. Radiating from the pool of blood lay several streams of it which had squirted from the inmate's head and face, hitting the walls about six feet from the point of the assault.

Ralston was a big man, well over six feet tall and weighed more than two hundred pounds. The severity of his injuries, the position of blood on the floor and walls, and the quantity of blood raised the possibility that more than one convict had assaulted him. The severity of Ralston's injuries also suggested to some onlooking staffers that a blunt weapon was used to beat him. "He was probably sitting and watching television," said a lieutenant, "when he was attacked. Looks like they used something on him, maybe a chair. Check 'em for blood." The television was still on, blaring early afternoon soap operas.

In several minutes the room was filled with hacks, lieutenants, and unit management staffers. Ralston was taken to the hospital, and John

Sams ordered me to "rack them all in their cells, right now." A formal investigation was beginning.

I walked down each range, beginning on E-range, telling each inmate to get in his cell: "Let's go, get in your cell!," I said over and over. Inmates responded, "What happened?" "What's going on?" "Nothing," I said, "Let's go, get in your house." They all went peacefully and without too much hesitation. After I got a range of inmates in their cells, the CC racked the cells closed.

Remarkably, of the 40 to 50 inmates who were in K-unit at the time of the assault, not one of them knew anything at all, most didn't know that an assault had occurred, they said. Then I joined a team of staffers shaking down all public areas of the unit, searching for a weapon. We looked behind vending machines; behind and under the washer and drier; in the shower room under sinks and in shower drains; in full trash cans that were dumped out on each tier; and, in every possible place where a pipe or a shank could be hidden. We found nothing.

After finishing this, I walked into the K-unit office. "That fucking thug is a chicken-hawk," exclaimed a staffer, who was reading Ralston's jacket. "He was picking up kids on the street and molesting them in the back of his van. That slimy fuck deserved what he got. They should'a killed him."

Captain Collins, John Sams, Gene Gill, and Rudy Marks discussed proceeding to the next step of the investigation, which was to interrogate all inmates who were in K-unit during the assault. Four two-man interrogation teams were assembled from various unit management teams. I worked with Carl Lowen.

Once interrogation teams were assembled, we decided among ourselves how inmates would be selected for each team's interviews. We went range by range, cell by cell, until all the inmates had been interviewed.

Lowen and I sat in his office. Each interview team used a standardized interview form. Inmates weren't told what had happened in the television room. They were asked, Where were you at approximately 11:50 a.m.? Whom were you talking to? Did you see any one standing near the television room entrance? and so on. As each inmate sat in front of us, we scrutinized the skin on his face and hands, looking for bruises, scratches or blood, and we looked carefully at each man's clothing and shoes, looking for blood stains.

As the interrogation teams worked, about six hacks, each working alone, went from cell to cell. Each inmate was ordered to strip to his underwear, to raise his arms straight out to the side, and to stand with his legs spread. The officer checked for visible fresh scratches and bruises on the inmate's, chest back, arms, and legs.

After this, each inmate was ordered to stand on the tier outside his cell, as the officer shook down the cell, looking for bloody clothes, a weapon, or both. According to lieutenants, inmates at USP-Lompoc have flushed bloody clothes down their toilets and have tried to flush assault weapons. Lt. Baker said that, in some serious cases, officers have been stationed at the penitentiary's sewer outlet pipe, waiting for evidence to flow by.

After the interviews, data sheets were collected. Those inmates who seemed to know more than they were willing to discuss in the interrogation were earmarked for later interviews. The investigation lasted several hours, and K-unit remained locked down for the remainder of that afternoon, opening again after the four o'clock count.

Lowen's intuition was that one of our interviewees, convict Clyde, was probably the assailant, and he suspected that convict Motta, a known partner of Clyde's, was his jigger. Carl was right. During our interview with Clyde, he was calm, but a bit more impatient than other interviewees, claiming he disliked being in Carl's office. He said, "I don't want any of them guys to think I'm telling you anything." Carl said, "How are they going to know what you say?" "They'll know," said Clyde.

Within hours of the assault, Clyde and Motta (with the help of snitches) were serious suspects, and were locked away in I-unit pending SIS investigation. Over the next several days staffers picked up information silently from K-unit inmates. When the details were collected, including the motive, Clyde was charged with assault.

Sex is the first motive cited by most staff and inmates as the explanation for inmate-inmate brutality. The next most common explanation is bad debts. Clyde wasn't talking, though. I asked him about it: "It's something that happens, that's all."

For days afterward, staffers talked about this incident. Men described and redescribed Ralston's injuries, and some men compared this assault to others: "That was the worst beating I've ever seen without a weapon. He must have used his boots on that guy's face to split it open that way. About 15 years ago in [Texas], I saw one that was close to this, but the convict's head wasn't split open like this guy's was," said Unicor staffer.

Lower-I didn't stop Clyde's violence. While in a rec cage several months later, he punched inmate George in the face, "exploding" (shattering) his cheek bone, causing one eye to hang from its socket. George's surgeon, a friend of mine, told me that George's injuries would require extensive reconstruction of the cheek, and that there was a high probability that George would lose his vision in the injured eye. After months of medical care, George's vision was restored. Despite the seriousness of George's injuries, one staffer at the scene described it this way: "He just got smacked. He'll [George] be all right."

On March 6, 1986, a Marielito killed another Marielito. The victim, Julio, was murdered when Bernardo shoved a foot-long shank under Julio's rib cage, pushing into his heart. Bernardo also shanked Julio's side, stomach, arm, and chest.

The F-unit killing occurred between E-range and F-range. I was there just after it happened, and I got a chance to talk to the FBI agent. Apparently, Bernardo and Julio were playing dominoes. Their fight began in the E-range dayroom, but only a few drops of blood were on the dayroom floor. During their initial struggle, Bernardo and Julio overturned a very heavy wooden table, which took up most of the space in the dayroom. Their fight moved to the E-range tier, and ended in death at the tier's front end. A thick pool of blood lay on the concrete floor, where it dripped and oozed from Julio's chest wounds. After shanking Julio, Bernardo ran down to his cell on A-range. On his way down, Bernardo passed his CC, who was running up to the third tier, after he heard the ruckus while working in the unit office.

We followed the same procedure here as we did in the Ralston assault. A new hack (in his late twenties, with three years of military corrections experience) and I worked separately, shaking down convicts in their cells and searching each cell for bloody clothes and a murder weapon; a weapon wasn't found that day. My partner was first on the scene. He said, "I seen him laying there. He had a big hole in his stomach on the side opposite to the appendix. I looked down and seen it and couldn't believe it at first. He was breathing, he took one big breath. I knew he was going to die. I wish I didn't run up here so fast."

Carrying Julio in a blanket, three staffers brought him down the narrow, winding staircase connecting each tier, to a waiting stretcher and a physician's assistant. He died in the penitentiary hospital about an hour later. His body was taken to the Lompoc Community Hospital, where he was pronounced dead by a physician (an FPS physician's assistant can't sign a death certificate). A staffer told me that Julio was handcuffed when they rolled him outside the perimeter of the penitentiary, since he wasn't "officially dead" yet. A penitentiary hospital employee said that was "stupid."

It was discovered later that Bernardo dropped his shank into his cell's heating duct outlet. It took several days to dig it out from the heating system under F-unit. Investigators said, incidentally, that a victim's shank wounds can sometimes identify the killer as Marielito. Their shanks are bifacially sharpened, whereas Havana Cuban criminals' shanks are unifacially sharpened; each type of weapon leaves a distinctive wound.

After our work was done we all stood around, telling stories, joking and laughing, not about the killing, but about anything else. "I'm my best at times like these," said one staffer. "If an outsider had walked in and watched us, he never would have guessed that this was a murder scene and that we had just been involved in a murder investigation." There was no sense of violence or killing or death at the scene. Once the victim had been taken to the hospital, a procedure had to be followed. Policy had to be maintained, work had to be done.

Inmates milling around outside the cellblock knew there had been a killing. Their mood was light, excited, cheerful, airy, and friendly, almost as if to express a sense of relief, knowing that now a murder might not happen again for quite some time.

Why did Bernardo kill Julio? Sex, drug debts, and sex and drug debts were the first rumors circulating among staff and inmates alike. Slim, who lives across the corridor in C-unit, told me his version of the killing. He sounded as if he had seen it on video tape. "They got into a little beef over their dominoes; some guys take it real serious, you know. Julio had a pipe and Bernardo pulled his shit. These things happen. I hear Julio was getting out in June. He got out all right, but he went through the door, flat and feet first."

A final rumor came from a senior custody staffer: "Bernardo was supposed to be transferred to Atlanta, on his way back to Castro's prisons. I guess he didn't want to go, huh? You know, Julio was going to be paroled this June [1986]. Tough break, huh. Ah, shit, we got a lot of Cubans."

Bernardo was housed in lower I-unit. Not long after arriving there, he tore his way through a rec cage's anchor fence which forms its perimeter. After getting out, he scurried to the roof of the main penitentiary building, where he was spotted by a rookie tower officer. A call for assistance went out. We chased him around the rear compound and cornered him within minutes. When he was asked why he ran off, he smiled and said, "I was testing institution security." During the rest of my research, Bernardo was relatively quiet—he didn't kill or assault anyone.

But on July 4, 1987, Bernardo, now back on the mainline, tried to kill convict Bobby. A staffer gave me this account:

> Bernardo had a shank hidden in the gym toilet. He got into a skirmish with a black [Bobby] in the gym, over basketball or something. He went after Bobby and tried to stab him. Bobby ran out of the gym and down the gym corridor, heading for the main corridor. As Bobby ran, Bernardo kept swiping at him with the shank. Bobby ran into the main corridor, but Bernardo still came at him. Bobby ran into the lieutenant's office, but Bernardo didn't stop. He ran in after him, and even tried to stab him in front of the lieutenants. They grabbed him and got the shank.

TESTING METTLE

A penitentiary culture systematically excludes outsiders, and in doing so creates an ethos among staffers. This ethos forces staffers to prove their worthiness. It binds men to other men who are in the same situation, and it keeps them from sharing their lives and stresses with noncorrectional people. Even their wives, who, they say, can't possibly understand what it's like on the inside, are excluded (see Blau et al., 1986: 148, on marriage and correctional officer stress). "Wives don't understand," said Lt. Brooks. "They don't know what a triple deuce is or a body alarm; forget about the shank that's got your name on it. As wives grow older, they begin to understand. New hacks' wives don't understand anything."

A penitentiary culture also systematically isolates insiders from insiders. The time-honored inmate expression, "do your own time," also applies to line staff. This isn't a "sharing" culture: close personal relationships (both among correctional staffers and inmates) aren't easily formed or maintained. A penitentiary culture compartmentalizes people, isolating staff and inmates alike from interpersonal relations and from counsel. These men don't freely allow other men to enter into their personal lives unless they have earned their way in. Violence opens the door.

"Working in this penitentiary," said a line hack, who had come to USP-Lompoc from a California prison, "is just babysitting a bunch of thugs, until the shit hits the fan." Experienced staffers understand that "new men don't know what's going on, for the first few months," said Gary Charles. "But they better learn in a hurry. If a hack doesn't respond to an emergency or if he backs away from action at the scene, he's a wimp, a coward, a chicken-shit."

Charles continued:

Trust in fellow officers is a fragile thing. You're trusting them with your life. I know that two men here are cowards. I've seen them back off. One guy did it in two fights and the other in three fights. Then you have untried rookies. I have four and a half years in the Arizona State Prison, and I still had to prove myself to my fellow officers here. It's a great thing here. Out in the corridor, Larry [Bert] is a man I'd trust with my life. Everybody was a rookie, but they got to prove themselves. It's like being blood relatives. Experience trusts experience. If you've got seven or eight years in federal institutions, it follows you along. Rookies have to prove that you can trust them: his actions, his willingness to work; he isn't bashful, he'll give orders; how he looks and how he acts when inmates are around. You know [GS-6 hack] Mahony in H-unit? An inmate will deck him, then he'll be an outstanding officer.

Testing a new hack's mettle begins with blood. GS-8 George Sand:

> Hacks have to earn their bones. I don't respond to [new] guys until I see blood on them—his or an inmate's. I want to see blood. Older hacks have been around for the trash truck escape and killings. The new guys are untested. New guys are stuck in towers or units. They may look good, but you can't trust them until there's an emergency, when you can see them in action. Emergencies aren't common, but when they come, they hit hard and heavy.

In the man's world of the penitentiary, the unwritten rule among the keepers and the kept is simple: Anybody can work in prison, but only "men" should be on the line in a penitentiary. Because of the organizational culture's emphasis on avoiding conflict, GS-8s and lieutenants don't talk openly about men who don't jump into a convict melee or men who subtly encourage and instigate fights with convicts.

Cowards and chicken-shits are quietly evaluated and discouraged informally, and with negative performance evaluations, from pursuing a career in correctional services. There is always competition for prestige among aggressive hacks. If a hack wants to stand out during a fight, all he has to do is wait around long enough; violence will find him.

Leon Mahony waited for months to earn his bones. Even before he got involved in his first knockdown, drag-out convict brawl, he had already been judged as "a good one," by Charles and by other lieutenants, who had seen him react to several triple deuces. Mahony always reacted quickly; he ran fast at the head of the pack; and he never failed to talk about how much he enjoyed the action, and how disappointed he was about missing "the good ones," the bloody fights/assaults.

Mahony let everyone know that he was ready at anytime, to "rock'n' roll with thugs." After a few months on the job, he got his first chance. This story of the J-unit brawl was told to me the next day by the participants: Lt. Houser, Charles, and Mahony.

It was early evening, around 6:15, during an up-to-then-quiet weekday evening watch. As the J-unit officer was walking on E-range, he passed a cell and spotted four inmates, hanging around inside. There was a "smell of homebrew and they sounded loaded," said the unit hack.

J-unit's new hack called central control, saying that he had two drunken convicts in cell E-10, E-range. Lt. Houser, the operations lieutenant, walked out of the lieutenant's office and told Charles, who was main corridor officer, to come with him. They walked into J-unit. Charles said that "Seventy-five, eighty inmates were hangin' off the tiers, hootin' and hollerin', so it had to be handled carefully without any extra-curricular activities."

They walked up three flights of dimly lit steps, arriving at E-10 to find the rookie unit hack standing in front of now empty E-10, pointing to the drunks, standing on F-range. Houser yelled to convicts Leiser and Peltzer: "Stop." They ignored the order and started walking down the tier. Again, Houser ordered them to stop and again they refused his order.

Houser and Charles then walked around to F-range. Charles approached Leiser: "I ain't gonna be here long. I'm gonna make the big time," said Leiser, according to Charles. "What's the big time? He thinks he's hot shit. He wants to make [USP] Marion. Ah . . . they think it's good for their reputations to do time in the control unit. He's a punk." Charles continued:

I ordered Leiser to turn around to put on cuffs and he refused. I ordered him for a second time to turn around and again he refused the order. Leiser pushed me backward and tried to get away from me and Houser. Houser grabbed his right arm and I grabbed his left arm and tried to put handcuffs on him.

By this time, Leon Mahony was on his way up to the third tier, from his corridor two post, outside J-unit.

I was walking down the flats. Then I looked up and saw Houser and Charles on E-range. I went up the F-range side and by the time I got there, Houser had Leiser. The three of us grabbed him. He was fighting, screaming and kicking. Peltzer came towards us and Charles said, "Stay back," and he said, "Fuck you, I'm gonna kill you motherfuckers" and jumped on Charles's back and punched at me [hitting him in the eye]. By then there was a pile of us on the tier, stacked four high. [Another officer] was holding one cuff. Leiser broke free and tried to kick me, and they jacked his ass on the wall.

Charles continued: "I broke the glasses off Peltzer's face and I wanted to break his fuckin' neck. I had a four-battery Mag Light on my hip. I reached for it once and chose not to go after it. If I used it, we might have had to fight 85 other convicts."

By then, yet another officer appeared, cuffing inmate Peltzer. Houser and Charles cuffed Leiser.

Mahony took Peltzer, walking him down from the third tier, followed by inmate Leiser, who was guided by Charles. On the way down the steps, Leiser again started to fight. Charles said that "Peltzer tried to kick Mahony in back of the legs on the way down the steps. I jammed him up against the wall. Then he tried to break away from me and jump Mahony who was about three stairs ahead of us. I put him on the wall to regain control."

The melee ended. Inmates Leiser and Peltzer were locked away in I-unit. Mahony had a nasty black eye, Charles had been kicked several times in the ribs and armpit, but he loved every minute of it, he said. Charles talked about Mahony. "I told Mahony he was gonna get his cherry broke before too long. That was 15 minutes before it happened. Mahony got a big shiner; he was proud of it. It was hard, hot, and heavy, that's how violent it was up there. It was fun!"

Mahony thought about the fight, too.

> The next day, I'm working I-unit rec yard. Whenever I turned my back somebody yelled, "Please don't hit me again, officer" or "What did they teach you at Glynco?" A couple of guys just came up and laughed at me. [Convict] Donnie came up and said, "Can I touch it [the black eye]?" and "What's the matter with you, hurt your neck, too?"

Mahony continued: "So I had to look at 'em and listen to it. They gave me a Peanuts cartoon of Charlie Brown with a black eye, lying on the ground, asking "Why?""

As he thought about the night before, Mahony commented:

> It was loud in there, ninety of them screaming and hollering. We got the guys and Charles said, "Let's get the hell out of here!" It was exciting. A sense of camaraderie with the three of us. Charles is a wild man, he loves it. I wanted to beat the shit out of them. Charles had boot prints on his shirt, and I didn't feel getting hit. I almost rolled off the tier, I reached up and grabbed a bar [of the tier's rail] and held on.

The result: no deaths and only minor injuries. The next day the convict rumor mill buzzed about the brawl. Rumor had it that it was a good, fair fight. According to Slim, who had an acquaintance in J-unit, a bunch of J-unit convicts were armed and prepared to attack and kill the officers if they thought that the fight had been conducted with unnecessary staff brutality. Slim's comment, even with its apocryphal origin, suggests a prevailing attitude held by inmates and staff: a prison fight like this one should be conducted by fair fighting rules.

Staff and inmate spectators enjoyed this one. Both staffers and inmates bolstered their prison reputations. The inmates may have gotten their wish, to be transferred to USP-Marion, and they will carry with them a proud record of assaulting staff.

Staffers were satisfied, too. Charles added new bruises and scars to a body and face already scarred and damaged from countless brawls with convicts. Houser improved his prestige as a knowledgeable supervisor by handling a potentially dangerous situation professionally. And Mahony strutted amid inmates and peers, exhibiting his shiny black eye proudly, a valuable badge of courage among rookie hacks.

An upper-echelon administrator, on the other hand, wasn't happy with the way the officers had handled that volatile situation. "With all the experience those guys have, they should have known better than to chase down drunks with 80 or 90 convicts hanging over the rails and yelling and screaming. They should have locked down the unit before dealing with the drunks. They could have gotten really hurt in there." "Yeah," I said, "but it sounds like they had fun, huh?" With a slight smile on his face, he said: "I bet they did, too."

Unlimited macho talk floats around the mainline after a cellblock brawl. According to Charles, after the J-unit fight "a couple of convicts came up and told me that guys think I'm a bad motherfucker. They think we did a good job down there [J-unit]." I replied: "You are a bad motherfucker, huh?" "I can be!" said Charles. Such a reputation can lead to yet another way of proving one's macho qualities.

wow!

CONTRACTS

Within several weeks of this fight, Charles told me that the "ABs have a certified contract on me." Several snitches independently identified the hitters and the contract's source. The validity of the contract was verified by the SIS and the FBI, according to Charles. "The captain wanted to pull me [off the main corridor] and stick me in 1-tower for about a week until things calmed down. They've tried this before. When it gets tough, I don't want to be pulled out. I told the captain: 'Cap, either play me or trade me!'"

Charles didn't want to hide from the convict hitters. "I asked around and I found out who was going to try to take me out. I stopped each one in the corridor, and I told him, 'If I see you coming up behind me or near me with a hand in your pocket, I'll take you out right then.' I love this. My wife thinks I'm crazy."

Murder contracts on staffers are powerful messages. If a convict wants to kill a staffer or an inmate, and can't or doesn't want to do it himself, he may "put a contract" out on the target. The target may be in the same or different prison, on the street, or anywhere in the country.

Big Brother describes the contract arrangement:

Say I put out the word that I want that some dude hit and will give $1,500. I'll send my ol' lady to see a hitter [in another prison]. Or the word can go out by telephone, in a letter or to your ol' lady in the visiting room. You got to be real careful when you talk on the phone or mail out a letter. They listen to calls and the SIS reads the mail. If the FBI finds out you set up a contract, you'll never get out of here. The best way to do it is send the word with some dude who's being transferred to the joint where the guy is, who you want hit. He can set it up, and you pay him. After the hit, you have your ol' lady put the money in the hitter's account.

The cost of a contract varies according to target (convict or staffer), social status of the target, and expertise of the hitter. At USP-Lompoc, "some ol' dope head will do it," said Slim. "It'll cost you one half ounce of heroin. Some guys might charge $500 to $1,000, or less, a couple hundred. A slight professional would cost $1,000 or a bit more. They use discretion." A contract "on the inside [penitentiary] may go $200," said a senior lieutenant, "but in the [FPC] camp, it may cost $1,000 to $2,000," since camp inmates, who don't have histories of violence, will have to contract with someone else who will do the hit at the camp.

As deadly as contracts can be, they are factors in mettle testing and sources of prestige for hacks, who take a sense of pride in being considered a worthwhile target. Once a contract has been verified, hacks take an even greater risk by remaining on the mainline. But greater risk yields greater prestige.

ASSAULTING EACH OTHER

Do you ever wonder why staff run in an emergency? Do you ever think about if a convict or staff is down? No one gives a shit if convicts kill each other, but it's scary to think that a staff member is down [A line hack].

In the 50-year history of the Bureau of Prisons, five staffers have been killed by inmates. Three of the five killings occurred between 1980 and 1985. These killings, particularly the two correctional officers killings at USP-Marion, are still on the minds of USP-Lompoc's line staff. Of these three convict killers, two were housed at USP-Marion, and the third coperpetrator in the "piping" (bludgeoning someone with a piece of pipe) and near decapitation of an FCI correctional officer is housed at USP-Lompoc.

Charles:

We don't give a shit if they kill each other, but the golden rule is, "They don't touch me and I don't touch them." 'Cause if they do, we go to the dirt. When something is done to a staff member, something got to be done to the convict. I don't mean beat the hell out of them. They got to know that staff members are off-limits: they can do what they want to each other, but they've got to leave staff alone, physically.

The few serious inmate-on-staff assaults at USP- and FCI-Lompoc are remembered well. Two serious assaults are noted here, one in 1982 at USP-Lompoc and the earlier one in 1978 at FCI-Lompoc. The staff victim of the 1982 attack, a J-unit counselor, has since retired, but a staffer who responded to the body alarm offers his own account.

> The counselor was piped by a convict because his transfer was turned down and it was handled by the counselor. We went in and found him on the tier, his head was caved in and he was in a big pool of blood. An inmate pushed his body alarm, he came up behind him and pushed his button; the convict saved his life. The next day they bused him [the attacker] out. The staff were serious about killing him.

The victim of the 1978 incident, correctional officer John Burland, now a case manager at USP-Lompoc, had his throat cut by a convict assailant on January 30, 1978. Burland recalls,

> I had been out of the institution for two weeks with walking pneumonia. I worked D-unit for two days and was assigned to L-unit to cover sick and annual post on evening watch. I hadn't worked L-unit in a long while. When I checked in, no one told me about [the attacker]. He had giant eyes, he had been burned out from drug usage. In those days they had a racking system: A guy could put his name on a chart to be racked out to watch TV after the 10:00 p.m. count. Some other inmate put [his] name on this chart and I racked him out. He thought that devils were after him and other inmates. I was raising the door on the lock box, and I felt a brush, like hair, on the side of my neck. I turned around and I could see blood hitting the wall, about five feet away. At first, I though an inmate had been cut on the third tier. I saw this inmate standing in front of me with two razor blades in leather thongs, and a crazed look in his eyes. I said, "What the hell are you doing?" He lunged at me again and that's when he cut my little finger all up. I backed up and hit my alarm button. I heard the keys in the corridor. He dropped the weapons to his side, turned around and walked to his cell. He put the weapons in his locker, took all his clothes off and went to bed.

Assaults without weapons occurred in a variety of situations during my research. In one incident, a convict, later reported to have been high on a hallucinogen, was frantically trying to escape from his cellblock, claiming spacemen were outside the cellblock and were coming for him. He smacked a rookie hack in the side of the head, when the hack refused to give the inmate his security keys. In another incident, an emotionally unstable inmate punched two staffers who tried to stop him for a shakedown.

In the only armed assault, convict Julian tried to stab George Sand, the main corridor officer. It happened just before noon on a weekday, directly in front of the mess hall.

According to Lt. Houser,

He tried to get into the mess hall, wearing a headband, two or three times. We stopped him at the door, and told him to take that thing off. He turned around and walked back to his unit. Then the last time, he came back again, still wearing that headband. I followed him into the mess hall and got him up by the steamline. I escorted him out, and turned him over to Sand for a shakedown. We were going to lock him up.

Officer Sand said: "I had him against the wall with his hands up against it, shaking him down. There was no problem, then he broke. He spun around and I pushed up against him and held him against the wall. I didn't know he had a shank, until Mike grabbed him."

And Mike Rizo added: "I was walking down the corridor and saw Julian up against the wall with a shank in his hand. I ran down there and grabbed his arm."

The details of this event remain fuzzy. No one knew if Julian had the shank on him or if someone handed it to him as he spun around. Because of the attack's high visibility, some staffers thought that it was a "lockup" move (an attempt to get off the mainline and subsequently transferred). (Toch, 1977, p. 125, suggests that inmates remove themselves from the mainline population to seek safety and privacy, and to find their way out of stressful situations, p. 193; I've seen this happen repeatedly, and some inmates talk about I-unit as a "vacation.") Said a GS-8: "It was a lock-move all the way. His fucking ugly brother is in [USP] Marion and that fucking slime wanted to join him. Fuck him, get him out of here."

A unit staffer told me: "Julian had just gotten a letter from [a relative] telling him that his brother had been killed [in a shoot-out]. He tried to get an emergency call, but no one would give him one, so he went off."

Slim had a version, too.

Mark, did you see that? Just like "Miami Vice." That guy came running down the corridor and grabbed that shank just in time. Sand would have got it good, man. Just like TV, huh? Julian was paid off by [convict Grey Feather] to off Sand. Yeah, they don't give a shit about Sand. He wanted to get the warden. They're still pissed off about the headbands. Eagle didn't have the balls to do it himself, so he got that crazy fucking Julian to do his shit for him.

The formal penalties for assaulting staff are serious: loss of all good time, disciplinary transfer, and an additional sentence of one to five years. Why do convicts assault staff? Slim said,

An officer could have disrespected you or the officer could be an asshole and you get fed up with it, and it get to the point where you want to do something to him. Some of them have a shitty attitude or think you a lower form of dude 'cause you're on this side of the wall. It's petty stuff, really. Let's say the phone. You call your people, they accept the charges, then hacks cut you off. If they're so tough, let them take off that radio and let's step in that little room; then they not be tough.

Slim said he had a run-in with his black supervisor in food service, who called him a "nigger." Slim said he recognized his supervisor's friendly intention, and, even though they had a good relationship, up to that point, he became angry. "If I've got to go to I-unit for busting you in the motherfucking mouth I'll do that," Slim said he told his supervisor. "I guess I can't blame him. Association brings on simulation," commented Slim about a black hack's use of the epithet.

Slim suggested also that convicts who have done time before have learned to distrust staff in situations like this one:

When I was down in [state prison] in '79, we did a racial thing. A white guard let whites get to the bats, and they rolled on us. What we did was get strapped down. We were in a dorm. They rolled off in the dorm and was swinging bats. They locked us down for couple of weeks. We got out and decided we were going to ride. We rode on two white guys watching TV. We rode on them and one of the them died, and the other was pretty bad. Imagine yourself in that situation. That you got buddies laid up in the hospital and you got a few bruises. You roll up on these guys, your buddies got knives and you say, "Let's hit these motherfuckers." Anger leads you. You got anger out front there. You try to hit them a multitude of times. They curl up in a ball and you hit them from every angle. We don't know if they were involved in the original thing or not; they were vulnerable, two of them, eight of us. If you leave yourself vulnerable, you're an easy mark. They had a lot of guards that keep stuff stirred up between tips. One guard might like the ABs more than Nazis. The guard who let them get the bats was a white broad too, a sergeant's wife.

Frankie was the only inmate who agreed to discuss an assault on staff that he himself had committed. This event happened at USP-McNeil Island.

In 1975, I caught a beef, a hassle with inmates and staff. Since then, when they read my jacket, they see me as a different dude. Five convicts moved on a partner of mine; they came up on him, and I got into it. We wiped a couple of them, others ran off. My partner was stabbed through the mouth into his neck, his tooth was missing and he was bleeding. I didn't know he was hit in the neck. I didn't know it was that serious until the blood came squirting out his mouth. When staff came, they broke it up, but they didn't take him to the hospital. So in the scuffle, we were busted for fighting with staff. I got six years for it, but they wanted to give him 45 years for assaulting staff and conveying a weapon.

Lt. Baker talked about working the line in USP-Marion's control unit. As America's only penitentiary monitored by Amnesty International, reports of occasional staff-to-convict abuse reach the media.

"Baker, did you ever abuse any convicts at Marion?" I asked him. He thought quietly about his answer for quite a while: "No, I wouldn't call it abuse. We didn't abuse them; we adjusted their attitudes."

Abuse is one thing, convict attitude adjustment is another, according to custody staffers. They talk of attitude adjustment in other institutions when an assaultive convict "accidently" hits his head on a wall or "trips" going down steel steps or has his cuffs put on too tightly.

Experienced men don't talk about "abuse." Conventional wisdom on the subject is: "equal force for equal force," "deadly force for deadly force," and "once a convict is in control, don't use force."

If an inmate claims that excessive force was used against him, he has the option of filing an administrative remedy against the offending officer(s). During my research, there was one case of alleged excessive force. Since I didn't see the event, I compiled the story from details discussed at a meeting of the American Federation of Government Employees.

A struggle occurred in the hospital between an inmate and several hacks and a physician's assistant. This inmate was being placed in soft restraints: leather cuffs for wrists and ankles. As the physician's assistant leaned over the inmate to fasten the final restraint on his wrist, the inmate spat in his face. The physician's assistant responded by stepping on the side of the inmate's face, pushing his head aside as he fastened the leather cuff on his wrist.

A lieutenant, who was supervising the event, reported it. After an investigation, it was concluded that the physician's assistant had used excessive force in controlling the inmate.

"This is a complex situation governed by the heat of the moment and the convict's frame of mind," said an experienced custody staffer who was familiar with this case. He agreed that the physician's assistant's behavior was inappropriate for that particular situation. In a broader sense though, he asks,

> If you're fighting a convict who has a shank and you throw him into a wall, is that excessive force? Is he threatening my life, or is that just part of my job? Some guy throws shit on me, so I smack him. He files against me. We go to court and the jury finds that convicts throwing shit on hacks is part of the job, an occupational hazard. Is stepping on the face of an inmate who just spit on you, an appropriate control mechanism? Was it

excessive force? When in this situation here was the inmate controlled? Do you mean to tell me that being spit on or having shit and piss thrown on you by some convict in I-unit is part of a correctional officer's job? If people on the street or people in courts think that catching shit and piss on your face and all over your clothes should be part of our job, then let *them* come in here and watch these convicts!

—10—

MAINLINE TALK

MACHO TALK

The prison's main players, its convicts and hacks, talk about toughness, machismo, and bravery as their primary form of self-expression (see Campbell, 1986: 119). Their macho talk is a metaphor of the prison's dominant values and their social roles in prison life. Macho talk creates, molds, nurtures, perpetuates, and protects players' often-brittle prison self-images. Not a single player, convict or hack, wants an outsider to think, even for a second, that daily life in "The Pen," isn't as depraved, as continuously dangerous, and as perpetually life-threatening as they say it is. But it usually isn't.

On Friday night, March 18, 1988, "20/20," a television news documentary program, ran a story about USP-Marion, "The Toughest Federal Penitentiary in the Country." Lompoc's hacks often told me that their penitentiary is the toughest. *Newsweek's* cover story on October 6, 1986 was titled "Inside America's Toughest Prison," and described life in Eastham Prison in the Texas Department of Corrections. The assault data shown in Table 1.1 show that USP-Lewisburg might actually be the toughest Federal prison. Are state prisons tougher than federal prisons? The answer depends on whom you ask. In the prison business, every joint is the toughest, every convict is the "baddest dude on the mainline," and every hack is "John Wayne" (Cheek and Miller, 1983). Hacks say they "take no shit from thugs," and, they add, they are usually "stressed out by the job." Just ask them, they'll tell you (see Crouch and Marquart, 1980; Cullen et al., 1985). When macho talk (verbal data) is understood in its natural, or "unselfconscious," social contexts, it becomes clear that players create their own versions of prison life for other players, as well as outsiders, to hear.

TALKING ABOUT VIOLENCE

GS-8s and GS-9/-11 lieutenants have to know how to control violent convicts and how to manage and supervise a crime scene. But a

220

potentially dangerous confrontation such as Mahony's J-unit brawl is "valueless" in developing his career in custody unless his account is told and retold with the right listening audience. Then, it can become valuable "property," which can be transformed into prestige by a verbally skillful and well-liked hack like Mahony, and prestige may lead to promotions and pay increases. After a hack has already acquired a "no bullshit rep," telling stories about bloody, brutal violence (the "good" kind), without actually facing the actual danger of it, may also be effective in further promoting his career (see Marquart, 1986b: 359-360).

Formal records don't show who acted at scenes of violence, but that doesn't matter since everyone remembers. Staffers who ran quickly, and those who ran slowly; those who arrived first, and those who arrived last; those who got involved, and those who backed away, are all included in hacks' stories. These details are always remembered and retold in good stories of violence, but not always to a general audience.

Over time and countless retellings, a staffer uses stories of bloody violence as a part of his own penitentiary experience. I found that staffers who missed good violence, like the Willie Free-Lady Claudine killing, tell someone else's eyewitness account in the "first person," embellishing it with their own realistic details. Following this pattern, I found that some macho-minded staffers told and retold their own Vietnam war experiences, while others, who didn't fight there, told, retold, and embellished someone else's Vietnam experiences.

Staffers and administrators are aware of all this, but no one talks about it, and no one ever "calls bullshit," as hacks say, at least not for hacks who are well liked. On one occasion, I learned how difficult it is, particularly for a new man, to distinguish "real" eyewitness accounts from penitentiary folklore. One morning not too long after I started work, three senior correctional staffers told me stories about violence and tales about convicts for almost three hours, and I naively believed every word of their colorful, first-hand stories. Several days later at a prison-staff beer party, Lt. Baker approached me. "Remember the other day when we were telling you all those stories? Most of it was bullshit. I didn't want you to think that all that stuff was true." Now what should I believe?

Some stories are obviously embellished and everyone knows it, but everyone loves to listen to them anyway. Hacks smile and laugh, joke among themselves, slap each other on the back, and everyone drinks another beer. Very personal experiences with violence (in prison or in Vietnam) are told by senior custody staffers only to their closest companions; here is where the details of other staffer's behavior "under fire," as they say, come out. Accounts of serious assaults on staff are never funny and are never told lightly; these tales are told only among men who share good rapport.

Most stories are about violence, such as the Willie Free-Lady Claudine killing. When I was told that story the first time in February 1986, I believed "my" storyteller's firsthand account of this killing. Why not believe him? He had more than ten years of line experience in the Bureau; he was a Vietnam veteran; he was trusted by everyone; his story seemed credible; and I heard numerous similar accounts later from other staffers. I had no reason to disbelieve him.

But in May 1987, just before Willie Free's trial in a federal court in Los Angeles, a Bureau legal specialist told me that my storyteller wasn't in the penitentiary on the day of the killing. If I couldn't believe the trusted staffers, who could I believe?

FOLKTALES

Folklore, verbal metaphors, and humor are forces counterbalancing the policies and unalterable schedules of maximum-security prison life (see Fernandez, 1974). Folklore includes stylized accounts of violence and tales of the institution, its staff and convicts. Verbal metaphors are staffers' caricatures of convicts' noteworthy features. Humor safely toys with racism, prison sexuality, staff sexism, and with changes staffers perceive in themselves brought by years of penitentiary work. But in the natural flow of penitentiary talk, it's often difficult to place folklore, humor, and metaphors in separate categories.

USP-Lompoc's social history is its folklore. Lompoc folklore is rich and varied and includes many tales of violence and near violence. These include mishaps with convicts and comic errors of staff; inmates' attempts at suicide and self-mutilation; adventurous fights and near riots during which convicts hurt convicts or staff hurt convicts. At beer parties, usually in late evening, old-timers tell stories to new men who huddle around.

"Good ol' days" tales of prison work are favorites over beer. Then, hacks were screws, turnkeys, and guards, and convicts didn't have rights and weren't worth the time of day. Those were times when only tough screws made it on the mainline. In the good ol' days, convicts and staffers walked on different sides of Lompoc's main corridor. In the good ol' days, the lieutenants's office was off-limits to line screws, and lieutenants ruled the roost with an iron hand. In those days, staffers could bounce a convict's head on a steel staircase, teaching him manners without worrying about grievances filed against them. Today, said a hack, "the BOP almost apologizes to them puke motherfuckers. 'We're sorry we have to put you in prison. Now here: you can take this and take that, too.'"

Even a story of an occasional supernatural cellblock apparition has its place in Lompoc's folklore. There is a recurring tale of a C-unit ghost whose presence was reported on a morning watch by a rookie hack who felt he was being followed, range by range, as he made his early morning rounds. The ghost appeared twice during my research, and, in each case, the unit hack (a different one each time) reported hearing a faint sound of keys jingling behind him.

In one case, as the day watch began after the ghost had appeared hours earlier, I heard lieutenants talking about the apparition, and, after discussing whether the hack was drunk or stoned, they acknowledged hearing a similar story at other times. Apparently, the C-unit ghost had been sighted many times before, by different hacks each time. The C-unit ghost is a convict who was killed at FCI-Lompoc.

Accounts may be told from several viewpoints, with differences signaled by storyline introductions. First, there are "I remember . . ." or "When I worked at . . ." stories, which come from a person's experience, either as an actual participant in the event or as a listener to a story told by a firsthand participant. Second, there are "There used to be a [staffer or convict] here who . . ." stories, which tell some aspect of Lompoc's social history. Third, there are "I was there when . . ." stories, which tell the details of some incident which the teller alleges to have seen firsthand. These tales are usually stories of brutal and bloody violence, the ones which carry the greatest value in correctional culture. They demonstrate a man's versatility in handling adversity as well as his courage—as when he stood close to a convict who was stabbing to death another convict.

Elders of the custody tribe—the highly experienced GS-8s and lieutenants—are carriers of correctional culture (prison knowledge, tradition and folklore), and many are wonderful storytellers. Their best tales are told at home among friends, over bourbon and Monday night football.

"Violence," said a 20-year veteran of custody, "gets the adrenaline flowing, it's a high, that's why men go to work. Why go to work if you're just going to sit around staring at your shined shoes? Action is a high."

"Violence is the glory subject," says Tony Halpin, a slight smile creasing his face. Six years at USP-Lompoc has put Halpin face to face with violence, but not too often.

I remember back about 1981 or '82. I had just come to work on the evening watch, when there was a triple deuce. We went running out to industries. There was [convict Brown], who had taken a pipe about two

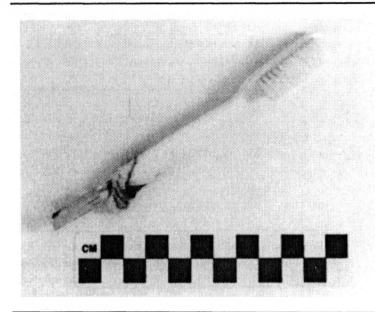

Figure 10.1 "Sissy" Shank

feet long and hit [convict Terry] unconscious. Brown, he took a sissy shank and cut off Terry's head, damn near. There was blood everywhere. His head was hanging on by a little piece of flesh. There was blood everywhere. The PA was there. He tried to save him. They got him on a gourney and the PA held his head on, while they carried him in. The work corridor and the main corridor were covered in blood. What a mess!

The "sissy shank" shown in Figure 10.1 is similar to the murder weapon used by Brown in 1981; his sissy shank had two single-edged razors attached to the end of its handle. It's called a sissy shank because it's small and rather harmless looking, as compared to large shanks. Staffers said Terry was killed because he snitched off Brown; others said sex caused it; and some staffers insisted that Brown "was just a stone-cold killer," who found "some excuse to kill."

Stories about close brushes with "good violence," especially incidents like the Brown tale, boost men's prestige, and prestige is held at a premium. "Fuck money, give me prestige," said Sammy Marino, a Lompoc food-service steward, former federal hack, and former big city street cop.

Gary Charles loved telling prison war tales and had a long inventory of fight and riot stories, and scars and healed broken bones to accompany them, he said. Charles said that "97% of the tedious, repetitive aspects of the job are worthwhile because of the 3% fighting. I've had a fractured skull, broken ribs—twice—three concussions, a broken nose, 26 bones broken on one hand in a fight, two missing knuckles and a bum knee from a fight down in L-unit."

Over the years, like other senior staffers, Charles has accumulated prestige in riots, near riots, cellblock brawls, and confrontations with armed convicts. Charles recounts the L-unit rumble:

> Down in L-unit I faced an inmate with a knife. It was a handle off a ten oz. ladle he got in food service; he sharpened it on a rock. I told him two, three times to drop it. He said, "No fucking way." He lunged at me; I stepped back out of the doorway and hit my body alarm and called for help. He came running out the door and I tried to grab him. He hit me in the chest with his shoulder and drove me back about two to three feet. I ran after him and ran up a stairway and I tackled him. He broke away and kicked me in the collar bone and ran away up to C-range and ran into the shower. There was a white inmate in the shower and he tried to hand the shank to him. The guy was standing there buck-ass naked. He said, "Get that knife away." I told him to give me the knife, he said, "No fucking way." He lunged at me again and I backed out the door. I jumped out the door as he ran past me. I got him in a bear hug, he flipped the shank; it went from C to F-range. He rammed me against the corner of the door. Finally, help got there. He was trying to throw me off the tier.

Figure 10.2 shows several shanks made from ladle handles.

Lt. Larry Thomas told me a hair-raising tale from the days of FCI-Lompoc in 1979. Thomas was then a line hack.

> I was working in L-unit. I was on the third tier and I heard these guys running up the stairs. I walked toward the staircase and two guys ran by, out of breath. I asked what was going on and they told me they had just come in from the yard and were running before the movement ended. I heard a ruckus outside the door. I went downstairs and looked out the door. I saw about 75 convicts standing on the east end. I went out of the unit and locked the door. I pushed through the group, and guys told me to go back inside. They were Mexicans and I'm Mexican; I got along well with them. I had been working L-unit for more than a year, and I knew all the guys in J and K. Anyway, they told me to go back inside, but I couldn't do that. I pushed through and saw two guys standing like this [in fighting posture with hands up under coats]. I pushed the body alarm. I knew they had knives. They saw me and started running. I waited for help, but no one came. I hit the body alarm again; finally, a lieutenant and an officer came running down the corridor, puffing, out of breath and covered with blood. What happened was that a guy in C-unit was piped real bad, so they were up there. At the same time, I saw a guy lying [dead] in the corridor near the

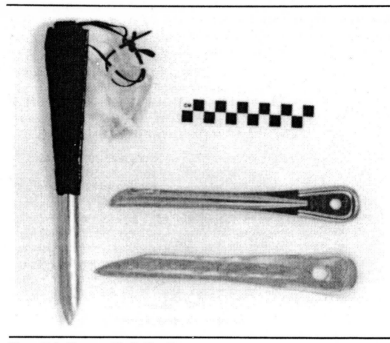

Figure 10.2 Sharpened Ladle-Handles

dining hall. The thing at the end of the hall was probably a diversion for what went on. [What killed the inmate lying in the corridor?] The investigation found out that one of the guys who ran up the stairs in my unit did it. He was probably wearing double clothes and after he killed him, he took off the bloody clothes and gave them to a friend who flushed them or whatever. You don't have much time to think [in a situation like that]. The first thing you do is try to control it. It's scary all right.

As hacks get older, they say they get mellower and their attitude about fighting convicts changes from "I" to "We." Gary Charles said, "I'm not brutal. Until about a year and a half ago, if an inmate wanted to fight, I'd jump right in. Now, I'll ask him two or three times, then if he wants to fight, we jump into it." He smirked.

Good stories like these L-unit tales are told and retold. For days after the K-unit Ralston assault, I heard staffers all over the prison telling their versions of it, and some of them weren't at the scene. This also happened after the F-unit Marielito killing, and also after each fight and assault, during my research. Cellblocks, like hacks, gain reputations this way, too.

Folkloric accounts about Lompoc's notorious criminals are often humorous. Hacks like to talk about notorious criminals who have done time there: Christopher Boyce (The Falcon; he escaped from FCI-Lompoc using a dummy like the one shown in Figure 6.1, according to a lieutenant who was on duty then); Dalton Lee (The Snowman, crime partner of the The Falcon; he was transferred to an FCI in fall 1985); the American Indian Movement's activist leader, Leonard Peltier (also escaped from FCI-Lompoc); Eddy Sanchez, who had his personal story told on the 60 Minutes television show; and Anthony Provenzano, "Tony-Pro," who was allegedly involved in Jimmy Hoffa's disappearance.

"Hey, know who we got in today," or "Hey, guess who I heard is in X-unit," always signaled the beginning of new convict folklore. In some folktales, convicts are attributed near superhuman strength or powerful social negotiability among other inmates; these are usually tales about inmates who are no longer housed in USP-Lompoc. Eddy Sanchez, said Lt. Baker, "beat through two cell walls in I-block, clawing his way from cell one to cell four in lower I-unit so he could attack the convict in cell one who said 'Sanchez you're a punk, and I'm going to fuck you in the ass.'"

"Sanchez got so angry," said Baker, "that he ripped off his cell's sink, using the porcelain to carve through the cell walls. When staff arrived, Eddy was in cell three, tearing at the last wall."

Tony-Pro, said a staffer,

> hasn't been to the mess hall for a meal since he got here. That's a year and a half. He gets his meals from inmates who steal his food and deliver it to him. He never gets his own clean clothing, sheets, newspaper or mail, and he always walks with several inmate bodyguards. And every year when the FBI comes in to interview Tony-Pro, they say: "Ok, Tony, where's Jimmy Hoffa?" Tony says: "Fuck you!" The FBI says, "OK, Tony, see you next year." I heard that Hoffa was ground into hamburger at one of the union's meat plants.

Then there's the Spider Man, said a lieutenant, who could "walk up" his cell walls to the ceiling by positioning himself across the cell, feet on one side, hands on the other. By using his incredible strength, he moved himself upward like a spider.

> Some rookie hack was working lower I-unit, and we had this guy down there. The kid walked over to his cell, shined in his flashlight, and yelled, "Lieutenant, better come down here, he's missing." I ran down range and we looked in, and that crazy bastard jumped down at us from the ceiling. Damn near gave me a heart attack.

This same story is also told in the first person by a disciplinary segregation inmate in "Other Prisoners," a 1987 television documentary, by Stephen R. Roszell, about daily life in the Kentucky State Reformatory.

A violent convict, Punchy, earned a reputation as a vicious killer among staff and inmates alike. "Inmates say that Punchy enjoyed it when he did [convict Sergeant] in I-unit. Inmates say he had a smile on his face," said Danny Crafter, a former hack, now a counselor, and Vietnam veteran. According to prison records, Punchy did kill two convicts in 1981, one in January and another one in August, with a weapon, staff say, like those shown in Figure 10.3; the middle shank is made from a bed spring. These stickers can be deadly.

Red Hog said Punchy "was a nut. He killed a cop in a state joint and three or four convicts. He killed [an inmate] in I-unit, and he killed another one. He killed the last one because he didn't like the idea that [the convict] was going home. Nuts, you can't trust them."

Then there was the "Ice Man" who, said a mechanical services staffer,

> had eyes as black and as cold as coal. You know, he could curl 480 pounds, and deadlift more than 600 pounds. I saw him do it. I stood right there on iron pile and watched him. There was a fight in I-unit, long ago, and Ice Man fought junior hacks half his size. He threw them around like they were dolls. When he got tired of playing with them, he just gave up. They were lucky they had handcuffs big enough for him.

On my second day of on-the-job training, a staffer went out of his way to introduce me to Spanish Eddy, who claimed to have been a technical adviser on the production set of *The Great Brinks Robbery,* starring Peter Falk. Spanish Eddy took me into his cell to show me his 8 x 10 color prints, proudly displayed on his bulletin board. There were several photos of Spanish Eddy standing on the production set, watching the actors at work. Among the half-dozen prints, he was especially proud of the photo showing him posing next to Peter Falk, and of another photo, showing him embracing the mayor of Boston.

VERBAL METAPHORS

Metaphors are used by correctional workers, particularly experienced custody staffers, as a way to distance themselves from prison violence and from convicts. These men use metaphors, often dark, personal ones, to describe how correctional work has changed them. I find that staffers sometimes attribute qualities to themselves that they see in convicts: They say they are "getting cold," they are "becoming hard," they are losing compassion. Some men attribute their coldness to prison, while others attribute it to Vietnam. Some men say they enjoy prison work

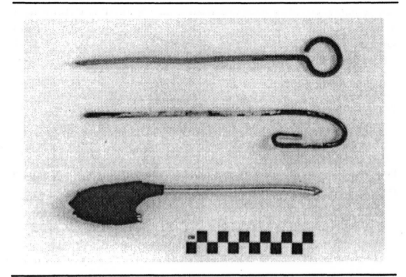

Figure 10.3 "Stickers"

and prison violence because of their Vietnam experiences. Danny Crafter put it this way:

> Shit, in '79, it seemed like there was a sticking and a killing every week around here. I got off on it. It reminded me of Vietnam, all that·blood around got me excited. Some new guys couldn't handle it. This place has made me cold. Even my old lady gets on me for it. My kid will fall and get hurt and start to cry. I'll tell him "stop sniveling and get up." Some guys come to work and see the ambulance parked at 1-tower, and the first thing they do is call and ask for [hospital] overtime [guarding the injured convict]. There'll be a convict down and bleeding and guys will be standing around laughing and waiting for overtime.

After the Marielito killing, some staffers at the scene did, in fact, complain jokingly that "there won't be no OT this time."

Simple metaphors describe and refer to inmates: thugs, punks, lowlife, scum-bags, assholes, dirt-bags, trash, and slimeballs. Thug is by far the commonest term of reference used for inmates by staff. Thug and convict are used as near synonyms. All these terms of reference, except thug, are insults; no convict or street person wants to be called a scum-bag or lowlife.

Inmates refer to themselves as thugs. Being a thug isn't good or bad; it's a neutral label of their social role in the institution. When talking among themselves, and when convicts became comfortable talking to me, they often referred to themselves as "'victs." Use of the term "thug" helps create social distance between staff and inmates. It is more difficult to have a personal relationship with a thug than with John Smith from Los Angeles, who has a wife and two children.

Inmates refer to correctional officers as hacks (the commonest term) and cops. Some old-time inmates even use the terms screw and turnkey for hacks. A convict who said he began his prison life just after World War II, and who said his father was a warden at the North Carolina State Penitentiary in the 1930s, told me that "in the old days of prisons, guards could hack time off a con's sentence. That's how they got to be called hacks." Correctional officers don't object to being called hacks, and being called cops gives them more power and authority than the FPS gives them; they don't complain about it. But no hack will stand for being called a pig; that's an insult. They also don't like being called guards.

Emotional relationships, positive or negative, can't be tolerated in correctional culture. So creating a thug places social and emotional distance between staffers and inmates. After spending years together inside the penitentiary, staffers and inmates would otherwise know each other too well.

When thugs are injured, no staffers or convicts admit to being emotionally hurt. Gary Charles:

> I worked at a slaughterhouse for five years when I was growing up, and when violence goes down, I turn myself off, and don't relate to them as human beings. I really started doing that when I was in Vietnam. I saw a lot of death and destruction over there, and it's a lot harder to relate to a friend that way than to a thug who's done something wrong.

George Sand put his feelings this way. "Thugs are not human beings. If you start thinking about inmates as humans, you can get killed. Fucking thugs aren't human beings."

In metaphoric imagery and folklore, convicts have these features: They are hard and emotionless; they are faceless, but have dark, coal-like eyes; they are muscular, very strong, and rather clever; they can sometimes be pleasant, but they are always deceptive and potentially violent; and if one dies, another will be along to take its place. That is a thug.

Several thugs tried to escape in October 1983, by driving a garbage truck through the west fences of the rear compound (see Canon, 1988b). As they attempted their escape, tower officers shot at the truck with their carbines. The garbage truck bogged down and stopped in the soft earth around the fences. Figure 2.2 is an FBI photo taken after this attempted escape; look at the northwest corner (upper left) of the rec yard, and you'll see where the garbage truck drove into the perimeter fences.

When the shooting ended, officers approached the truck and found a dead convict, shot through the back of the head. A staffer, who claims to have been one of the first men on the scene, told me that another staffer looked at the dead inmate and said: "That's the best I've ever seen you look, you thug piece of shit!"

A 20-year custody veteran put his feelings about violence this way: "Violence bothers you. No one likes to see the mess or stand in the blood, but you can't talk about it that way. You have to act like it doesn't bother you."

HUMOR

Humor is a legitimate means of raising sensitive topics in a public forum—topics like homosexuality, race relations, and hack-convict conflict—and it is often expressed in joking relationships among staff and between staff and inmates. Joking relationships may include limited touching between staff and inmates.

In a "humorous" anecdote like this one, told by a GS-11 lieutenant, violence becomes demystified. "The institution needs to pick a Correctional Officer of the Month and a Convict of the Month. And, on a nice day, in rec yard, the CO will hang the inmate. Nothing brutal, a good clean drop."

Blood and violence and humor are commonly expressed together in penitentiary humor. A senior lieutenant told this tale:

Shit, I don't even remember when it was. I think this happened when I was here, back in the '70s. I responded to a body alarm in L-unit, with, uh, I forgot his name. The unit officer found a convict under his bed. He was stabbed pretty good. It looked like somebody had thrown the blood in buckets; it was everywhere—the floor, walls, ceiling. We carried him to the hospital in our arms; we got covered with blood. I had blood all over my pants and covering my white shirt. After we left the hospital, we walked up the corridor to go to the lieutenant's office before we went home to change clothes. We were up by the gym corridor when two convicts came around that corner—you know where I mean [connecting the gym corridor to main corridor]. They saw us and fainted; they just stopped in their tracks, looked and fainted right there in the corridor. I called the hospital for some smelling salts. It was the funniest thing you ever seen.

Senior officer specialist Larry Bert recounted this incident at the FPC-Boron, California:

Two officers responded. One of them stepped in blood and tracked it all around, down steps and up steps, all over. The FBI investigated and wanted the shoes which made the bloody tracks, thinking that the owner was the perp. They searched everywhere and they couldn't be found. One week later, while sitting in the office and looking at a photo of the footprints, Lt. Cook looked up and saw the shoes on the feet of the officer who was sitting at a desk with his feet up. The hack had seven pairs of shoes, and it wasn't until a week later that he wore the shoes again!

Racial jokes are surprisingly rare. Jokes with a racist twist aren't told by white staffers to black convicts or to black staff. And when they are told among whites, they are told quietly.

Just after a noon meal one day, an experienced white hack said to me: "What's long, black, and stinks?" I said, "I don't know." Smiling, he look at me: "Diet line at Lompoc!" Then he asked: "What do you call a white man surrounded by a thousand blacks?" "Warden," he said. I didn't hear any jokes, told by black hacks or white hacks, about white convicts.

No one wants racial trouble among staff, or between staff and convicts. Lompoc's convicts know that racial violence can quickly get out of hand. Frankie:

> A black may get into it with a Mexican or a white. Then it leads to retaliation and random violence. A black hits a Mex, then a Mex hits the first black he sees. It's silly sick shit. Look, man, when your name is good, there's respect in spite of race. A stand-up dude reputation carries from the street to the joint and back to the street. Some guys come up together through juvie [juvenile hall] or may be from different sets [gangs], but now [in USP-Lompoc] they have a mutual respect for each other. You gotta remember . . . even if you can righteous whip a guy's ass, he's always a threat to you. So if you don't want to take him out [kill him], leave him alone.

Convicts, including Eddie, said interethnic or interracial convict fights were usually founded on personal issues. "I don't like niggers," said a white convict, "but being a nigger doesn't make a dude an asshole or a punk, and that's what's gonna get 'em hit." Frankie added that "hot-nose'n [meddling] and disrespect will get a dude in trouble, not his skin color."

Rapport among staffers is often expressed as humorous sexual banter, but, on one occasion an inmate was involved. About 7:45 a.m., the main corridor officer was shaking down Gorgeous, a well-known homosexual and drunk, "who is so ugly they call him Gorgeous," said a line hack. Gorgeous had joking relationships with several staffers.

After leaving his food service job, Gorgeous was walking down the main corridor. Thinking that Gorgeous might be carrying stolen food, the main corridor officer stopped him for a shakedown. The officer was standing behind Gorgeous, bent over and patting down his legs. Another employee walked by and goosed the officer, causing him to quickly straighten up. As he did, the jokester yelled to Gorgeous: "Hey,

Gorgeous, he almost stuck his dick up your ass." Sexual joking like this is uncommon between correctional staffers and convicts, but nonsexual joking is common between inmates and their unit officers, unit team members, and work-crew supervisors, usually signaling good rapport.

Similarly, the use of obscenities is verbally stylized in conversations between inmates and staffers who share good rapport. Kidding, laughing, and joking between them ends when a staffer says, "Get out of here, you fucking asshole!" or "Get the fuck out of here!" or "Get the fuck out of my face!" Then, after the inmate has walked away, the staffer may add, "He's not a bad guy . . . for a convict." In serious conversations, line staffers (including work-crew supervisors) never use personal obscenities with inmates; there is no name calling.

This type of verbal banter rarely occurs between inmates and low-ranking line staff or between inmates and UMs and CMs or between inmates and administrators; it only occurs between inmates and work-crew supervisors, counselors, and senior correctional staff.

Line hacks or lieutenants never shake hands with convicts. Should a line staffer get too chummy (as signaled by too much touching or by hand shakes), people might think that he is too close to convicts, and thus too susceptible to manipulation. Although hand shaking between correctional staff and inmates is rare, unit management staff do shake hands with unit inmates.

Staff-convict verbal joking is sometimes accompanied by very slight hand gestures, which fall just short of touching. Even if inmates and staffers don't share a joking relationship, slight nonaggressive hand movements signal good rapport or the amiable resolution of a staff-inmate problem. Otherwise, a cautious staffer will touch an inmate only after telling him that he is going to be touched and what is to happen. Unannounced touching may set off serious trouble.

CUSTODY
A Growing American Industry

HUMANE PRISONS: OUR ONLY CHOICE

As a cultural anthropologist, my interest in prisons stems from a major cultural fact in American society: America produces a lot of violent people. No other advanced industrialized society, except for South Africa, suffers from violence as America does (Currie, 1985: 19).

Almost six million people were victims of violent crime in both 1984 and 1985 (Bureau of Justice Statistics, 1986a and 1986b). The risk of homicide in America is seven to ten times higher than it is in Japan or in most European countries (Currie, 1985: 5). In America everyone, regardless of race, ethnicity, or sex stands a good chance of being murdered (see Langan and Innes, 1985).

Americans have been surrounded by criminal violence and have reacted to it by imprisoning violent people to a greater and greater extent. This is perfectly understandable, because positive community-level efforts to curb crime haven't worked. America imprisons criminals at a higher rate than any other Western industrialized society (Currie, 1985: 28). Since 1850, America's incarceration rate has increased over 700%. In a little more than a century, America has gone from a scant 6,737 inmates, and an incarceration rate of 29 per 100,000 people (Cahalan, 1986), to 570,519 inmates in 1987, and an incarceration rate of 220 per 100,000 (Bureau of Justice Statistics, News Release, 1987). From 1980 to 1986, America's state and federal prison population increased by 65.7% (Greenfeld, 1987: 1). Between 1985 and 1986 alone, the state prisoner population grew by 8.6%, and the federal prison population grew by 11.7% (Greenfeld, 1987: 2). Even so, Assistant Attorney General in the Department of Justice Lois Haight Herrington wrote in the *Washington Post* (February 15, 1986), that America's justice system is sending too few felons to prison. It is depressing that we have no reason to believe that the crime or imprisonment rate will decline in the future.

Americans show righteous indignation when it comes to criminals, brutal crime, and the use of prison to keep violent criminals off the street (see Irwin, 1985: 73). When they see the bloody mess and the destruction of families left behind by wanton violent crime, Americans react with horror and shock. "Lock up the bastards, and throw away the key . . . let 'em suffer, like they made other people suffer . . . who cares if they are in inhumane, overcrowded, and filthy prisons?" Their reaction might be understandable, but it's irrational.

America needs a rational approach to imprisonment. When our tax dollars are used to build prisons, we are buying shares in the business of custody. Over recent years, we have been making a substantial investment. As of July 1987, there were approximately 600 state prisons, under the jurisdiction of state and territorial governments, and 46 federal prisons. Despite this, prison overcrowding remains the greatest concern of state and federal correctional officials. At the end of 1986, the overcrowded conditions in state prisons forced 17 states to house 13,770 in local jails (Woldman, 1987:3). The federal prison system is 56% over capacity, and state and federal prisoner populations continue to expand (Woldman, 1987: 2). By 2002, the federal prison population may be as high as 156,000 (Block and Rhodes, 1987: 6).

Thirty-nine states are spending approximately $3 billion in prison building programs, with each new cell costing between $15,200 and $15,700, depending on land costs and institution security level; 15% to 20% of inmates require high cost, maximum-security facilities (Woldman, 1987: 5). A maximum-security prison cell costs $75,000 or more to construct; conservatively estimated, yearly operating costs per maximum-security inmate are $15,000 to $20,000 (Currie, 1985: 89). Despite these high costs, we need high-security cells.

Irwin and Austin (1987: 12) suggest that "30 percent of those now sent to prison have been convicted of crimes of violence." And that is the low estimate. The Bureau of Justice (1987) estimated that 95% of state prisoners in 1979 were convicted of a violent crime or were recidivists. DiIulio (1987) reported that 90% of prison inmates and almost half of all jail inmates are violent criminals, recidivists, or violent recidivists.

If criminals are caught and imprisoned, they serve very little time. Even when serious-felony offenders are taken off the street and sent to prison, they do an average of about two and a half to four years of actual prison time (Koppel, 1984; also see Martin, 1988). In 1981, about two-thirds (67.1%) of the murderers released from state prisons served less than 7 years; rapists served a median sentence of 33 months, and only one in every 28 rapists served more than 10 years (Greenfeld and Minor-Harper, 1984).

In 1983, state inmates released from life sentences served median sentences of eight years and seven months, including jail time; 20% of lifers served less than three years. Almost 25% of inmates released from a life sentence had served time before on a felony conviction (Bureau of Justice Statistics, 1987; also see Klein and Caggiano, 1986; Petersilia et al., 1986; Petersilia, 1987).

Recidivism is a recurring problem in the crime-and-prison cycle, and recent high incarceration rates and longer sentences have created a large population of middle-aged convicts, which has added to the problem (Austin and McVey, 1988: 5-6). (For example, almost 80% of USP-Lompoc's inmate population is between 30 and 69 years old.)

In America, where few people have lifetime job security, middle age is a tough time to change careers. It's even more difficult for released convicts who are in their 40s, 50s, 60s, and 70s (see Blumstein and Cohen, 1987: 991; also see Blumstein et al., 1988; Gottfredson and Hirschi, 1986; cf. Flanagan, 1983; Jensen, 1977; Petersilia and Honig, 1980; Wolfgang, 1961). It is doubtful whether hundreds of thousands of former convicts can compete successfully in the job market.

America is now in the costly, risky, and big business of custody. On any day, 3.2 million people are held by America's criminal justice system—on probation or on parole, in juvenile institutions, in city and county jails, and in state and federal prisons (Irwin and Austin, 1987: 7; also see Austin and Tillman, 1987).

Prisons are service businesses (Grosser, 1960: 130), serving 850,000 imprisoned people: 530,000 prisoners are in federal and state prisons; 235,000 other criminals are in city and county jails; and another 85,000 young criminals are housed in juvenile facilities (Irwin and Austin, 1987: 7). All prisoners must be provided with housing and food, security, medical and dental care, education, recreational facilities, and work ("rehabilitation") opportunities.

High prison costs, along with evidence that imprisonment probably doesn't deter serious crime (Currie, 1985), have moved people to consider alternative forms of sentencing, particularly for nonviolent offenders (Petersilia et al., 1985; Petersilia et al., 1986; Jamel, 1987; Etzioni, 1987). Even so, there are still tens of thousands of violent criminals who do require maximum-security treatment.

What will America do, in coming decades, with tens of thousands of seriously violent, high-risk criminals who commit armed robbery, murder, and rape in American communities? What will America do with its high-risk criminals who have already spent years or decades in penitentiaries, serving time for violent crimes? The fact is that, no matter what we do, prisons just keep returning violent criminals to the streets. Some of these men should not get out of prison.

As difficult as it may be to provide *objective* answers, one thing is certain: It costs less to have state and federal prisons that are professionally managed and that provide humane conditions for offenders than to have abusive prisons. We have no other rational choice. Housing criminals in inhumane prisons is too costly to sustain, and, moreover, our inhumane treatment of criminals violates their constitutional rights. It's simply illegal to mistreat America's miscreants.

Contrary to the popular but incorrect belief, a miserable prison doesn't "teach 'em a lesson." Abusive prisons don't reform (rehabilitate) convicts into living straight lifestyles, nor do they scare (deter) convicts into becoming decent people. Abusive prisons do, however, eventually release a majority of their convicts back into communities all over America. And when they do, the results are dreadful—to the rest of us.

> Increasingly, the realization is dawning, even in these conservative times, that not only inmates, but citizens also, pay too high a price for a system that brutalizes the people who live in it. . . . When brutalized prisoners are eventually released, they may take out pent-up anger and frustration on innocent, law-abiding citizens [Lerner, 1986: 44].

America's prisons must stop being "black holes" on our landscape. Except perhaps for those in the corrections business, Americans don't know what happens inside maximum-security prisons; they don't understand the serious, even fatal consequences of failed correctional management, particularly among violent criminals.

Blunders in correctional management are highly visible and always costly (see Corrections Compendium April, 1985). In late 1986, a House Judiciary Subcommittee ordered a $40-million renovation at the USP-Atlanta to improve living conditions for the institution's Mariel Cuban detainees (*Newsweek,* December 7, 1987). On November 21, 1987, 1,104 Cuban detainees at the Alien Detention Center, Oakdale, Louisiana, rioted, holding 26 hostages for 8 days. A State Department announcement that many detainees would be deported to Cuba allegedly prompted the riot. Two days later, another 1,100 Cuban detainees at USP-Atlanta rioted during lunch and took 90 hostages for 12 days. One Cuban was killed and 30 were injured. A $40-million renovation project went up in smoke. According to a Bureau official, in an interview with me, the Cuban riots caused $137 million in damage.

Wholesale destruction of prison facilities is dramatic and costly, but it is rare, and it is not the reason that prisons have failed to become the cost-efficient, humane, and nonviolent institutions they should be. Rather, recurring small-scale social violence often squelches efforts to operate prisons (particularly maximum-security penitentiaries) as anything but violent, high-cost human warehouses. Fights, inmate assaults on staff and inmates, inmates killing inmates and staff, prison gang and contract killing, and staff malfeasance (food and property theft, weapon and drug smuggling to inmates, staffers' inattention to inmates' social and emotional problems, staffers' physical abuse of inmates, and racial and ethnic discrimination), seriously hamper administrative and legislative efforts to operate prisons as cost-efficient, humane institutions.

Simply building more prisons doesn't ensure their professional management. Effective correctional ("custodial") cultures must be carefully planned and sculpted with the same degree of concern and thoughtfulness that guides corporate strategic planning, where profits are a measure of success. In the business of custody, however, the currency of success is not profit. Successful prisons are silent: no riots, no killings, and no escapes. There is also an informal measure of correctional success, but one less easily discernible to prison outsiders: it is "felt in the air" by the men and women who work inside maximum-security penitentiaries every day. Success for them is walking alone through a cellblock, night or day, and knowing that there is only a slight chance of being assaulted; success is looking forward to each day's work, instead of dreading it; and success is knowing that they can talk to an inmate without being insulted, spat on, or punched.

Positive advances can be made in the management of maximum-security penitentiaries, as well as in the management of jails, juvenile institutions, and minimum- and medium-security prisons, but first legislators and upper-echelon correctional administrators must accept the responsibility for having promoted prison mismanagement. They have allowed prisons to be overcrowded and have tolerated inadequately trained prison managers. Unless we take positive steps toward curbing correctional mismanagement, tens of billions of Americans' tax dollars which are now being spent on prison construction will eventually be wasted.

IT'S TIME FOR PROGRESSIVE CHANGE

Conservativism is the hallmark of correctional culture, and it has been contributing to failures in prison management. We must become more progressive in hiring, training, retaining, and compensating employees at each staff level. Correctional systems, like companies, prefer to promote from within, but in the business of custody, this custom often promotes stale management ideas and very often promulgates destructive attitudes in correctional cultures.

A senior administrator in one of America's largest state correctional systems told me, "The problem in our major institutions is in middle-level management and upper-level administration. Our system promotes internally, so guys who were guards 15 and 20 years, who came up in the system beating convicts and thinking inmates were shit, are now running the prisons. And we can't get rid of them!"

It's time that correctional agencies, like private businesses, open themselves to new, highly experienced talent for upper-level positions. And, too, correctional systems must compete more actively for top students, coming from colleges, universities, and the military. Energetic, intelligent people are out there, but violent prison stereotypes deter those young men and women from pursuing careers in the business of custody.

Changes in management practices and in a prison's organizational culture must begin at the top of the prison hierarchy. Regaining and maintaining administrative and managerial control of a prison have to begin and end in the warden's office. Wardens are slumlords if they allow rats and high levels of violence in their prisons.

Daily operations in a prison or jail are highly personal and often highly emotional. Because of that, staff objectivity is the single most important organizational value in correctional management, especially among inmate supervisors at the line-staff level. But prisons and jails are often so desperate for line staff that they'll take virtually anyone. "If a person can walk in, sign his name, and put on a uniform, he's got a job," said a manager in a large state prison. I've heard exactly the same sentiment from managers and line staff in major jails. This must end. When a personnel net is cast over all unemployed people, it catches racists, among others. A racist line staffer in a prison is a short fuse on a big bomb.

Good prison management, as well as a change of attitude about using prisons to America's advantage, can transform costly abusive joints into financially self-sustaining, humane communities of streetmen and streetwomen who, for whatever reason, use crime as their form of self-expression. America has hundreds of prisons, and hundreds more are now being constructed. Let's think of how to use prisons creatively in order to benefit free society, serve the hundreds of thousands of inmates who already live in prisons, and attend to the needs of the tens of thousands of men and women, hacks and convicts alike, who will be part of prison life in the future.

Despite arguments over the usefulness of imprisonment as a mechanism of crime control, it is imperative to transform awful and costly prisons into productive and financially self-sustaining institutions, like USP-Lompoc. Prison industries can play a role in that transformation. I completely agree with Funke (1986): "Prison industries are not the cure-all for the correctional ills that plague this nation. . . . We believe that prison industries can significantly improve the quality of life in a correctional system, with benefits for staff, victims, taxpayers, and offenders" (p. 22).

Industry in prison is in its formative stages (Funke, 1986; Mullen, 1985; Sexton et al., 1985). USP-Lompoc is an example of how prison industry can make sound financial and social sense. But if prison industries are to grow successfully in popularity and in profitability, a growing work force of professional administrators and managers will be required in all future industrial state prisons and jails.

We don't need private organizations to manage and operate our prisons (see DiIulio, 1988). We do need strong recruitment programs and stronger financial incentives to get the best business students and social science students to accept career positions in the business of state and federal custody. State correctional agencies can benefit by actively recruiting retired Unicor employees and retired federal administrators and managers for responsible in-prison positions. The federal prison system can benefit by lifting its age-35 hiring restriction (all employees must be hired by their thirty-fifth birthday), and by offering market-competitive salaries for business and professional positions, especially in high-cost-of-living urban areas.

The financial and social benefits of prison industries are now obvious. Effective use of inmate labor can cut yearly in-prison operating costs; it can be used to generate funds for criminals' victims; it can be channeled to alimony and child-support obligations; and it can help finance youth rehabilitation programs for urban, poverty-level children. Perhaps, with a well-organized federal and interstate effort, profits from factories with fences can generate funds to shore-up social programs for youth job training and education programs. In the long haul, profits from inmate labor can save many lives, including those of the men who generate those profits.

In factory-prisons such as USP-Lompoc, long-term incarceration of high-risk, violent criminals is cost effective and humane. If prisons aren't already humane places, then we must now devote our attention to transforming the awful ones into productive social institutions. Putting factories in prisons is a great way to begin.

Glossary

AB. *Aryan Brotherhood.*

ARS. *Administrative Remedy System.*

AWO. *Associate warden for operations.*

AWP. *Associate warden for programs.*

Beef. *A new legal charge or a personal gripe against someone. Used in the expressions, "to have a beef [with someone]," and "to caught a new beef," or "to caught a beef," used by inmates to mean "acquiring a legal charge."*

Bloods. *A Los Angeles street gang composed of numerous local neighborhood groups, each called a "set." At USP-Lompoc, there were several Bloods of the Piru set.*

Blue Book. *A blue vinyl notebook, kept in the lieutenant's office, which compiles mug-shots and brief criminal histories of the penitentiary's highest-risk inmates, those who have had histories of prison violence, or escape.*

Body Alarm. *A method of emergency communication. A body alarm is a device, about the size of a two-way radio, which transmits an electronic signal, received in the institution's central control room on a body-alarm board which gives a precise location of the point of origin of the signal. This red device is carried by all staffers who supervise inmates and by women work within the confines of the inmates' living, working, and recreation area.*

Brew. *Prison made wine. Also called "homebrew" or "pruno."*

Camper. *An inmate in a federal prison camp.*

CC. *Correctional counselors.*

CCS. *Chief of Correctional Services. The "captain."*

CM. *Case manager.*

CO. *Correctional officer.*

CIMS. *Central Inmate Monitoring System.*

Commissary. *Inmate store.*

Compound. *The area within the secure perimeter of the penitentiary.*

Rear Compound. *Often used to designate the yard area, Unicor, and mechanical services.*

Club Fed. *Used commonly by inmates and staff to refer to Federal Prison Camps. Also used by staff to refer to the Federal Law Enforcement Training Center at Glynco, Georgia.*

Control Unit. *The highest security cellblock at USP-Marion.*

Corridor. *The main corridor is the penitentiary's principal thoroughfare. The work corridor leads from the main corridor, at its far east end, to the Unicor factories and mechanical services shops in the penitentiary's rear compound.*

Crime Partner. *A person with whom an inmate committed a crime.*

Crips. *A Los Angeles black street gang, composed of numerous local, neighborhood groups, each called a "set." At USP-Lompoc, there were several Crips of the Compton Crip set, also known as "CCs."*

Custody Level. *A measure of an inmate's dangerousness to himself and to others. Inmates in a federal penitentiary are either "Maximum" or "In" custody; in federal correctional institutions, inmates are "In" custody; and in the federal prison camps, inmates are "out" or "community" custody.*

Disruptive Group. *The Federal Prison System's official designation for a prison gang. The Federal Prison System recognizes five disruptive groups: the Aryan Brotherhood; the Mexican Mafia; La Nuestra Familia; the Black Guerilla Family; and the Texas Syndicate.*

Dry Cell. *A cell in the hospital where inmates who are suspected of smuggling drugs into the penitentiary from the visiting room are sequestered.*

Eme. *Mexican Mafia, classified by the Bureau of a Disruptive Group.*

FCI. *Federal Correctional Institution. A federal prison of "medium" security.*

Fish. *A new inmate or staffer.*

Flats. *The first, or ground, level of a cellblock.*

FLETC. *Federal Law Enforcement Training Center at Glynco, Georgia.*

FPC. *Federal Prison Camp. Federal prison of minimum security.*

FPS. *Federal Prison System.*

Gang-Banging. *Term used by street gang members designating gang membership and alluding to intergang fighting.*

Grill. *A iron-bar door.*

Hack. *A correctional officer. The most common term used by Lompoc's correctional officers, particularly experienced men. Other terms, including turnkey and screw are also heard, but when they are used, they are used in stories or some other form of stylized verbal speech.*

Homebrew. *Prison-made wine. Also called "brew" or "pruno."*

Hype Kit. *An inmate-made hypodermic needle.*

IDC. *Institution Discipline Committee. The discipline committee that reviews all serious cases of inmate misconduct.*

IFT. *Institution Familiarization Training.*

In-Back. *Used by USP-Lompoc staffers to designate inmate living and recreation areas, Unicor factories, and mechanical services shops.*

Ink. *A slang term for a tattoo.*

Inside. *Staffers' term for USP-Lompoc which distinguishes the penitentiary from FPC-Lompoc. Also used by staff to designate the inmates' living, working, and recreation areas, as opposed to the penitentiary's "public," or up-front areas, where visitors are permitted.*

I-unit. *The cellblock housing inmates in administrative detention and disciplinary segregation.*

I-unit Trap. *A security entrance which separates the main corridor from the housing area in I-unit.*

Iron Pile. *The inmates' weight-lifting area.*

Jigger. *An inmate lookout.*

Joint. *A prison.*

Juice. *Used by inmates to refer to "homemade wine." Used by staff to refer to the political clout of administrators.*

Living Unit. *A cellblock.*

Lockup. *A term staffers and inmates use for I-unit, Lompoc's administrative detention and disciplinary segregation cellblock.*

Lockup Move. *An inmate's intentional violation of an institution rule(s) serious enough to have himself placed in administrative detention.*

Lockdown. *A time when all inmates are locked in their cells.*

Mainline. *A reference to the general inmate population, excluding those inmates in administrative detention and disciplinary segregation.*

OJT. *On-the-job Training.*

Outside. *Staffers' term for FPC-Lompoc.*

PA. *Physician's Assistant.*

PC. *Protective custody.*

PC-up. *An inmate's request to have himself placed in administrative detention; an inmate feeling that he is in jeopardy will "pc-up." Also, an inmate's intentional violation of an institution rule(s) serious enough to have himself placed in administrative detention. This case is more often called a "lockup move."*

Piru. *A Los Angeles street gang. A Blood gang, sometimes referred to as "Anti-Crips."*

Post. *A work location.*

Prohibited Act. *A regulation guiding inmate behavior.*

Pruno. *Prison-made wine. This term is used most often by former state prisoners. Also called "homebrew" or "brew."*

Rack. *"To open or close." Used as a request: "Give me a rack" or emphatically, "Rack me out," meaning, "open the grill." The emphatic expression, "Rack 'em," means, "Close the cell door(s)!"*

Range. *A row of cells in a cellblock.*

Rep. *Reputation.*

Road Dog. *An inmate's "street" companion, who also may be his crime partner.*

Roster. *A list identifying the staff and their institution jobs or posts.*

Sanction. *The formal "punishment" for violating a prohibited act.*

Security Level. *This refers to the architectural layout of a prison. High security level federal prisons, such as USP-Lompoc, are surrounded either by a wall or a double, sometimes triple, perimeter fence. Low security level prisons, such as FPC-Lompoc, have neither a wall nor a fence surrounding it.*

Set. *A neighborhood. A set designates membership in a street gang, as when inmates say they are "in the same set." Set is also used in the expression, "to fall back on the set," meaning, "to leave prison and return home."*

Shank. *A knife made by inmates. A shank which is made of heavy wire used for bed springs is often called a "sticker." Some inmates refer to shanks, and other prison made weapons, as their "shit," as in, "I'm going to get my shit." "Shit" also is used for "penis," as it is in street talk.*

Shot. *Incident report.*

SIS. *Special Investigations Supervisor.*

Team. *Unit team.*

The Board. *Federal Parole Commission. Inmates use "the Board" in the expression, "I've got to give [bring] the board ten," meaning he must serve ten years on his sentence before the parole commission will consider his request for parole. After an inmate has been in prison for many years, he might use the expression, "I've got ten to board," meaning he has already served ten years, and must serve more time before parole.*

The Street. *Commonly used to refer to the urban neighborhood where an inmate grew up or hangs out.*

Tier. *The upper floors of a cellblock.*

Tip. *A tip is a group of two or three inmates who enjoy "hanging out" together (see Irwin 1980: 60). Tips are informal, loosely arranged groups. Tips don't have a charter and they break up often, with inmates regrouping into different tips.*

Tower. *A perimeter guard tower manned by a correctional officer twenty-four hours a day.*

Triple Deuce. *A triple deuce is a method of emergency communication, deriving its name from dialing "2-2-2" on any telephone in a federal prison. Triple deuce calls are received on special, red telephones in the prison's central control room, the lieutenant's office, the associate wardens' offices, and the warden's office.*

UDC. *Unit Discipline Committee. A discipline committee hears all cases of inmate misconduct, referring the most serious cases to the Institution Discipline Committee.*

UM. *Unit manager.*

Unicor. *A U.S. government-owned, profit-making corporation of light industries.*

Up-Front. *The penitentiary's public areas in which visitors are permitted, including inmate visiting areas and the administrative and business offices.*

USP. *United States Penitentiary. A high-security-level federal penitentiary housing the most violent inmates or inmates who are security risks, such as inmates who have already escaped from one or more federal prison.*

Watch. *A work shift.*

References

Adler, Nancy J., and Mariann Jelinek (1986) "Is 'organization culture' concept bound?" Human Resource Management 25 (1): 73-90.

Adler, Patricia A., and Peter Adler (1987) Membership Roles in Field Research. Qualitative Research Methods, Series 6. Newbury Park, CA: Sage.

Austin, James, and Aaron David McVey (1988) The NCD Prison Population Forecast: The Growing Imprisonment of America. San Francisco: National Council on Crime and Delinquency.

Austin, James, and Robert Tillman (1987) Ranking the Nation's Most Punitive States. San Francisco: National Council on Crime and Delinquency.

Beck, James L. (1981) Employment, Community Treatment Center Placement, and Recidivism: A Study of Released Federal Offenders. Federal Probation (December): 3-12.

Bernard, H. Russell (1988) Research Methods in Cultural Anthropology. Newbury Park, CA: Sage.

Blau, Judith R., Stephen C. Light, and Mitchell Chamlin (1986) "Individual and contextual effects on stress and job satisfaction. A study of prison staff." Work and Occupations 13 (1): 131-156.

Block, Michael K. and William M. Rhodes (1987) The Impact of Federal Sentencing Guidelines. Report 205. National Institute of Justice. (September/ October): 2-7.

Blumstein, Alfred and Jacqueline Cohen (1987) "Characterizing criminal careers." Science 237 (August): 985-991.

Blumstein, Alfred, Jacqueline Cohen, and David P. Farrington (1988) "Criminal career research: its value for criminologists." Criminology 26 (1): 1-35.

B'nai B'rith (1986) Extremism Targets the Prisons. Special Report. New York: Anti-Defamation League, Fact-Finding Department, Civil Rights Division.

Bowker, Lee H. (1980) Prison Victimization. New York: Elsevier.

Bowker, Lee H. (1986) "The victimization of prisoners by staff members," pp. 134-157 in Kenneth C. Haas and Geoffrey P. Alpert (eds.) The Dilemmas of Punishment. Prospect Heights, IL: Waveland.

Bureau of Justice Statistics (1986a) Criminal Victimization in the United States, 1984. A National Crime Survey Report. Washington, DC: Department of Justice.

Bureau of Justice Statistics (1986b) Criminal Victimization 1985. Bulletin. Washington, DC: Department of Justice.

Bureau of Justice Statistics (1987) News Release. Washington, DC: Department of Justice.

Bureau of Justice Statistics (1987) BJS Data Report, 1986. Washington, DC: Department of Justice.

Burger, Warren E. (1986) "Factories with fences," pp. 349-356 in Kenneth C. Haas and Geoffrey P. Alpert (eds.) The Dilemmas of Punishment. Prospect Heights, IL: Waveland.

Cahalan, Margaret Werner (1986) Historical Corrections Statistics in the United States, 1850-1984. Washington, DC: Bureau of Justice Statistics.

California Department of Corrections (1985) Violence in California Prisons. Report of the Task Force on Violence, Special Housing, and Gang Management. Sacramento, CA.

Camp, George M. and Camille Graham Camp (1985) Prison Gangs: Their Extent, Nature and Impact on Prisons. U.S. Department of Justice, Office of Legal Policy. Washington, DC: Government Printing Office.

Campbell, Anne (1984) The Girls in the Gang. A Report from New York City. New York: Basil Blackwell.

Campbell, Anne (1986) "The street and violence," pp. 115-132 in Anne Campbell and John J. Gibbs (eds.) Violent Transactions: The Limits of Personality. New York: Basil Blackwell.

Canon, Scott (1988a) $17 Million Operation Exerts Moderate Impact. Santa Barbara News-Press, March 27.

Canon, Scott (1988b) Many Have Tried, But Few Have Escaped. Santa Barbara News-Press, March 27.

Canon, Scott (1988c) Inmate Families Get a Helping Hand. Santa Barbara News-Press, March 28.

Carroll, Leo (1974) Hacks, Blacks, and Cons: Race Relations in a Maximum Security Prison. Lexington, MA: Lexington.

Cheek, F. E. and M. D. Miller (1983) "The experience of stress for correctional officers: a double-bind theory of correctional stress." Journal of Criminal Justice 2: 105-120.

Clemmer, Donald (1958) The Prison Community (1940). New York: Holt, Rinehart & Winston.

Cloward, Richard A. (1960) "Social control in the prison," pp. 20-48 in Donald Cressey (ed.) Theoretical Studies in Social Organization of the Prison. New York: Social Science Research Council.

Cohen, Albert K. (1976) "Prison violence: a sociological perspective," pp. 3-22 in A. K. Cohen et al. (eds.) Prison Violence. Lexington, MA: Lexington.

Cohen, Albert K., George F. Cole, and Robert G. Bailey [eds.] (1976) Prison Violence. Lexington, MA: Lexington.

Corrections Compendium (1985) Reported Riots/Disturbances, Vol. 9, no. 10. Lincoln, NE: Contact Center, Inc.

Cressey, Donald (1968) "Contradictory directives in complex organizations: the case of the prison," in Lawrence Hazelrigg (ed.) Prison Within Society. Garden City, NY: Anchor.

Crouch, Ben M. [ed.] (1980) The Keepers: Prison Guards and Contemporary Corrections. Springfield, IL: Charles C Thomas.

Crouch, Ben M. (1986) "Prison guards on the line," pp. 177-206 in Kenneth C. Haas and Geoffrey P. Alpert (eds.) The Dilemmas of Punishment. Prospect Heights, IL: Waveland.

Crouch, Ben M. and G. Alpert (1982) "Sex and occupational socialization among prison guards: a longitudinal study." Criminal Justice and Behavior 9 (2): 159-176.

Crouch, Ben M. and James W. Marquart (1980) "On becoming a prison guard," pp. 63-106 in Ben M. Crouch (ed.) The Keepers: Prison Guards and Contemporary Corrections. Springfield, IL: Charles C Thomas.

Cullen, Francis T., Bruce G. Link, Nancy T. Wolfe, and James Frank (1985) "The social dimensions of correctional officer stress." Justice Quarterly 2 (4): 505-533.

Currie, Elliott (1985) Confronting Crime. New York: Pantheon.

Curtis, Lynn A. (1975) Violence, Race and Culture. Lexington, MA: Lexington.

Dave Bell Associates (1980) Hard Time. Mag-net Distributors. Los Angeles: RKO General.

Davidson, Theodore (1974) Chicano Prisoners: The Key to San Quentin. New York: Holt, Rinehart & Winston.

DeCordoba, Jose (1987) "White-collar inmates find that tennis and good food do not a prison unmake." Wall Street Journal, June 9.

DiIulio, John J. (1987) "True penal reform can save money." Wall Street Journal, September 28.

DiIulio, John J. (1988) Private Prisons. National Institute of Justice, Crime File. Washington, DC: Department of Justice.

Duffee, David (1980) Correctional Management: Change and Control in Correctional Organizations. Englewood Cliffs, NJ: Prentice-Hall.

Ekland-Olson, Sheldon (1986) "Crowding, social control, and prison violence: evidence from the post-Ruiz years in Texas." Law & Society Review 20 (3): 289-421.

Elder, Glen (1985) Life Course Dynamics. Ithaca, NY: Cornell University Press.

Ellis, Desmond (1984) Crowding and Prison Violence. Criminal Justice and Behavior 11 (3): 277-307.

Emerson, Ryan Quade (1985) "Black/White/Latino: prison gangs." American Survival Guide (August): 14.

Etzioni, Amitai (1987) "In praise of public humiliation." Wall Street Journal, April 2.

Farrington, D. P., and C. P. Nutall (1980) "Prison size, overcrowding, prison violence and recidivism." Journal of Criminal Justice 8 (4): 221-231.

Federal Bureau of Prisons (1981) Program Statement 3420.5 (Standards of Employee Conduct and Responsibility).

Federal Bureau of Prisons (1982) Program Statement 5270.5 (Inmate Discipline and Special Housing Units).

Federal Bureau of Prisons (1984) Anniversary Celebration. Unicor: USP-Lompoc.

Federal Bureau of Prisons (1984) Program Statement, USP-Lompoc, Supplement 5511.2 (Inmate Accountability).

Federal Bureau of Prisons (1985) Introduction to Correctional Techniques. Federal Law Enforcement Training Center, Glynco, GA.

Federal Bureau of Prisons (1985) Program Statement 5100.2. CN-8 (Custody/Security Classification).

Federal Bureau of Prisons (1986) Statistical Report, FY86. Washington, DC: Department of Justice.

Federal Bureau of Prisons (1986) Report 80.51 (Demographic Data for USP-Lompoc).

Federal Bureau of Prisons (1986) Correctional Services Report Comparison Report for July, August 26, 1986.

Ferdinand, Theodore (1987) "The methods of delinquency theory." Criminology 25 (4): 841-862.

Fernandez, James (1974) "The mission of metaphor in expressive culture." Current Anthropology 15: 119-145.

Fishman, Laura (1986) "Repeating the cycle of hard living and crime: wives' accommodations to husbands' parole performance." Federal Probation 50 (4): 44-54.

Fishman, Susan Hoffman and Albert S. Alissi (1975) "Strengthening families as natural support systems for offenders." Federal Probation (September): 16-21.

Flanagan, T. (1983) "Correlates of institutional misconduct among state prisoners: a research note." Criminology 21: 29-39.

Fleisher, Mark S. (1981) "The psychosocial dynamics of prison inmate families." Paper presented at the 80th American Anthropological Association conference.

Fleisher, Mark S. (1982) "The socialization of women and children into prison society." Paper presented at the 81st American Anthropological Association conference.

Fleisher, Mark S. (1983) "Review of 'who rules the joint? The changing political culture of maximum-security prisons in America.'" American Anthropologist 85 (3):716-717.

Fleisher, Mark S. (1985a) "Learning whose rules? Strategies of married life in a maximum security prison." Paper presented at the 84th American Anthropological Association conference.

Fleisher, Mark S. (1985b) Incident Report Handbook. USP-Lompoc.

Fleisher, Mark S. (1986a) Correctional Officers: Identification of Issues and Development of Intervention Strategies to Increase Morale and Reduce Resignations and Terminations at the United States Penitentiary, Lompoc, CA. Final Report. Bureau of Prisons, Research Office, Washington, DC.

Fleisher, Mark S. (1986b) Report Writing in the Legal Process. Annual Training Lesson, USP-Lompoc.

Fleisher, Mark S. and Dan McCarthy (1988) "The effects of wage earning on reducing serious violence among maximum-security federal inmates." Paper presented at the 40th American Society of Criminology conference.

Fox, James G. (1982) Organizational and Racial Conflict in Maximum-Security Prisons. Lexington, MA: Lexington.

Fujisaka, Sam, and John Grayzel (1978) "Partnership research: a case of divergent ethnographic styles in prison fieldwork." Human Organization 37 (2): 172-179.

Funke, Gail S. [ed.] (1986) National Conference on Prison Industries: Discussion and Recommendations. The National Center for Innovation in Corrections. Washington, DC: George Washington University, Division of Continuing Education.

Gaes, Gerald G. and William J. McGuire (1985) "Prison violence: the contribution of crowding versus other determinants of prison assault rates." Journal of Research in Crime and Delinquency 22 (1): 41-65.

Galan, Hector (1988) Shakedown in Santa Fe. Frontline.

Giallombardo, Rose (1966) Society of Women: A Study of a Women's Prison. New York: John Wiley.

Glaser, Daniel (1969) The Effectiveness of a Prison and Parole System. Indianapolis: Bobbs-Merrill.

Gleason, Sandra E. (1978) "Hustling: the 'inside' economy of a prison." Federal Probation (June): 32-40.

Goodstein, Lynne (1979) "Inmate adjustment to prison and the transition to community life." Journal of Research in Crime and Delinquency 16 (2): 246-272.

Gottfredson, Michael R. and Travis Hirschi (1986) "The true value of lambda would appear to be zero: an essay on career criminals, criminal careers, selective incapacitation, cohort studies, and related topics." Criminology 24: 213-233.

Greenfeld, Lawrence A. (1987) Prisoners in 1986. Bureau of Justice Statistics. Bulletin. Washington, DC: Department of Justice.

Greenfeld, Lawrence A. and Stephanie Minor-Harper (1984) Prison Admissions and Releases, 1981. Washington, DC: U.S. Department of Justice.

Greenwood, Peter W. and Susan Turner (1987) Selective Incapacitation Revisited: Why the High-Rate Offenders Are Hard to Predict. Santa Monica, CA: Rand Corporation.

Grosser, George H. (1960) "External setting and internal relations of the prison," pp. 130-144 in Donald Cressey (ed.) Theoretical Studies in Social Organization of the Prison. New York: Social Science Research Council.

Hagan, John and Alberto Palloni (1988) "Crimes in the life course." Criminology 26 (1): 87-100.

Harris, Marvin (1981) America Now: The Anthropology of a Changing Culture. New York: Simon & Schuster.

Hass, Kenneth C. and Geoffrey P. Alpert [eds.] (1986) The Dilemmas of Punishment. Prospect Heights, IL: Waveland.

Herrington, Lois Haight (1986) "Do we have enough prisons?" Washington Post, February 15.

Hershberger, Gregory L. (1979) "The development of the federal prison system." Federal Probation (December): 13-23.

Hilbert, Richard A. (1980) "Covert participant observation: on its nature and practice." Urban Life 9 (1): 51-77.

Hofer, Paul (1987) "Thematic apperceptive responses of two psychopathic groups." Ph.D. dissertation, California School of Professional Psychology, Berkeley, CA.

Holt, Norman and Donald Miller (1972) Explorations in Inmate-Family Relationships (January). Number 46. Sacramento, CA: California Department of Corrections.

Homer, Lee Eva (1978) "Inmate-family ties: desirable but difficult." Federal Probation (March):47-51.

Irwin, John (1970) The Felon. Englewood Cliffs, NJ: Prentice-Hall.

Irwin, John (1980) Prisons in Turmoil. Boston: Little, Brown.

Irwin, John (1985) The Jail: Managing the Underclass of American Society. Berkeley: University of California Press.

Irwin, John and James Austin (1987) It's About Time: Solving America's Prison Crowding Crisis. San Francisco: National Council on Crime and Delinquency.

Irwin, John and Donald Cressey (1962) "Thieves, convicts and the inmate culture." Social Problems 10: 142-155.

Jackson, Bruce (1984) Law and Disorder. Urbana: University of Illinois Press.

Jacobs, James B. (1974a) "Street gangs behind bars." Social Problems 21: 395-409.

Jacobs, James B. (1974b) "Participant observation in prison." Urban Life and Culture 3 (2): 221-240.

Jacobs, James B. (1976) "Prison violence and formal organization," pp. 79-87 in A. K. Cohen et al. (eds.) Prison Violence. Lexington, MA: Lexington.

Jacobs, James B. (1977) Stateville: A Penitentiary in Mass Society. Chicago: University of Chicago Press.

Jacobs, James B. (1983) New Perspectives on Prisons and Imprisonment. Ithaca, NY: Cornell University Press.

Jacobs, James B. and Mary Grear (1977) "Drop-outs and rejects: an analysis of the prison guard's revolving door." Criminal Justice Review 2 (2): 57-70.

Jacobs, James B. and Lawrence J. Kraft (1978) "Integrating the keepers: a comparison of black and white prison guards in Illinois." Social Problems 25: 304-318.

Jacobs, James B. and Lawrence J. Kraft (1983) "Race relations and guards' subculture," pp. 160-177 in James B. Jacobs (ed.) New Perspectives on Prisons and Imprisonment. Ithaca, NY: Cornell University Press.

Jamel, Latique A. (1987) "For many criminals, incarceration is not the answer." Wall Street Journal, April 2.

Janus, Michael, Jerome Mabli, and J. D. Williams (1986) "Security and custody: monitoring the Federal Bureau of Prison's classification system." Federal Probation (March): 35-41.

Jennison, Karen M. (1986) "The violent older offender: a research note." Federal Probation (December): 60-65.

Jensen, G. (1977) "Age and rule-breaking in prison: a test of sociocultural interpretations." Criminology 14: 555-568.

Klein, Stephen P. and Michael N. Caggiano (1986) The Prevalence, Predictability, and Policy Implications of Recidivism. Santa Monica, CA: Rand Corporation.

Koppel, Herbert (1984) Time Served in Prison. Bureau of Justice Statistics, Special Report. Washington, DC: U.S. Department of Justice.

Kotlowitz, Alex (1987) "Day-to-day violence takes a terrible toll on inner-city youth," Wall Street Journal, October 27.

Langan, Patrick A. and Christopher A. Innes (1985) The Risk of Violent Crime. Bureau of Justice Statistics, Special Report. Washington, DC: U.S. Department of Justice.

Lansing, Douglas, Joseph B. Bogan, and Loren Karacki (1977) "Unit management: implementing a different correctional approach." Federal Probation (March): 43-49.

Lasky, Gareth L., B. Carl Gordon, and David J. Srebalus (1986) "Occupational stressors among federal correctional officers working in different security levels." Criminal Justice and Behavior 13 (3): 317-327.

Lerner, Steve (1986) Bodily Harm: The Pattern of Fear and Violence at the California Youth Authority. Bolinas, CA: Common Knowledge.

Levine, Robert (1973) "Outsiders' judgments: an ethnographic approach to group differences in personality," pp. 388-397 in R. Naroll and R. Cohen (eds.) A Handbook of Method in Cultural Anthropology. New York: Columbia University Press.

Levinson, Robert B. and Roy E. Gerard (1973) "Functional units: a different correctional approach." Federal Probation (December): 8-16.

Levinson, Robert B. and J. D. Williams (1979) "Inmate classification: security/custody considerations." Federal Probation (March): 37-43.

Lindquist, Charles and John T. Whitehead (1986) "Burnout, job stress and job satisfaction among southern correctional officers: perceptions and causal factors." Journal of Offender Counseling, Services & Rehabilitation 10 (4): 5-26.

Lockwood, Daniel (1980) Prison Sexual Violence. New York: Elsevier.

Lockwood, Daniel (1982) "The contribution of sexual harassment to stress and coping in confinement," pp. 45-64 in Nicolette Parisi (ed.) Coping with Imprisonment. Beverly Hills, CA: Sage.

Lockwood, Daniel (1986) "Target violence," pp. 116-133 in Kenneth C. Haas and Geoffrey P. Alpert (eds.) The Dilemmas of Punishment. Prospect Heights, IL: Waveland.

Lombardo, Lucien X. (1981) Guards Imprisoned. New York: Elsevier.

Lompoc Record (1985) "Prison headband ruling stands." November 6.

Los Angeles Times (1986) "Sex, drugs and death: testimony in prison killing." January 26.

Mabli, J., C. S. Holley, J. Patrick, and J. Walls (1979) "Age and prison violence: increasing age heterogeneity as a violence-reducing strategy in prisons." Criminal Justice and Behavior 6 (2): 175-186.

MacKenzie, Doris Layton (1987) "Age and adjustment to prison: interaction with attitudes and anxiety." Criminal Justice and Behavior 14(4): 427-447.

Mahan, Sue (1982) "An 'orgy of brutality' at Attica and the 'killing ground' at Santa Fe: a comparison of prison riots," pp. 65-78 in Nicolette Parisi, (ed.) Coping with Imprisonment. Beverly Hills, CA: Sage.

Marquart, James W. (1986a) "Doing research in prison: the strengths and weaknesses of full participation as a guard." Justice Quarterly 3 (1): 15-32.

Marquart, James W. (1986b) "Prison guards and the use of physical coercion as a mechanism of prisoner control." Criminology 24 (2): 347-366.

Marquart, James W. and Julian B. Roebuck (1986) "Prison guards and snitches: social control in a maximum security institution," pp. 158-176 in Kenneth C. Haas and Geoffrey P. Alpert (eds.) The Dilemmas of Punishment. Prospect Heights, IL: Waveland.

Marsh, Peter and Anne Campbell [eds.] (1982) Aggression and Violence. New York: St. Martin's.

Martin, Dannie (1986) "AIDS: the view from a prison cell." San Francisco Chronicle, Sunday Punch, August 3.

Martin, Dannie (1987) "A place to shake the gloom of the cage." San Francisco Chronicle, Sunday Punch, October 18.

Martin, Dannie (1988) "The elusive 52-month killer." San Francisco Chronicle, Sunday Punch, April 10.

McArthur, Virginia (1974) "Inmate grievance mechanisms: a survey of 209 American prisons." Federal Probation (December): 41-47.

McCarthy, Dan (1986) Demographic Unit Custody/Security Analysis (July 1, 1986). Research Office, USP-Lompoc.

McCarthy, Dan (1987) Report on the Administrative Remedy Process (ARP) at USP-Lompoc. Research Office, USP-Lompoc.

McCleery, Richard (1960) "Communication patterns as bases of systems of authority and power," pp. 49-77 in Donald Cressey (ed.) Theoretical Studies in Social Organization of the Prison. New York: Social Science Research Council.

McVicar, John (1982) "Violence in prisons," pp. 200-214 in Peter Marsh and Anne Campbell (eds.) Aggression and Violence. New York: St. Martin's.

Megargee, Edwin I. (1976) "The prediction of dangerous behavior." Criminal Justice and Behavior 3 (1): 3-22.

Megargee, Edwin I. (1977) "The association of population density, reduced space, and uncomfortable temperatures with misconduct in a prison setting." American Journal of Community Psychology 5: 289-298.

Melnichak, Joseph M. (1986) "Chronicle of hate: a brief history of the radical right." Police Marksman (September/October): 42.

Miller, Jerome G. (1988) "Address given in acceptance of the August Vollmer Award." Criminologist 13 (1): 713-14, 18.

Minor, W. William and Michael Couriander (1979) "The postrelease trauma thesis: a reconsideration of the risk of early parole failure." Journal of Research in Crime and Delinquency (July): 273-293.

Moore, Joan (1978) Homeboys: Gangs, Drugs and Prison in the Barrios of Los Angeles. Philadelphia: Temple University Press.

Morris, Pauline (1965) Prisoners and Their Families. New York: Hart.

Mullen, Joan (1985) Corrections and the Private Sector. National Institute of Justice, Research in Brief. Washington, DC: National Institute of Justice.

Nacci, Peter L. and Thomas R. Kane (1982) Sex and Sexual Aggression in Federal Prisons. Office of Research, Progress Report. Washington, DC: Federal Bureau of Prisons.

Nacci, Peter L. and Thomas R. Kane (1983) "The incidence of sex and sexual aggression in federal prison." Federal Probation (December): 31-36.

Nacci, Peter L. and Thomas R. Kane (1984) "Sex and sexual aggression in federal prisons." Federal Probation (March): 46-53.

Nacci, Peter L., Hugh E. Teitelbaum, and Jerry Prather (1977a) "Population density and inmate misconduct rates in the federal prison system." Federal Probation (June): 27-38.

Nacci, Peter L., Hugh E. Teitelbaum, and Jerry Prather (1977b) Violence in Federal Prisons: The Effect of Population Density on Misconduct. National Institute of Justice/National Criminal Justice Reference Service.

National Law Enforcement Institute (1986) Gang Manual. Santa Rosa, CA: Author.

Newsweek (1986) "Inside America's toughest prison," October 6.

Newsweek (1987) "A Cuban explosion," December 7.

Newsweek (1988) "A 'west coast story,'" March 28.

Nowicki, Ed (1987) "Marielitos: the Cuban connection." Police (April): 38-40, 67, 69.

Olivero, Michael J. and James B. Roberts (1987) "Marion Federal Penitentiary and the 22-month lockdown: the crisis continues." Crime and Social Justice 27-28: 234-255.

Parisi, Nicolette (1982) "The prisoner's pressures and responses," pp. 9-26 in Nicolette Parisi (ed.) Coping with Imprisonment. Beverly Hills, CA: Sage.

Park, James W. (1976) "The organization of prison violence," pp. 89-96 in A. K. Cohen et al. (eds.) Prison Violence. Lexington, MA: Lexington.

Petersilia, Joan (1980) "Career criminal research," in N. Morris and M. Tonry (eds.) Crime and Justice, Vol. 2. Chicago: University of Chicago Press.

Petersilia, Joan (1987) "Probation and felony offenders." Federal Probation, (June): 56-61.

Petersilia, Joan and P. Honig (1980) The Prison Experience of Career Criminals. Santa Monica, CA: Rand Corporation.

Petersilia, Joan R., Susan Turner, James Kahan, and Joyce Peterson (1985) Granting Felons Probation: Public Risks and Alternatives. Santa Monica, CA: Rand Corporation.

Petersilia, Joan R. and Susan Turner, with Joyce E. Peterson (1986) Prison Versus Probation in California: Implications for Crime and Offender Recidivism. Santa Monica, CA: Rand Corporation.

Philliber, Susan (1987) "Thy brother's keeper: a review of the literature on correctional officers." Justice Quarterly 4 (1): 9-37.

Piliavin, Irving, Rosemary Gartner, Craig Thornton, and Ross L. Matsueda (1986) "Crime, deterrence, and rational choice." American Sociological Review 51 (February): 101-119.

Poole, E. and R. Regoli (1980) "Role stress, custody orientation and disciplinary actions." Criminology 18: 215-227.

Potter, Constance (1976) "The federal prison system, 1926-1932." M.A. thesis, Washington State University, Pullman, WA.

Powdermaker, Hortense (1966) Stranger and Friend: The Way of an Anthropologist. New York: Norton.

Read, Kenneth E. (1980) Other Voices: The Style of a Male Homosexual Tavern. Novato, CA: Chandler & Sharp.

Reimer, Hans (1937) "Socialization in the prison community," pp. 151-155 in Proceedings of the American Prison Association. New York: American Prison Association.

Rhodes, Lorna Amarasingham (1986) "The anthropologist as institutional analyst." Ethos 14 (2): 204-217.

Rockey, Alexandra (1987) "Special report: highway to hell." Police (May): 34-38, 62-64.

Roszell, Stephen R. (1987) Other Prisoners. A Film Documentary of the Kentucky State Reformatory. A production of WTTW/Chicago.

Rothman, D. B. and J. R. Kimberly (1975) "The social context of jails." Sociology and Social Research 59: 344-361.

Schafer, N. E. (1978) "Prison visiting: a background for change." Federal Probation (September): 47-50.

Schafer, N. E. (1982) "Good time and prisoner misconduct: a preliminary examination," pp. 147-158 in Nicolette Parisi (ed.) Coping With Imprisonment. Beverly Hills, CA: Sage.

Schein, Edgar H. (1984) "Coming to a new awareness of organizational culture." Sloan Management Review (Winter): 3-16.

Schmalleger, Frank (1979) "World of the career criminal." Human Nature (March): 50-56.

Schwartz, Mary C. and Judith F. Weintraub (1974) "The prisoner's wife: a study in crisis." Federal Probation (December): 20-26.

Sexton, George E., Franklin C. Farrow, and Barbara J. Auerbach (1985) The Private Sector and Prison Industries. Research in Brief. Washington, DC: National Institute of Justice.

Silberman, Matthew (1986) "The dynamics of social control in a correctional setting." Paper presented at the American Sociological Association conference.

Standing Deer et al. v. Carlson, Christensen, LaRoe 831 F. 2d 1525 (9th Cir. 1987)

Stastny, C. and G. Tyrnauer (1982) Who Rules the Joint? The Changing Political Culture of Maximum-Security Prisons in America. Lexington, KY: Lexington.

Sykes, Gresham M. (1958) The Society of Captives. Princeton, NJ: Princeton University Press.

Sykes, Gresham M. and Sheldon L. Messinger (1960) "The inmates' social system," pp. 5-19 in Donald Cressey (ed.) Theoretical Studies in Social Organization of the Prison. New York: Social Science Research Council.

Sylvester, Sawyer F., John H. Reed, and David O. Nelson (1977) Prison Homicide. New York: Spectrum.

Thornberry, Terence P. (1987) "Toward an interactional theory of delinquency." Criminology 25 (4): 863-891.

Toch, Hans (1969) Violent Men: An Inquiry into the Psychology of Violence. Chicago: Aldine.

Toch, Hans (1975) Men in Crisis. Chicago: Aldine.

Toch, Hans (1976) "A psychological view of prison violence," pp. 43-51 in A. K. Cohen et al. (eds.) Prison Violence: A Sociological Perspective. Lexington, MA: Lexington.

Toch, Hans (1977) Living in Prison: The Ecology of Survival. New York: Free Press.

Toch, Hans (1978) "Social climate and prison violence." Federal Probation (December): 21-25.

Toch, Hans and Kenneth Adams (1986) "Pathology and disruptiveness among prison inmates." Journal of Research in Crime and Delinquency 23: 7-21.

Toch, Hans, Kenneth Adams, and Ronald Greene (1987) "Ethnicity, disruptiveness, and emotional disorder among prison inmates." Criminal Justice and Behavior 14 (1): 93-109.

United States Department of Justice (1986) "AIDS in prisons and jails: issues and options." National Institute of Justice. Research in Brief (February).

United States Department of the Treasury (1986) Illegal Tax Protester Information Book. Internal Revenue Service, Criminal Investigation, Office of Intelligence. Document 7072 (1-86). Washington, DC: Government Printing Office.

United States Penitentiary at Lompoc, CA (1985) Incident Report Logs.

United States Penitentiary at Lompoc, CA (1986) Lompoc Freeway. January 15.

United States Penitentiary at Lompoc, CA (1986) Lompoc Freeway. September 18.

United States Penitentiary at Lompoc, CA (1986) Internal Memorandum. January 10.

United States Penitentiary at Lompoc, CA (1986) Incident Report Logs.

United States Penitentiary at Lompoc, CA (1987) Inmate Handbook for Federal Prisons.

Van Maanen, John (1981) "The informant game: selected aspects of ethnographic research in police organizations." Urban Life 9 (4): 469-494.

Walkey, Frank H. and D. Ross Gilmour (1984) "The relationship between interpersonal distance and violence in imprisoned offenders." Criminal Justice and Behavior 11 (3): 331-341.

Wall Street Journal (1987) "Cuban prisoner riots followed seven years of U.S. ambivalence," December 1.

Wall Street Journal (1988) "Los Angeles seeks ultimate weapon in gang war," March 30.

Ward, David (1986) "Control strategies for problem prisoners in American penal systems." (unpublished)

Weber, Tad (1988a) "Penitentiary neighbors enjoy crime-free streets." Santa Barbara News-Press, March 28.

Weber, Tad (1988b) "Penitentiary or camp: inmates' lives differ." Santa Barbara News-Press, March 27.

Weintraub, Judith (1976) "The delivery of services to families of prisoners." Federal Probation (December): 28-31.

Williams, Virginia L. and Mary Fish (1974) Convicts, Codes and Contraband. Cambridge, MA: Ballinger.

Wilson, James Q. (1985) Thinking About Crime. New York: Vintage.

Wilson, James Q. and Richard J. Herrnstein (1985) Crime and Human Nature. New York: Simon & Schuster.

Woldman, William (1987) Prison Conditions: The Congressional Response. Government Division, Congressional Research Service. Washington, DC: Government Printing Office.

Wolfgang, Marvin E. (1961) "Quantitative analysis of adjustment to the prison community." Journal of Criminal Law, Criminology and Police Science 51: 608-618.

Wolfgang, Marvin E. and Franco Ferracuti (1982) The Subculture of Violence: Towards an Integrated Theory in Criminology. Beverly Hills, CA: Sage.

Wooden, Wayne S. and Jay Parker (1982) Men Behind Bars: Sexual Exploitation in Prison. New York: De Capo.

Zemans, Eugene and Ruth S. Cavan (1958) "Marital relationships of prisoners." Journal of Criminal Law, Criminology and Police 49 (1).

About the Author

Mark S. Fleisher (Ph.D., 1976) is Associate Professor of Criminal Justice Sciences at Illinois State University. He is a cultural and linguistic anthropologist and has conducted linguistic research in Mexico, Guatemala, Indonesia, and on the Northwest Coast of the United States among Salish and Nootkan peoples.

Fleisher has more than 20 years experience studying prisons and criminals, has been a research and an evaluation consultant to federal, state, and county correctional systems, and has been a consultant to the National Institution of Corrections Academy. He was employed from 1989 to 1993 by the Federal Bureau of Prisons as Special Assistant to the Regional Director (Western Region & North Central Region) and as a Correctional Programs Specialist (Assistant Designator) and Strategic Planning Coordinator (North Central Region).

His latest book, *Beggars and Thieves* (1995), is a comprehensive ethnography of the life trajectory of chronic urban street criminals, funded by the U.S. Census Bureau and the Harry Frank Guggenheim Foundation.

Printed in the United States
43173LVS00002B/151-180

9 780803 931237